The NAGA Society

Attention Authors

The NAGA Society

Dr. Chandrika Singh

Head: Department of Political Science
Nagaland University (India)

Manas Publications
New Delhi - 110002

MANAS PUBLICATIONS
(Publishers, Library Suppliers, Importers & Exporters)
4402/5-A, Ansari Road (Opp. HDFC Bank)
Darya Ganj, New Delhi-110 002 (INDIA)
Off. ✆ 23260783, 23265523, Res. ✆ 23842660
Fax: 011-23272766
E-mail: manaspublications@vsnl.com
manaspublications@yahoo.com

2nd Impression 2012 (FP – 2008)

ISBN 81-7049-333-1

₹ 495/-

Designed by
Manas Publications

Printed in India at
RK Offsets, Delhi
and published by Mrs Suman Lata for
Manas Publications, 4402/5-A, Ansari Road
(Opp. HDFC Bank),
Darya Ganj, New Delhi-110 002 (INDIA)

Preface

The story of the strife-torn state of Nagaland is sadistic, pathetic, painful, heart-rending and full of thorny problems. The Naga society, while comprising various tribes and sub-tribes that belong to Indo-Mongoloid race, is an ancient one. The Nagas carry a prolonged and chequred history, which bespeaks of their origin, migration, confrontation, internecine war-fares, etc. The Naga people developed independent socio-political systems based on their customary laws that reflect their ancient wisdom and ability to manage their affairs and survive independently. However, the Naga society remained stagnant, confined to villages, isolated from the civilized world, relied on minimum needs of the life based on tribal customary laws and conventional practice till the British subjugated the Nagas and seized their territory. Various tribes inhabiting different mountainous regions remained free from foreign occupation due to difficult mountain ranges and dense forest that defend as a shield to these people. The Nagas, were proud of their supremacy and independence, but were separated, disintegrated and were inimical to each other with no reason or rhyme. Their political consciousness was limited; social behaviour was conventional and thinking attitude was parochial. Life of the early Nagas was community based where individualism had absolutely no role to play. The Nagas were brave no doubt, but their bravery was chauvinistic. Their parochial thinking and chauvinistic behaviour hardly allowed them to come together and form a society comprising the tribes belonging to the same blood. The tribes living adjacent to each other had no intention at all to subjugate others. Each of them had gathered sufficient strength to defend their earmarked territory. They totally disliked any outside intervention in their internal affairs.

Each Naga tribe was a society in itself in the sense that it was socially integrated, politically organised, and economically viable with limited needs. If they had any outside link, it were the Ahoms with whom the Naga's living near the boundary of Assam had some sort of relations. It is true that the Ahoms, sometimes, forced the Naga people to pay some sorts of tributes as a token of Ahom's suzerainty, but the Ahom rulers could establish their permanent suzerainty over the Nagas. With the fall of the Ahoms, the Nagas who were directly or indirectly influenced by the former, regained their previous position. It were the British who successfully made a breakthrough in the defence mechanism of the Naga tribes, destroying their prolonged isolation and forced them to accept supremacy of the British government willingly or unwillingly. Thereafter, the British applied the forces to subjugate the Nagas and put them under a single administrative pattern.

Penetration of the Western Baptist missionaries into the northeastern region of India, their cordial relations with the animist Nagas, spread of new faith and establishment of churches and missionary schools are the historic events that changed the traditional outlook of the indigenous people and opened a new avenue for social as well as political changes destroying Naga's age-old cultural and social values. The Nagas no doubt, in the beginning, protested the missionary activities, but the mild behaviour and sympathetic attitude of the missionary people towards the natives won over the heart of the war-like Naga tribes who gradually accepted Christianity as their religion.

Every thing began to change in the Naga society with the changes in their concepts when they came close to the foreigners. Introduction of new political structure and laws, the setting up of new administrative headquarters in towns, new economic order and new fiscal practices brought the Naga society near to the threshold of modernity and served as tools to transform the traditional Naga society into a modern society. Administrators, bureaucrats, businessmen, contractors, engineers and host of government servants who appeared with the creation of Nagaland state gave further impetus to the growth of modernization and urbanization in Nagaland. Industrial products easily available in new markets with the growth of trade and commerce increased the needs of the Nagas making them prone to the habit of consumerism. Spread of education broadened their mind making them curious about new knowledge and technology. A tendency and temptation to adopt new style of life, which developed among the educated Nagas, made them averse to their ancient culture and civilization. Under such growing consciousness the Naga intellectuals formed a social as well as political common platform where they thought of future political shape of their nation and began to act to achieve the decided goal which was Naga's freedom. The Naga intellectuals, without making any delay, commited themselves to pay for the cost of achieving the right to self-determination.

Not long before India's independence, the issue that agitated the mind of the Nagas, was not their economic problem, but their future political status. Despite their will and efforts, they were put under the constitution of India with some special autonomy, but without any change in their previous political status. They were denied even a separate political unit which compelled the Naga leaders to begin agitation, which ultimately resulted in armed conflicts between the Indian armed forces and the Naga freedom fighters. It is unfortunate that the political turmoil, which took place in Nagaland soon after India's independence caused great hindrance to economic growth of the state and its people. The territory of the Nagas became the bed-rock for armed struggle between the Indian armed forces and the Naga freedom fighters where a number of Nagas lost their lives and people in general faced harassment, torture, humiliation, intimidation and much more.

The bitterness of memory of the Nagas of their sufferings during the days of armed struggle is still fresh and hurting the mind of the people. The scars of the wounds the Naga people had suffered for decades, have not yet dried up. The problems and pangs of the Nagas are still painful. The nightmare, through which the Naga people have passed not for a month or a year, but for decades, has not yet disappeared. The Naga society has witnessed so many ups and downs in a very short span of time. Blood has been shed profusely on the soil of the Nagas. It is sad to note the political future of the Nagas is yet uncertain despite tough struggle and immense sacrifices of six decades.

The Naga society is still reeling under the wounds.

The Naga Hills, which was simply a district of province of Assam, became a full-fledged state in 1963 having all infrastructural facilities. Due to the sincere efforts of the moderate Naga leaders and also the kind cooperation of the government of India, the state moved towards the path of prosperity despite constant confrontations and conflicts. Today, the Naga society may be called as a modernized society because the traditional attitude of the people has changed. The Nagas have moved fast towards modernity. Immense changes have taken place in economic, political, social and administrative fields. The state has all the ministries, departments and non-governmental agencies to administer the people and help them in their efforts for self-development. Numerous educational institutions, right from primary to the post-graduate levels, are playing the role of enlightening them with wide and broad conceptual framework with a view to link them to the modern world of science, arts, technology, architecture, etc. These all have transformed the Naga society to a large extent. There is no village which is not electrified today. There is no village which lacks the educational facility at least at primary level. Literacy of the state has gone very high (69%). Light of education has made people more aware of their future. The society is prospering and people are developing. The broadened consciousness has increased the aspirations of the Nagas to such an extent that knows no bounds. Each conscious guardian is worried about the better education facilities for their children and wards. These all indicate that how the modern Nagas are actively conscious for better life and better living.

A modern society is an industrial society. Modernization is a continuous and open-ended process.

"Modernization is not for once and for all-time achievement. There seems to a dynamic principle built into the fabric of modern societies that does not allow them to settle or to achieve equilibrium. This development is always irregular and uneven." Moreover, modernism has two main phases. First, it carries the institutions and values of societies that are regarded as progressive upward movement. Secondly, it 'brings new social and material structures that may threaten the very growth and expansion on which modern society is founded'.

In the second phase modern societies find themselves faced with an array of new problems whose solution often seems beyond the competence of the traditional nature state.

So far the case of Naga society is concerned it has not yet entered into the second phase. The dynamics of social and material structure of the society are very slow due to lack of industrial base and also to some extent traditional base of the Naga society. The old social institutions and their values still have relevance with traditionality. It would be better to say that the Naga society is a progressive society. Its social structure is changing, no doubt, but traditional outlook of the general mass has, not changed much. Modernity has brought about changes in the mental attitude of the educated and rich Nagas, but the longing of the Nagas for their past values has not yet disappeared totally. That's the reason why the culture and civilization what the Naga people have today are neither purely western nor indigenous. Rather these are the mixture of modernity and traditionality. An inclination of the educated Naga people towards westernization may easily be discerned, but at the same time they are not ready at all to give up wholly their ancient cultural values. This is because the culture of a social group is related to the heart and thinking process of the members of the group, to which they are accustomed. Culture is not the subject to imitate or to copy. However, it is true that a culture specially traditional is influenced by modern culture and civilization. The impact of modern culture and civilization tempts the people to adopt new and drop the old one, but the old one cannot be destroyed in toto.

The Naga culture is very old and stable. The arrival of new culture in Nagaland along with the western people influenced the indigenous culture of the Nagas, no doubt, but it could not exterminate it. Moreover, growth of modernity in Nagaland has brought about changes in various aspects of the Naga society along with the living style of the people, but reminiscence of the past social as well cultural values is still fresh in the mind of the Nagas. And so the Nagas who are yet proud of their indigenous culture are found worried when modernity wants to prosper at the cost of their old social and cultural values. However, the young generation is more inclined towards new civilization. The mighty wave of modernization that came in Nagaland from the west, has not only changed the social and material fabrics of the Naga society making the youngsters more prone to new style of life and new values but has also brought about numerous problems in the society. The society, which was once casteless and classless, has been stratified on the basis of division of power, status and prestige. The elements who were conscious and smart loose no time in availing of the new opportunities to enrich themselves.

Under the influence of modernization the Naga society has lost its collective character and moved fast towards individualistic feature where the vested interests have enough scope to successfully manage to achieve power, wealth and prestige. The conscious Nagas in pursuit of availing of the opportunity to enrich themselves left no stone unturned to change their lifestyle indulging themselves in modern luxuries and comforts. But the people, who remained far behind even in getting even their marked share of benefits of modern development, are subject to miseries and sufferings. In other words, the uneven distribution of benefits coming out of different development schemes and programmes has divided the Naga society into two sharp divisions—the rich and the poor. The rich people on whose door the modern material facilities are abundantly available, have become the leaders of the society. The trend of present Naga culture, which has been shaped by the forces who are rich enough materially and cultured enough educationally on the western line, is getting dominance. This culture is based on self-adoration and self-perfection. It hardly cares for those who are far behind in the race of development. Such culture, in the words of the Governor of Nagaland, Mr. Thomas, has brought "Wide-spread corruption" which "has hindered economic development seriously and brought about class differences destroying the traditional egalitarianism of society and a culture of consumerism and easy money".

Though the general mass has developed the feeling of negligence, they lack ability and desire to revolt against social and economic injustice, which they are getting from their own leaders. Perhaps their consciousness is still in the infant stage. Leaders of various unions and associations who stand to fight for justice and protect the interests of the people are either silent spectators or lack the required quality and ability to act against the social as well as political injustice. The Naga society has numerous unions, associations and non-governmental organizations, no doubt, but their role to fight with the anti-social elements and protect the interests of the people is not much viable. The primary purpose of their leaders is to obtain money. In Nagaland all actions are justified in the name of the people, but reality is that there is hardly any one to care for the people. As it generally happens in India, the leaders of the unions and associations fall easy prey to the politicians and they are used as a tool to serve their vested interests.

The current of 'westoxication' in Naga society "determines the psycho-historical factors governing basic principles". The external forces have "consistently shaped historical accounts" and have managed to shift the focus from becoming a gradual process to "acquiring as an escalating process". What good the Nagas has adopted today are the copies of westernization where there is enough scope for class formation, class antagonism and class conflict. The rise and growth of secularism and materialism in the Naga society has given a severe blow to the philosophy of religion and moralism "where the moral aspect of life is completely ignored and as a result of this the society is dragged into atheistic culture where the purpose of life is largely ignored". The old values of the Naga society like honesty, sincerity, simplicity, straightforwardness, traditional arts, techniques and social commitment etc., are eroding paving the way to the growth of individualism, self-centralism, egoism, dishonesty, fraud and violence.

The serious problems which have engulfed the modern Naga society today are lust for alcohol, drug-addiction, growing number of victims suffering from AIDS, HIV, violence, goondaism and pauperism. Swelling number of unemployed youths, unchecked growth of money extortion drive, imposition of heavy taxes by underground factions etc., are the features of today where people find themselves helpless and hopeless. Bitter and unending bloody factional feuds and fighting among underground factions have not only delayed permanent solution of the Naga issue but also have divided the society in the name of tribalism creating tension and fear. Declining morality of the Naga politicians and bureaucrats, who are more interested in self-development rather than for the development of the society and its people, is another hurdle, which has brought mass corruption in the society.

The state has developed and the society has changed, but real beneficiaries are those who have successfully maneuvered to exploit political, administrative and economic mechanism of the state to serve their ends. The poor sections are yet deprived of even essential daily needs. No doubt, the group standing between the rich and the poor, namely, the white collar workers like teachers, doctors, small rank officers, small businessmen, pastors etc., has managed to meet their minimum needs by developing links with the people who are well-to-do in the society. Though they are conscious of such unjustified development and economic injustice, they have not yet developed the courage to raise their strong voice against the existing corrupt scenario and protest against injustice. In other words, it may be said that the Naga society lacks the quality of revolutionary zeal and ability to begin and continue protest movement against the elements, which are directly or indirectly acting against the general interest of the society and its people as a whole.

Thus the march of the Naga society from traditionality to modernization carries numerous wonderful histories, which need thorough investigation, close observation and critical interpretation. The present work, which presents a critical account of the dynamism of the Naga society, is an exercise in this direction. The work explores the origin of the Nagas, growth of the Naga society and activities of the Naga people. It further examines and analyses the factors, which are responsible for transformation of the society. The book thoroughly investigates and examines various critical circumstances and embarrassing situations through which the society had passed. It also interprets and examines the events responsible for creating the confusing and complex circumstances which added more miseries and troubles to the people. Efforts have been applied to examine the influences of modernization and its consequential impact upon the people.

For the last six decades the Nagá society and its people have been living in perpetual affairs of disturbance, bloodshed, fear and fraud. Since I have been living in Nagaland for more than three decades in the capacity of a teacher, I have not only been the silent spectator of the events of the society, but I have also suffered the pangs and problems of the society along with the people. My stay in Nagaland as a teacher for more than three decades and my close association with the Naga people have enabled me to understand the problems of the Nagas from a very close angle. While discussing and analyzing the factors relating to the Naga society I have applied the efforts to remain unbiased throughout my investigation and interpretation of its various aspects. I hope this work would be of immense help to those who have the curiosity to know the Nagas and their struggle for peace and development. This will also help the general readers to have a clear concept about the Naga society and its people. I hope each section of the society would appreciate the work. However, I beg forgiveness of those whose feelings have been hurt due to free and frank description of the problems of the Nagas society. Before my retirement and return back to my home town, I dedicate this work to the Naga people in fond memory of my living with them.

I am thankful to all those authorities and friends who have helped me in completing the work with their valuable suggestions.

Dr. CHANDRIKA SINGH

***

Abbreviations

ADC	Additional Deputy Commissioner
BDO	Bloc Development Officer
CAD	Constituent Assembly Debates
D.C.	Deputy Commissioner
DPB	District Planning Board
DP	Democratic Party
EAC	Extra Assistant Commissioner
FGN	Federal Government of Nagaland
GB	Gaon Baurah
GRPN	Government of the People's Republic of Nagaland
INC (I)	Indian National Congress (Indira)
IAY	Indira Awas Yojana
IRDP	Integrated Rural Development Programme
ISR	Industrial Service and Business
JRY	Jawahar Rojgar Yojana
LS	Lok Sabha
LP	Legislature Party
NA	Naga Army
NC	Naga Club
NEC	North East Council
NGO	Non-Governmental Organization
NMA	Naga Mothers' Association
NNC	Naga National Council
NDA	Nagaland Democratic Alliance

NBCC	Nagaland Baptist Church Council
NISC	Naga Internationl Support Centre
NHD	Naga Hills District
NHTA	Naga Hills Tuensang Area
NLA	Nagaland Legislative Assembly
NPC	Nagaland People's Council
NPF	Nagaland People's Front
NNDP	Naga National Democratic Party
NNO	Naga Nationalist Organization
NPCC (I)	Nagaland Pradesh Congress Committee (Indira)
NPP	Nagaland People's Party
NPMHR	Naga People Movement for Human Rights
NREGP	National Rural Employment Guarantee Programme
NSF	Naga Students' Federation
NSCN (I-M)	Nationalist Socialist Council of Nagaland (Isak-Muivah)
NSCN (K)	Nationalist Socialist Council of Nagaland (Khapalang)
PC	Privilege Committee
PCBH	Procedure for Conduct of Business of the House
PCI	Planning Commission of India
RC	Reformation Committee
RD	Rural Development
SDO (C)	Sub-divisional Officer (Civil)
UDF	United Democratic Front
UDF (P)	United Democratic Front (Progressive)
UF	United Front
UG	Under Ground
ULP	United Legislature Party
VC	Village Council
VDB	Village Development Board
VLW	Village Level Worker

***

Contents

1

A Unique Profile

The Naga society, proud of its historical base, is tribal in nature. The people of this land have been carrying out some notable sets of social values and good principles. The Naga society is unique in the real sense of the term, as it has been maintaining its social norms and values independently despite various inconveniences and difficulties. Before the arrival of the British in the land of the Nagas, the Naga society was unknown to the outside world. It succeeded in maintaing its separate identity because of its existence in the mountainous ranges covered with dense forests that served as a protective cover zone. No doubt, the early Nagas living near the foot-hills of Assam had some sort of relations with the Ahom rulers who tried to subjugate the Nagas, but the latter never allowed the Ahoms to establish their sovereignty over them and destroy their social as well as cultural norms and values. The relationship with the Ahoms and the Nagas proved short-lived and the Nagas maintained their own systems and values independently. History bears the testimony that many old cultures and civilizations lost their identities in the mighty wave of subjugation and assimilation by the powerful forces. However, in the case of the Naga society and its cultural as well as social norms and values, it never happened that the Naga people lost their identity. Even during the British rule the Naga society preserved its social norms and values and kept the social identity intact with the exception that it was affected by the current of modernization. This chapter traces out the origin and growth of the Naga society and evaluates and examines customs, traditions, cultural as well as religious ethos and political system of the early Naga society.

Society—Its Meaning and Nature

Before giving a description of the ancient Naga society, it would be convenient to have a cursory look at the meaning and nature of society. The word 'Society' is generally used to refer to an encompassing network of a social relationship that encloses some more specific phenomenon, which forms the object of the analysts. Analytical definitions of a society usually treat it "as a relatively independent or self-sufficient population characterized by internal organization, territoriality, cultural distinctiveness and sexual recruitment—self-sufficient group remains a constant element in most concepts of society."* According to Abere and his colleagues, a society is a group of human beings sharing a self-sufficient system of action which is capable of existing longer than the life-span of an individual, the group being recruited at least in part by the sexual reproduction of the member. It means a society is not a temporary existence. A society is destroyed under two conditions—first, by a war of all against all and secondly by subjugation by another powerful society. For permanent existence of a social group the following elements are essential.

1. **Sexual Recruitment**—Sexual recruitment means blood relationship, the members of a social group should not be alien, but reproduced by the members of the same society.
2. **Adequate Relationship with the Environment**—A society exists in a territory, which has its environmental situation. The members of the society should not only be fully acquainted with the environment but also absorbed to the environment. His relationship with the existing environment must be adaptable to the group members.

---

* David L. Sills (ed), *International Encyclopedia*, vol. 13/14, pp. 577-78.

3. **Assignment of the members**—The members of the group must have assigned roles to support the society. Their performances must yield goods not only to the group members, but also to the whole world.
4. **Normative regulations of means and emotional expression**—For survival of the society certain normative regulations are needed to adjust the mutual relationship of the members and also the establishment of ways and means to express emotional feelings.
5. **Socialization**—Socialization is to train the members of the group towards adopted values of the society. It also means to persuade the members to believe in the adopted social norms and follow the social systems and perform the duties to strengthen them in the greater interests of all.
6. **Control of disruptive behaviours**—A society is a living being which has its growth and development. If there are some anti-social elements whose behaviour harms the society, it must be controlled. Social norms, which are established, must not be destroyed by some vested interests. Society needs to be governed in a full-fledged way so as to protect the social interests and create favourable circumstances for the growth and development of the society and its members.

The clear concept of society emerged during the eighteenth century with the rise and growth of rational liberal views. The liberal thinkers placed the society prior to the state. It was John Locke who separated society from the state and propounded that society has its independent existence before the state. State appeared in support of the society. Time came when the Church (religion) was also separated from the state. Philosophy of romanticism developed the theory of society based on conventionalism and put stress on the unity of the integrated whole. Society came to be viewed as organic growth, embodying the practical and profound wisdom of conventions and traditions. Abstract analytical segments cannot be separated from the whole and changed arbitrarily. If it is done, it will have to destroy the complex interdependence of the web of the social life. This theory supported interdependent actions. In the early nineteenth century, August Comte developed the idea of cultural order as a constituent element of society. Comte argued reformation of society required the creation of a new scientifically based moral order. He liked reconstruction in religious, familial, educational and political institutions on scientific lines giving significance to moral order. He did not believe that barely a consciousness is a sufficient condition for organised collective life. The consensus must be organised in institutional order that symbolizes teachings, enforces and implements moral ideas and rules.*

Thus, it is very much obvious that the concept about the society has been changing. During early period the proper term was group or community of the people which is a territorially bounded social system or a set of interlocking or an integrated functional sub-systems serving a resident population. The community concept does not include such characteristics as harmony, law, "we-feeling" or intimacy, which are sometimes nostalgically imputed to idealized pre-industrial communities (Foster, 1960-61). However, it includes a minimum of consensus. It means it lacks social cohesiveness, ideological spirit and consensus base. People live together and follow established norms and values.

With changing of time the idea about society was totally transformed. Society emerged as a powerful identity covering every aspect of life. The relationship between the society and the individual was defined. Though conflicting ideas related to the boundary line between the society and the individual emerged, the individual was saved from the grip of the society. The ideal type of the society is that which permits the individual to prosper irrespective of sex, birth, race, religion, place, etc. Civil society is a term which includes civilization and culture. Civilization means sense of social orders, institutional base and zeal as well as strong desire to maintain the social order. A civilized people are those who are organised socially, politically, economically and religiously and have that common sense to live and let others live. The civilized

---

* David L. Sills (ed), *International Encyclopedia,* vol. 14/14: pp.579-80.

people have certain socially recognized and legally protected autonomies and freedoms to prosper. Culture is also a set of civilization which is related to living standard and way of behaviours. Culture of a society includes the elements like social behaviours, religious rituals, family norms, ethical codes and social organizations. It teaches manners. Literature, arts, social rituals, customs, traditional conventions etc. are the constituent elements of culture.

Early Naga Society

The question is whether the early Naga society was, in fact, a society or it was simply a group of people belonging to a particular tribe having blood relationship. Here opinions vary. The British authors who had closely observed the Naga society during early nineteenth century are of the view that the Nagas were barbarous and uncivilized or semi-civilized. The different Naga tribes were disintegrated and inimical to each other. Their world was very much limited and they knew nothing about the outside world. No doubt, each tribe had some sort of social norms, cultural values and political institutions, but their behaviours towards other people were non-friendly and harmful. The British authors like A. Mackenzie, Hutton Robinson termed them 'savage', 'uncultured' and semi-civilized. It appears that their perception about the indigenous Nagas was based on their war-like nature and famous tradition of head-hunting. There are British authors like V. Elwin, J.S. Mill and Robert Reid who appreciated the democratic spirit and political wisdom of the early Nagas.

No doubt, the early Naga people were divided into various tribes and sub-tribes and lived nearby, but they lacked the skill to form a bigger polity to live together. However, to be true the early Naga people were not savage and uncivilized. Though their world was separate and limited, they knew how to live and how to prosper. If society means the set of social norms, cultural values, economic support, a zeal for survival and a desire for having independent social as well as political status, the early Naga society must be termed a society because they possessed all these requisites for a society. Their traditions, conventions, customary laws and social rituals etc., substantiate the fact that the early Nagas were not vagabonds or nomads.

The Naga society, a tribal one, consists of various tribes, sub-tribes and clans differing basically in their respective social and customary behaviours as well as their dialects. The common characteristics of the Nagas are their strong will to have and maintain their separate identity, dauntless courage to fight difficulties and face the enemies, a desire strong enough to have a free life and a bitter disliking for meddling of others in their internal affairs. It was the longing of the indigenous Nagas to have their own separate identity, which enabled them to overcome a number of difficulties and problems while searching for a permanent abode. The early Nagas lacked the knowledge of script and literature, no doubt, but they carried some sort of mythological tales of their past life, origin and development. Since there are no written documentary proofs about the past life of the Nagas, nothing scientifically and authentically can be said about their ancient life and behaviour. Written history of the Naga society begins with the arrival of the British and Christian missionaries in the land of the Nagas. Undoubtedly some mentions about the Naga people are available in the Ahoms' Buranjis. But it hardly speaks of the social, customary and religious behaviours of the Naga people. Various diverse viewpoints related to the origin, migration and nomenclature of the Nagas have been produced by different scholars. The fact that nothing can be ascertained who the Nagas are, why they are called the Naga and when did they arrive to the territories they are occupying presently. Their mythology and tales indicate that they possessed some values and norms, which enabled them to form a society of their own and maintain it in the greater interest of the community as a whole including the individual. The society was not open and the community was treated as the supreme. However, it does not mean that individual has no place in the community. Like early Greek society it was difficult to distinguish between the individual and the society. Both stood for each other.

Some Features

The Naga people as a whole are simple, friendly and hard working. They are brave and have the courage to face the enemies. They love freedom and liberty. By nature they are straightforward, jolly and cheerful. The society had been classless and casteless during its early phase, but their association with the British and Christian missionaries and also the arrival of modernity have stratified it creating a gap between the rich and the poor. Economic standard of the people has developed and their political consciousness has been sharpened. Advent of schools, colleges and university have helped the people to enrich themselves in the field of education and opened new avenues for employment. Traditionality, which was the basic feature of the Naga society, has changed into modernity not only widening the understanding of the Nagas, but also increasing their needs and changing their lifestyle. Though Christianity is the accepted religion of the Nagas, inclination of the Naga people towards material prosperity has overshadowed spiritual aspect of religion.

Geographic and Political Features

The state of Nagaland, which is mostly hill territories, lies between 25° 60′ and 27° 40′ latitude north of the equator and between the longitudinal lines 93° 20′ and 95° 15′.[1] Nagaland covers an area of 16,527 sq. km. with a population of 19, 88,636 according to the census of 2001. Out of this, 82.26% of the population is rural. The average density of population is 120 per sq. km.[2] Besides the people living in Nagaland, many Naga people are living in Manipur, Arunachal Pradesh, Assam and Myanmar. The state is bounded by Assam in the north and west, by Myanmar and Arunachal Pradesh in the east and Manipur in the south and runs more or less parallel to the left bank of the Brahmaputra. The altitude varies between 194 meters and 3048 meters. The territory of the state is mostly hilly except some plain areas in Dimapur. The rolling mountains, the enchanting valleys, the swift flowing streams and the evergreen forests of the Naga Hills present scenic beauty. Its moderate climate and pollution-free environment attract visitors all round the year. It forms an irregular plateau with elevated ridges and peaks. The peaks of Nagaland vary in height from 350 meters to 3,000 meters above the sea level. The highest peak is Saramati (in Tuensang) with a height of 3,826 meters. The Dhansiri is the largest river of the state that flows through North Cachar and Kohima before it finally flows into the Brahmaputra in Assam. The soil is fertile and yields varieties of agricultural and horticultural products. The forests are evergreen and rich in bamboo and timber.

The state of Nagaland is divided into as many as eleven districts, namely, Kohima, Mokokchung, Tuensang, Mon, Zunheboto, Khiphere, Longleng, Dimapur, Wokha, Pheck, and Peren. The state carries a chequred history behind its evolution. Kohima is the capital headquarters. Kohima, Mokokchung and Tuensang are oldest districts while other districts came into existence later on. Each district has been divided in administrative sub-divisions administered by the Additional Deputy Commissioners, Sub-divisional Officers and Extra Assistant commissioners. Besides, each district has different supporting administrative offices for development of the state.

Origin, Migration and Permanent Settlement of the Nagas

The Naga people follow their different tongues, cultures, social behaviours and historical legends and mythologies, which help one to understand their early life. If the Naga people have something in common, then these are their physical appearance, customary laws, simplicity and generosity. They all belong to the same blood that is Indo-Mongolian. They migrated to the present territory in different phases from Central Asia. The tribes, who entered into the hilly region of the northeastern part of India crossing the rivers Chindwin and Irawaddi, "were not homogenous one, but deadly of different races divided into numerous tribes, sub-tribes and clans under the 'Mongoloid' race, different in origin, distinct in language, diverse in physique, character, culture and society, depending upon the peripheral geographical locality, although basically they were more or less the same having much in common affiliations, common heritage, religious values, norms, common ideas of liberty and decencies."[3]

The cause of multiplicity of tribes in the Naga society is, perhaps, due to their migration to the present geographical areas in different phases and in different groups and also their permanent settlement in different hilly terrains.[4] It seems that they migrated to the present place, sometime in B.C. era when other tribes like Caren, Shan,

Chin, Singpho and Koyans of Indonesia, Myanmar and Philippines who bear the similarity in physique with the Nagas, migrated from the same place (Central Asia) and settled where they found unoccupied lands. Smith is of the view that the Naga tribes belong to the same blood which is found in the people of Burma (Myanmar), Sikkim, Bhutan and other hilly areas of North East India.[5] Perhaps the Naga tribes were a bit late to reach the north eastern part of India. Before they reached, some other tribes like Ahom, Singpho and Miri had already settled in the plains of North East. It was the north east frontiers, which were still unoccupied with the result that the different bands of the Naga tribes found it convenient to occupy the unoccupied lands. After permanent settlement, they earmarked their respective occupied territories with stone, rivers and mountains as boundary lines. They established their respective tiny sovereign state-village maintaining separate identity. Though they were not yet fully civilized, they developed some common social norms based on their customary practices. Asoso Yonuo is also of the view that "These Nagas with a fairly well developed culture established permanently small village states similar to those of the Greek City-State in the hilly and mountainous ranges or spurs, high above the valley."[6]

The most lamentable part on the history of the ancient Nagas is that they lacked the skill of diplomacy and feeling of unity. All the tribes remained separate from each other and preferred isolation. Consequently, they remained far behind to form a nation-state comprising all the Naga tribes. This is because of the fact that the Nagas by nature are skeptical, suspicious and doubtful about the activities of others. They preferred separation and isolation because they did not like any sort of intervention in their internal affairs. To preserve their separate identity and meet the outside danger they maintained warriorship selecting young and brave youths. Since their needs were limited, they managed every thing for survival without outside contact.

The question whether the Naga people are original settlers of India or they migrated from different places to the part which they have been occupying since time immemorial, is still controversial. Several viewpoints have been developed in this regard.

Some Indian thinkers like S.K. Chatterjee are of the view that these Nagas are original settlers since the Vedic period and were known as the *Kiratas*. However, this view is not an authentic one.

The theories and facts related to the origin, migration, nomenclature of the term 'Naga', their settlement in the present territories, religion etc., are not dissimilar. The facts, which have been attracting others to know about the Nagas, are their traditional culture and social values and also their ancient political organizations. The various Naga tribes divided in sub-tribes and clans follow their respective traditions and social practices. What these people have in common are their history, feelings, aspirations and pains and pleasure, which they have experienced from time immemorial. Despite various anthropological and sociological researches about the origin of the Nagas, their migration, permanent settlement and nomenclature of their name as 'Naga', no reliable truth has been established so far. There are divergent views which lead nowhere in this respect. As a result, the past history of the Naga people is shrouded in mystery.

Despite all these, there is no denying the fact that the Naga society is one of the oldest tribal societies, carrying out notable set of customary practices with social, political and religious moorings. The expressions about the nomenclature, migration and occupation of the present territories by the Nagas are all based on legendary and mythological statements. The reality is that the different waves of the Naga tribes migrated to the northeastern part of India in B.C. era. Another established fact is that the Naga people belong to the Indo-Mongoloid race.[7] These Mongoloid tribes originally known as 'Non-Chinese Chiang Tribes', migrated from the central Asia in B.C. era due to inhospitable land and environment they had been occupying. First, they migrated to north-west border of China and later on they spread over to China, Indonesia, Philippines, Bhutan, Myanmar and Nagaland.[8] This view is evident from the fact that the Naga people bear similarity with some tribal groups like Dyaks and Koyans of Indo-Chinese countries. Supporting this view W.C. Smith says that the social customs and culture of the Nagas somehow resemble those of the Dyaks and Koyans—the tribal people belonging to Indonesia and Philippines. He also believed that the type of blood of the peoples of Burma (Myanmar), Sikkim, Bhutan and other hilly peoples of southern part of Asia, is akin to that belonging to the Naga tribes.[9]

Head-Hunting War and its Consequences

The head-hunting war among various ancient Naga tribes is the dark feature of the Naga society. It was this inhuman practice, which convinced the foreigners to call the Nagas uncultured, uncivilized and savage people. It is evident that various Naga tribes migrated to the hills of the northeastern part of India in different waves and occupied the vacant territories as per their convenience, earmarking the boundary lines. Though they lived adjacent to each other, they hardly tried to integrate various Naga tribes to form a common polity. Rather they remained separate and disliked each other, which indulged them in 'head-hunting wars' till the British occupied their land and forced them to stop such dirty and inhuman practice. At the same time the Christian missionaries taught them that there is no justice of murdering their own people. Perhaps it was the suspicious nature of the tribes and their separatist attitude, which could not allow them to live together. It is true that each tribe maintained its own political and social organizations based on its respective traditions and culture, but none of the tribes was ready to establish link with others and follow a common way of life. Rather they remained proud of their own respective traditional living and cultural values. Such parochial as well as separatist attitude of the ancient Nagas resulted in frequent head-hunting wars destroying the lives of thousands of innocent people.

Head-hunting war, a common feature among the ancient Naga tribes, was in fact, an ominous sign, which hardly allowed the indigenous Nagas to come together and unite to develop a common platform from where they could exercise their wisdom in the interest of the people of their own land. The head-hunting war among the Nagas was a traditional and customary practice. It was an established custom of taking human heads to prove the warriorship of the Nagas and also of the Naga tribe. The custom allowed the people of a tribe to hunt heads either in a regular warfare, raids or in a casual surprise. The custom was not only universal among the Nagas, but it had its historical base.

Such inhuman customary practice reflects two major facts. First, it reflects that the indigenous Nagas could hardly reconcile their rivals whosoever they might be. Secondly, such practice became a permanent feature due to the attitude of revenge. Peal, a British administrator, noted that there were certain causes of head-hunting war, but by no means always. According to Peal the major cause of head-hunting was: "The Nagas to obtain tattoo on body and to obtain this certificate of manhood, must present their Raja with a human head... belonging to a tribe, not related." In the opinion of Peal the purpose of the head-hunting was to establish bravery or warriorship. It had become a fashion among the Nagas having the support of the entire community. A tribe wanted to establish their superiority over others by creating terror and fear in the minds of others. It was this practice, which compelled each tribe to develop skill and tactics of warriorship to meet any such eventuality or to attack inimical tribes. Another cause of head-hunting may be to establish superiority over other tribes in the field of bravery. However, history bears the truth that no tribe attacked other tribes with a view to establishing their sovereignty over others. It shows that the early Nagas had either no idea of imperialism or disliked to assimilate with other tribes.

They practised "such inhuman act (head-hunting war) not as a part of barbarism, but they did it all to establish their warriorship over other tribes... . Moreover, such practice was followed as a part of tribal-rivalry and also to take revenge."[10] Dr Horam is of the view that the Naga used to commit head-hunting wars "to have his success first recognized, then praised, and finally awarded by the group." According to him the Nagas used "to take a head, bring it home in triumph, to be feted as a warrior, gain the privilege of wearing the coveted warrior's ornaments and at last having proved his worth and manhood, acquire a pride."[11] The practice of head-hunting never allowed the ancient Naga people to have peace. Rather it "drove them and their villages to greater isolation" and compelled them to fortify the villages for safety and security. It is evident from the fact that each early Naga village was set up at the top of the mountain well-bounded and protected by sentries who guarded the village day and night having close watch over outsiders.

The practice of head-hunting war among the ancient Nagas was, in fact, inhuman practice based on cruelty. It was this practice, which forced the Naga people to live in constant fear and terror. While attending their services in the agricultural fields, they were afraid of any eventuality and losing their heads. Even women were not spared. It was certainly a barbarous practice, which helped the British administrators and Christian missionaries to consider the Naga people uncivilized and barbarous. The ancient Nagas, no doubt carried too much social values, but such practice of head-hunting created the feeling in general that the early Nagas were uncivilized, uncultured, barbarous, rough, cruel and revengeful.

Barbarism has remained the part of the uncivilized community. A barbaric people are uncultured, cruel and shortsighted. They lack the vision. The practice of head-hunting war among the Nagas even after the arrival of the British in their land raises the question as to whether the early Nagas were really barbarous. The question is not so easy to answer. It is true that the cruel practice of head-hunting war by the Naga people forces one to form the opinion that they were barbarous. But at the same time the social organization of the Nagas and their democratic style of life overturns the former opinion. The early Nagas carried a lot of good habits and social values. Except the head-hunting war, the Naga people practised so many good things, which indicates that they knew the meaning of life and value of good life. They adopted the habit of head-hunting as a form of patriotic as well as chauvinistic heroism. It was the established means to prove heroism and earn reputation in the society. Head-hunting war was not a cause, but a fashion approved and supported by the concerned community. If there was any cause, it was to register the superiority of one tribe over others. It was this practice or habit, which made the Nagas brave and bold to fight fearlessly.

Nomenclature of the term 'Naga'

Behind the nomenclature of the term 'Naga' there are various beliefs and assumptions. According to John Butler, it was the people of the plains of India who used to call them Nagas because they were found naked. W.C. Smith is of the view that the root word of the Naga is 'Noga', which itself has been derived from the word 'Nok', which means people. It was the term Nok, which in due course of time became Naga. Sir Gait also agrees with the same view and regards the word 'Nok' as the root of the term Naga.[12] Butler and Hutton both relate the term Naga to the Hindi word 'Nanga' (naked) or the Bengali word 'Nangta'. Elwin finds the origin of the term Naga in the local tongue as 'Nok,' which means people, that is similar in Tibeto-Burman languages.[13]

However, all these views are non-acceptable to the Naga people because they were never naked. Phizo, the most prominent leader of the Naga people, believed that the word 'Naka" was the origin of the word Naga. In the Burmese language 'Na' means ear and 'Ka' means pierced—one whose ears are pierced or those who bear earrings. Since the Naga people during olden period used to pierce their ears for wearing flowers, as they were lovers of flowers, the term Naga is closely related to the Burmese word 'Noka'. This view, in fact, appears convincing and realistic.

Religious Faith of Indigenous Nagas

So far the religion of the Naga people is concerned, today, almost all the Nagas are Christian by faith. The Christianity came in North East India with the arrival of the western Christian missionaries and establishment of the British rule. It was the organized effort of the missionaries who took enough trouble and risk to bring the Nagas under the faith of the Christianity. Since there is an independent chapter on it, the facts would be discussed in detail there. Here it is notable that there is no village in Nagaland which has not got a church nicely organized and maintained. Today, the faith of the Nagas is fully determined in Christianity no doubt, but the Nagas before the arrival of the missionaries and the British in their land were animist by faith.

Animism is a kind of religion, which carries the ideal of soul or spirit. Soul has been the fundamental concept of the tribal religion all over the world. The animists are not atheists. They believe that every object has a soul. The myth, which teaches that the supreme being works and reveals mysteries through creation, is the base of animism. The ancient Naga people having strong faith in natural forces were animist by their faith. Each Naga tribe carried religious myth, which contained religious scriptures and creeds written in the minds and hearts of the people in the absence of any prescribed religion. The animism helped them not only to understand the environment and universe but also to shape their social and cultural life.

Tribal religion is basically a community religion, where individual life and community life is inseparable. Here both faith and action are interdependent. The rituals and religious practices, which developed among the different Naga tribes, are all based on the faith of animism. According to M.M. Thomas, the world view about the tribal religion is that "There is the sense of spiritual continuum within which the dead and the living natural objects, spirits and gods, the individual, the clan, the tribe, animals, plants, minerals and man form an unbroken hierarchical unity of spiritual force. The self of man is not an individual self, but an extended universal self present and actively participating in all the parts of totality."[14] Since the reasoned faculty of the tribal people under such situation was not sharp, they could hardly distinguish between sacred and the secular, between religious and non-religious, between spiritual and the material areas of the life. That is the reason that all of their cultural components were closely inter-related.

The Naga people while passing through the phase of animism, believed in a power superior to all and capable of doing anything for the good or bad. Since they believed that such power is omnipotent and omnipresent, they believed its reflection through various agencies and means such as trees, stones, ponds and mountains. That is why the ancient Nagas believed their origin through the stones or mountains and trees roots, etc. They realized the nearness of such power and adopted some forms of worship to please such force with a view to avoiding curse and obtaining blessing. That belief is floating among the Nagas even today. During the ceremonial festivals they still practise such things.

It was such belief or faith in supreme power, which moulded the Nagas towards a life of decency and discipline on the one hand and set up religious rituals and social functions on the other.

This made them habituated to worship gods, ancestral souls and natural objects. This formed the base of their moral and ethical conducts making them honest, sincere, simple and obedient. Robinson wrote that the faith of the Nagas in superior natural force brought for them "more just and adequate conceptions of the power that presided the nature." The Nagas began to feel that "There must be some universal cause to whom all things are indebted for their being. They also acknowledged the divine power to be the maker of the world and the disposer of all events."[15] The undeveloped reasoning faculty of the ancient Nagas was not in a position to enlarge the meaning of superior power and explain its manifestation. However, their faith was firm in the assumption that "If they had good and worthy lives on this earth and abstained from all coarse food and specially had abstained from eating flesh, after death their spirits would fly away into the realms above, and there became stars."[16] This statement clearly indicates that the ancient Nagas believed in continuation of the circle of life and rebirth. They also had the idea of salvation, for which one had to live the life of purity and prudence.

One of the common features of the ancient Naga people was celebration of religious rituals in common. That is why religious faith became a common faith, common practice and common celebration. While celebrating religious ceremonies all the members of a community joined their hands. They enjoyed celebrations in participating common singing and common dance, which is still practised. Common dance and common singing became common feature of the Naga community. Later on, singing and dancing became a way of life whether it was celebration of birth or marriage. Horam has rightly observed that "if dancing, singing, eating and drinking are minused from the Naga life, their life would be dull and idle."[17]

System of Governance

The basis of the ancient governing system of the different Naga tribes was the sovereign village state. Each village had developed the system of governance based on their customary laws with the purpose to manage common affairs, maintain law and order, provide justice and protect the people from alien aggressions. The political institutions, which they developed, were generally democratic in spirit because the Naga people from the beginning believed in equality, liberty and fraternity. The forms of the governance might be aristocratic, republican or monarchic, but the spirit of these governing institutions was democratic. Each village had a government comprising a Council of Elders which was chosen by the adult villagers. It was the Council which used to be responsible for village administration and to do justice to the people. The Council had the power of legislation and adjudication both. A village was established under a distinct leader who was a warrior and a man of capacity to command and protect the people.

A study of the ancient political system of the Naga people reveals the truth that they had enough wisdom to manage their affairs in the common interests and develop social values. Though they lacked the wisdom to frame a constitution, they used their customs as the code of the laws. The customs did not allow the people to defy authority. People were loyal and obedient to their rulers. This is all because the customs were based on long experienced wisdom containing enough social as well as political values. Being the head or chieftain of the village, he always remembered that he was the repository of God's favour and people's obedience. The behaviour of the rulers towards their subjects was sound and appreciable. As a custom the people obeyed the orders of the rulers "so far as they were in accordance with the customs and the wishes of the community at large." In the words of Asoso Yonuo the ruler acted "as the sagacious agent of the people". This was possible due to "age-honoured customs" which served as "a great measure of order, peace and stability to the Nagas." The customs, which were debased on collective wisdom, made the Nagas sane. Horam also writes that to the ancient Nagas "ethics were not different from religion." To the Nagas "to obey was piety; to destroy was impious, and the rule of obedience was enforced upon each individual by the will of the community to which he belonged".

There was no similarity in the system of governance among the Naga tribes. They practised different types of governance, no doubt, but they gave much significance to the spirit of democracy.

Among the Konyak, the Angs (king) possessed greater arbitrary powers whose words were treated as laws. Among the Semas, the monarchy was the form of governance. The king had the absolute power, no doubt, but there was a Council of Elders to assist him. The Angamis, Lothas, Rengmas etc., practised peculiar type of democracy with a little variation in the nature of composition of political institutions. According to Asoso Yonuo they were nominally governed by two kings or chieftains of their respective villages who were chosen for "their bravery in a war, skilful democracy, richness in the farm of cattle and land, or power of oratory in contrast to the hereditary system in which the office of the king passes to the eldest son on the death of his father."[18]

Among other Naga tribes the Ao people who are well known for the governing system based on purely democratic norms, were the first to develop well organized polity. The faith of the ancient Aos was unshakable in democracy. A study of ancient political institution of the Ao during the early period shows that among other Naga tribes the political system which the Ao community possessed, was more democratic and well advanced. It was all because their social culture was highly developed. The ancient Ao had staunch faith in the democratic principles like equality, liberty and fraternity. The ancient Ao villages were the symbols of republican form of the government. Entire social and political system of the Aos was structured under the system of Putu Menden (the Council of Elders). The system was so sound, democratic and attractive that various British administrators and authors have highly appreciated it. For instance, E. Elwin, wrote, "Each village amongst the Aos is a small republic, and each man is as good as his neighbours, indeed, it would be hard to find anywhere else more thoroughly democratic communities. Head men, Tatars, so existed but their authority are very small." Hutton, too, while appreciating the Ao's system of governance wrote, "The least that can be said of the Nagas is that in general he has mental outlook and mental process for more consistent with those of the Europeans than has the ordinary native of India."[19]

The Naga villages are the most permanent social and political unit for all practical purposes including the governance. In the past it was a miniature state having a republican form of government with a well-established Putu Menden by the chosen representatives of various clans. Among the Ao villages the Putu Menden had certain varieties, having much difference in their objectives and formations especially between the Chungli and Mongsen. Generally, the Chungli group follows a longer period tenure system based on a fixed duration of 30 years for its Putu Menden. On the other hand, the Mongsen's system of the Putu Menden is more flexible with tenure of six or five years. Moreover, in some villages of the Mongsen Ao group the Shamen Menchen system is practised which is like the Putu Menden.

Putu Menden is the highest authority of the Ao village. Putu Menden, Tatar Menden and Shamen Menden all are the same in meaning and objectives. The word Tatar means 'the chosen leader/ entitlement'. Putu means one generation that refers to a term of 30 years and Menden means a seat. Thus, the Tatar Putu Menden means "the persons who sit upon the seat of generation to rule for thirty years, where only the persons who are entitled can occupy that seat of administration."[20] The system of Putu Menden was started in the first Naga village, Chungliyimti, on the practice of meat sharing, which is followed even today among the Aos. To quote Talitemjen and Lanunungsang once more, "the fundamental basis of the Ao system of administration is based on the share of meat sharing system, which is entitled to every clan. Acceptance of a share of meat signifies the registration in Putu Menden."[21] The Mongsen group called the village governing institution as Shamen Tatar Menchen or Shamen Menchen, which means the seat of fundamental basis of meat eating/sharing.

Tatars are the members who are elected from within the village on the merit of their personal influence, ability to present a case in traditional manner and also from the 1st class citizen called 'impurchanu' (original settler) in Ao dialect. The meeting of the Putu Menden is held when majority of members is present. The continuous absence from the meeting makes him lose his seat and is replaced by others. All matters of common interests are placed before it and nothing can be done without its approval and sanction. It has the powers in various fields like legislative, executive and judiciary.

With the advent of the British rule and spread of Christianity in Nagaland, the significance of the village organizations including Putu Menden began to decline. Though the British administrators did a little interference in the local affairs of the Nagas, the new set of rules and administration, which was imposed on the Nagas by the British, attracted the Nagas towards them broadening their mind. Moreover, the Christianity which made a deep dent in the Naga society tried its level best to erode the customary practices of the Nagas making them more and more responsive to the new set of social organizations and religious faith. The new religion (Christianity) asked the Naga believers to part with all their old culture and follow the new European or American culture in almost all aspects of life. The missionaries "condemned our (Naga's) old culture as most sinful, godless and useless."[22]

Social Organisations

The Naga villages were well organized not only politically but socially also. Each Ao village had the *Ariju,* popularly known as 'dormitory' or bachelors' house, which is called as *Morong* in the Assamese language. Arr means enemies and Ju means to watch. Therefore Ariju means 'the watch place of enemy'. J.P. Mills called it as 'Public School' because it used to impart experiences of the elders and social values.[23] The institution (Ariju) served as the base of the learning place of the youths and also the meeting place of the people where they used to take vital decisions. This bears the significance of its popularity being as the oldest and strongest means of social control. It served as the agent of social security and was popular for training and disciplined personnel. That is why Talitemjen has termed it 'University or military headquarters' because of its functions, nature of training and propagation of ideas. It was also a bachelor's sleeping place where they used to get together and learn from the experience of each other. Asoso Yonuo observed the significance of the Morong as "an important educational, political and social institution" where the youngsters of the village "learn manners, discipline, art, stories, songs, war tactics, diplomacy, religious and customary rites and ceremonies living in it."[24] It had been a school for the young "to learn the art of livelihood, responsibility and cooperation before the Nagas came in contact with modern education and life."[25]

As the years rolled by and population increased, the number of the Morongs also developed. Its significance was so high that each clan developed its own Morong. Whenever a new village came into being, the Morong was constructed within the village circle and membership of this social institution was extended to all the members irrespective of their status who were at least 12 or 13 years old. Each Morong had certain groups of members according to their age group. The basic objectives of the Morong were to defend village for which training system to the youth was developed. Besides that, the members of the Morong had to perform various functions ranging from social security, civil administration, manpower training, personal development, promotion and preservation of culture, etc. The most notable fact is that the married person were not permitted to sleep in the Ao Ariju. The entrance to it for women was totally prohibited. Today, the need and significance of Ariju/Morong have declined due to changing social pattern of the Aos and also due to adoption of Christianity by them.

The most attractive social institution of the Naga people was the Morong, a commonplace of assemblage of the village youth. It also served as a village educational institution to impart social, cultural and educational values to the youth. The Morong was known by different names in different communities. In the southern group of western Angami it was called *Rensi* while in the northern group it was popular as *Azughu*. The Morong has remained the centre of traditional social life and fulfilling a number of purposes to the society. Morongs existed separately for the boys and girls. According to the practice the youngsters used to get together daily in the morong and they listened to the old legends told by the elders. The elders used to share their experiences and opinions with the young fellows. It served as a means to communicate the experience and knowledge of the people from generation to generation and prepare the youth to shoulder the responsibility in their life. For the womenfolk the morong was taboo. However, during festival days they would come with their children to the open ground in front of the morong and watch dancing and other performances from a distance.

In a real sense the Morong served multi-purpose services of the Naga society. In olden days when there was neither any school nor any educational institution, the Morong was the place of common sitting and teaching as well as meeting of the young generation. It was a sanctuary where the new young generation used to receive good sermons from their elders. The village elders used to not only tell the youngsters the happenings of the past but also teach some moral and ethical values for decent life. It was an established principle that no criminal whether of that village or a fugitive from another could be harmed in a morong. No insulting or abusive words could be used while talking in a morong. The morong was given high regard. It was like a temple of the village, which did not permit any kind of ill-will and violent acts. It was the place of piety and purity of thought and behaviour. Even a murderer could not be harmed in the morong. In the words of Malda Ganguli (1984), "Any stranger on entering a morong must be treated politely and cannot on any account be refused a night's shelter." Appreciating the value of the Naga morong, Asoso Yonuo (1975) writes that it is "an important educational, political and social institution" where the youngsters of the village "learn manners, discipline, art, stories, songs, war tactics, diplomacy, religious and customary rites and ceremonies living in it". It also has been the school for the youths "to learn the art of livelihood, responsibility and cooperation before the Nagas came in contact with the modern education and life".

Economic Base of Society

The Naga community has been rural based where cultivation and animal husbandry have been basic occupation of the people. In ancient society the land was considered as the gift of Almighty. The common properties were occupied by different villages and in due course of time those villagers who established their hold over the land and forests, claimed their private ownership. The private ownership of land in Nagaland emerged "when men cultivating plots of land obtained perspective rights for ownership of cultivable plots of neutral land. Some of the common lands were divided among the families of the clans enabling each family to have some plots of land.[26]

In the Ao area there are three types of land—common village-land, clan-land and individual family land. The common land was managed by the Putu Menden. The villageland holds large area of forest lands which are divided among each individual or every clan into specific tracts within their territory for the purpose of cultivation. Landless people are allowed to cultivate on such lands on payment of rent. Clanlands vest with the clan members of the village in perpetuity. The rights over the land pass from generation to generation and the land is held in common by the clan members as a whole. Allotment is made by the elders. The title to the individual land vests with the head of the family. These are self-acquired land. Hence the individual has the right of possession. After the death of the head of the family, the eldest son inherits the land in his capacity as the head of the family. Each type of land has its boundary. In case of any disputes regarding the boundaries of lands, the matter is referred to the Putu Menden in the presence of both the parties whose right is in jeopardy. The right to inheritance is also available among the Aos. The individual has his absolute right over his earned properties. When the individual migrate to another village permanently, he may sell his private property. However, he cannot sell out ancestral land because in such situation, he loses all his rights and title to it. But this rule is, however, not applicable to an Ao emigrant to towns and cities.[27] The notable point is that despite the right to individual land and also the right to inheritance, there was no scope for "big landlords, no extreme paupers, no millionaires, no slums and no beggars" because the concept of landlordism was yet far away among the people.[28] The society was still classless.

The Naga society has been rural based. Animal husbandry has been the basic side occupation of the people. The system of cultivation has been collective type. Barter system was rarely found. The people worshiped work and every one used to work in the field without any hesitation. No doubt, the system of private ownership existed, but not so strong. Most of the cultivated or waste land belonged to clans or villages in common. It was a belief that land was the gift of the Almighty. It was thought to be common property meant to be communally held. Due to rise and growth of more villages and increase in population the common land property was occupied by different villages and in due course of time those villagers who established their hold over the land and forests, claimed their private ownership. Thus the Naga economy, in the words of Yonuo "began with a measure of family communism and separated with a measure of rude capitalism". Among the Changs, Semas, Kukis, Lushais etc. the land belonged to the chiefs of the villages.

Private ownership of land in Nagaland according to Tajenyuba (1957) emerged: "When men cultivating plots of land obtained perspective rights for ownership of cultivable plots of neutral land. Some of the common clan-lands were divided among the family of the clan enabling each family to have some plots of land."[29] Some of the lands owned by a village became private property when the individual established his right by cultivating such land. Since there was enough land available at the time, there was no objection, which encouraged the conscious Nagas to establish his hold over such extra land. To quote once again Tajenyuba: "If any member of the family was heavily in debt and he had no personal property to pay up the debt, he transferred or mortgaged his share of common family property to cover his debt, which was thus an origin of private ownership."[30]

Thus, emergence of private ownership paved the way for growth of inequality in Naga society. Those who were landless were forced to depend upon the land-holders. On the death of the father his children were entitled to inherit the father's property equally. Hewer, this right is prohibited to the widows and daughters. The notable point is that despite the emergence of private ownership among the Nagas, there was enough scope for "big landlords, no extreme paupers, no slums and no beggers".[31] It was all because of non-existence of bourgeois nature of the property system and lack of industrialisation. Every Naga was self-sufficient. Their wants were limited and their conduct was yet honest and sincere. The concept like exploitation and high social dignity was not known to the ancient Nagas. They all were brothers and dedicated to the community life. They were God-fearing people and very much prone to the ethics like which ask us not to commit adultery, theft, robbery, stealing and speak lies. They were not cheaters. They have learnt to work hard, respect elders, help needy persons, worship God and live the life of decency. No doubt they were violent by nature, but not to the friends, but to the enemies. They practise head-hunting war, no doubt, but not against their villagers.

Mariage and Divorce

In the ancient society the husband had dominant position over the wife because the society was matrilineal and patriarchal. However, it does not mean that the position of the ladies was inferior. They were considered as the mistresses of the family. Again, monogamy has been the established norm of marriage system. Polygamy and bigamy both are totally prohibited among the Nagas. If such system is violated, the violator is severely punished. According to Talitemjen, the custom of compulsory marriage with a wife's sister or with the widow of a brother, older or younger, is not prevalent among the Aos, but the brother's widow can be married by his elder or younger brother. Similarly, a deceased wife's sister may be married by the widower.[32]

Divorce among the Nagas is permissible, no doubt, but on the valid reason. However, divorce is a rare case even today. J.P. Mills while writing about the system of divorce among the Ao Nagas, says, "Divorce is very rarely that one meets an Ao of any age who has been married only once."[33] Divorce is allowed on the grounds of death of the either party to the marriage or at the instance of the parties. The causes such as unsound mind, incurable disease, sodomy, rape, adultery, cruelty, desertion, barrenness, mutual incompatibility of temperament, taste, ideas, interest and careless management of households, are considered as the valid grounds for divorce. Adultery is regarded as a serious offence on the part of the wife as well as the husband. It is a punishable offence under the customary law. The customary law permits both the wife and the husband to look after the children after divorce, no doubt, but when they become grown up, they are regarded as the property of the father. The case of the divorce is decided first by the family members, then by the clan members in the presence of both the parties. An appeal lies in the hands of the Putu Menden who is the final authority in the matter. When the case is referred to the Putu Menden, the hearing is held in public. There is also a provision for re-marriage of the divorcee if he or she likes so. There is no fixed period to wait for re-marriage. Thus the way is opened to reunite the parties who divorced each other. The divorced women have the right to claim their maintenance.

Traditions, Customs and Rituals

Traditions, customs and conventions have remained the founding stone of the tribal society but a tribal society in which customs and traditions have been healthy and reasonable is regarded as the most advanced. In the case of the Ao tribal society it has the credit to claim its advanced and matured traditions and customs which were founded by their ancestors long ago. That is why the Ao people are proud of their traditions and customs. The whole fabric of ancient Naga society was woven in social, religious and political customs. The impact of such customs and traditions may easily be discerned even today upon the people. However, the rigidity of the customs, sometimes, creates problem. For instance, the practice of exogamy marriage among the Aos, in the words of Talitemjen, "It is a problem for young boys and girls of predominant clan to get suitable partners. And it is a fact that many of them spoil their life career."[34]

The crime of adultery and seduction are still treated with utmost severity. The offenders are brought before the assembly of the people to investigate the offence. But punishment is prescribed after full verification of the crime.

Religious customs or religious superstitions of the Nagas had no place for individuality. Participation in such ceremonies was essential for all. The faith in natural power paved the way for the emergence of various ceremonies among them where common dining, singing and dancing created the impact of unity and integrity. Such practices never disappeared from the Naga society as a whole. The Naga society which claims itself to be modern today has not separated itself totally from its ancient norms and practices, though the ancient good values have been missing to a great extent. The impact of early customary practices in their social, cultural and religious life may easily be marked even today. This is another fact that these practices are loosing the binding effect. The system of marriage among the Naga tribes has been modified, no doubt, but it still contains the relics of old practices.

Customary funeral practices among the Naga people are based on reason and religious faith. The people from the beginning believe in survival of souls even after death. That is why the dead body of a person is buried with honour and dignity. According to established practice the dead body of a man is washed by his son and then covered with white cloths. At the side of the dead body some baskets full of food-grains along with garlic are placed. Before disposing off the dead body a funeral feast is arranged generally in the afternoon. The dead body is put in the coffin along with some weapons like dao and spear. The coffin is carried to the burial place followed by the family members, relatives, friends and villagers. Besides these, many rituals are followed, which are participated by relatives and friends.

The cultural values what the Naga people have today are the common properties of their ancestral gifts. In the words of Horam, to the ancient Nagas, "Ethics were not different from religion... Every person was subject to law of tradition. To obey was piety, to destroy was impious and the rule of obedience was enforced upon each individual by the will of the community to which he belonged." The commitment to the community for the Ao was based on the idea that a community is the custodian of individual's security and safety. The community belonged to the individual and the individual belonged to the community. The community gave the individual the full freedom to express his/her will and act freely, no doubt, but at the same time every one was bound to obey the decision of the community, which was taken after full deliberations amid the presence of the elders. Describing the culture and habit of the Naga people, Puthenpurkal writes, "Once a decision is arrived at, a Naga is ready to obey it because he had great respect for his village elders and tribal chieftains."[35]

Thus, it is very much obvious that the ancestors of the Naga people possessed all the skill and arts to manage their social affairs living independently. The social and cultural values, which they possessed, were unique and useful to all. They believed in truth and honesty. Their life was simple and full of joys and enthusiasm. Cooperation, mutual understanding and straightforwardness were the way of the life of the early Naga people. They did possess neither any script for language nor any written set of religious scriptures and creeds, but they were more religious and ethical. The code of customary laws, which they had developed in due course of time, enabled them enough to live peacefully and happily. They were self-reliant and self-sufficient. They had developed the art to produce what they needed at the time. The evils like selfishness, greediness, avarice and jealousy had no place in the mind of the ancient Aos. Their wants were limited and their conduct was honest. The concept like exploitation, high social dignity and status did not exist at all in the ancient Ao Naga society. As a whole, they were God-fearing people. They were active, alert, brave, hard working and farsighted. They had no knowledge of the outside world, but they were satisfied with the world of their own.

All the cultural values and ethos of the Nagas began to disappear gradually with the arrival of the British rule and Christian missionaries in their land, which brought to them a new set of social, political as well as cultural values. In the words of Elwin, "The activities of the Baptist mission among the Nagas have demoralised the people, destroyed tribal solidarity and forbidden the joys and feasting, the decoration and romance of communal life."[36] According to Horam, Christianity while giving the Naga people new things damaged the old image and cultural values of the Naga people. It destroyed Naga's religious and cultural values, threatening family norms, social ethics and culturalreligious meanings in the name of modernisation.

With the arrival of the British rule and Christian Missionaries in Nagaland, which worked hard to modernise the Naga society, all the ancient cultural, social and religious values of the indigenous Nagas began to erode gradually. Practice of Christianity made the Naga people averse to animism, which they had been following and practising. New social values and western education damaged considerably the ancient values of the Naga society. The rise of new economic system and spread of modern education and western civilization changed the mind of new generation. The educated Nagas began to change their behaviour very fast with a view to catching up the race of modernization giving up their old social, religious and cultural values.

After India's independence and creation of Nagaland state, the scenario totally changed in Nagaland. The introduction of various Acts and Regulations by the government of Nagaland undermined the authorities of the traditional institutions to a great extent. The creation of Nagaland Village and Area Act, 1978 and the Village Development Boards Model Rules, 1980, brought about new agencies, which began to play better role than the traditional one with the result that people's faith and interest in traditional governing agencies began to decline. Today, the Putu Menden, Council of Elders etc., are still in existence, no doubt, but their earlier fervor and enthusiasm are not seen. Their roles and performances are limited to the field of welfare of the people and resolve the petty disputes in villages. The new order ushered in a period of tremendous changes. The main agent of such changes is the government itself. The impact of modernity on the Naga people as a whole has not only transformed the society affecting the old cultural values and traditional institutions but also changed the character, habits, behaviour and mind of the Nagas.

References

1. *Statistical Hand Book of Nagaland,* published by the Directorate of Information and Statistics, Government of Nagaland, Kohima, 2004, p.2.
2. *Ibid.*
3. Asoso Yonuo, *The Rising Nagas,* Vivek Publishing House, New Delhi, 1975, p.x.
4. S. Barkatki, *Tribes of Assam,* Shillong, 1968, pp.1-4.
5. W.C. Smith, *Ao Naga Tribe of Assam,* London, 1925, pp.153-60.

6. Asoso Yonuo, *The Rising Nagas, op. cit.*, p. x.
7. H.B. Horny, "The Wild Tribes of India", in Elwin's *The Nagas in the Nineteenth Century*, Oxford University Press, London, 1969, pp. 169-72.
8. *Burma Census Report*, 1991, p. 252.
9. W.C. Smith, *Ao Naga Tribe of Assam, op. cit.*, pp. 153-60.
10. Chandrika Singh, *Naga Politics: A Critical Account*, Mittal Publications, New Delhi, 2004, p.6.
11. M. Horam, *Social and Cultural Life of the Nagas*, New Delhi, 1992, p. 88.
12. W.C. Smith, *Ao Naga Tribe of Assam, op. cit.*, p.16.
13. H. Hutton, *The Angami Nagas*, Oxford University Press, London, 1969, p. 31.
14. M.M. Thomas, "Modernization of Society and Struggle for New Cultural Ethos", in *Ecumenical Review*, Vol. VII, No. 4, October 1969, p. 429.
15. W. Robinson, "A Descriptive Account of Assam", in Elwin's *The Nagas in the Nineteenth Century, op. cit.*, p. 502.
16. J. Butler, *A Note on Angami Nagas*, Vol. VI, No. 4, Calcutta, 1875, p. 504.
17. M. Horam, *Social and Cultural Life of the Nagas, op. cit.*, p.58.
18. Asoso Yonuo, *The Rising Nagas, op. cit.*, p.15.
19. V. Elwine, *Nagas in the Nineteenth Century; op. cit.*, p.324.
20. N. Talitemjen Jamir & A. Lanu Ao, *Naga Society and Culture*, Nagaland University Publication, Mokokchung, 2005, 38.
21. *Ibid.* p. 39.
22. Bendangnagshi, *Glimpses of Naga History*, Saraighat, Guwahati, 1993, p. 181.
23. J.P. Mills, *The Ao Nagas*, Oxford University Press, London, 1973, p. 5.
24. Aoso Yonuo, *The Rising Nagas, op. cit.*, p.11.
25. *Ibid.*
26. Tajenyuba, *Ao Naga's Customary Laws*, pp. 58-59.
27. N. Talitemjen Jamir, *Ao Naga's Cultural Heritage*, p. 80.

28. Asoso Yonuo, *The Rising Nagas, op. cit.*, p. 22.
29. Tajenyuba, *Ao Naga Customary Laws,* pp. 58-59.
30. *Ibid.* p. 59.
31. N. Talitemjen Jamir & A. Lanu Ao, *Naga Society and Culture, op. cit.*, 69.
32. J.P. Mills, *Ao Nagas, op. cit.*, p. 212.
33. Talitemjen, *Ao Nagas Customary Laws,* pp. 75-76.
34. Puthenpurkal, *Baptist Mission in Nagaland,* Shillong, 1948, p. 15.
35. V. Elwin, "The Aboriginals", published in the Oxford Pamphlets on *Indian Affairs,* Bombay, 1944, p. 14.

***

2

Anglo-Naga Relations

The arrival of the British and Christian missionaries in the land of the Nagas in the early 19th century ushered in a new era—a turning point in the Naga's socio-economic, political, religious and cultural history. The subjugation of the Nagas and integration of their territories to the British rule resulted in unification of the various disintegrated Naga tribes on the one hand, and spread of Christianity among the Nagas with organised churches that played greater role in transforming the early Naga society on the other. Though the British while introducing new administrative pattern interfered little in the internal affairs of the Nagas, the Naga society did not remain uninfluenced from the charm of new western pattern of life style. The confinement of the Naga people to their limited small world and their prolonged isolation from the rest of the world was for first time fully broken by the British invaders who had ventured into the hitherto forbidden land of the Nagas and command the war-like Naga tribes. No doubt, the Naga warriors tried their level best to stop the British advance in their land, but they failed because of their disunity and conventional weapons, which could hardly meet the British modern weaponry and advanced war technology. As a result, the Naga tribes, one after another, surrendered to the British forces and gradually adopted the administrative pattern imposed on them by the British rulers.

The western Christian missionaries who had already arrived in the plains of Assam made no delay to penetrate into the Naga villages and indoctrinate the animist Nagas with new faith that is Christianity. They took all the troubles in the name of Almighty to fulfill their mission. The mild and polite approach of the missionaries and their helpful and sympathetic attitude towards the semi-civilized and economically backward Nagas took not much time to befriend the war-like people and bring them under the religious order of Christianity. Thereafter, the whole matrix of the traditional Naga's concept and their social fabric began to change. This chapter presents a brief critical account of the arrival of the British in the Naga Hills and their relations with the Nagas. It also discusses about the process of modernisation of the Naga society during the British regime.

The British in Assam and their advance towards the Frontiers

The British arrived in the land of the Nagas and established colonial rule over North east India—a turning point in the political history of India. It was the Burmese invaders who provided an opportunity for the British to enter the valley of Brahmputra by invading the weakening Ahom kingdom during the first quarter of the nineteenth century. The British East India Company, which had succeeded in establishing its suzerainty over Bengal, had no mind to move towards North East India in the beginning, but persistent requests of the Ahom rulers to protect them from the onslaught of the Burmese, changed the mind of the Company's government. It was the famous treaty of Yandabo (1926) signed between the Burmese King of Ava and the British government, which forced the former to retreat from the land of the Ahoms on the one hand and paved the way for the British to extend their rule in both the plains and the hills of frontier of Assam on the other. So long as the British had not been aware of about the areas of North East India, their interest in that part was very little. Once they got acquaintance with the land and the people of the Assam, the interest of the government of the Company developed in these people and they soon decided to subjugate the people and bring their territories under the British rule. Thereafter, the process of colonization of North East India began, though slowly but steadily.

The process, which began in the early part of the 19th century, continued till it was completed. After ousting the Burmese from the land of Assam, the British government cornered the Ahom rulers on various excuses and accounts and, thereafter, they penetrated into the hills and subjugated the hill tribes one after another. It is true that in the beginning the higher British authorities sitting in Calcutta had no intention to penetrate into the interior of Assam and open new fronts with the war-like hill people, but their local officers working in Assam liked to enter into the frontiers and nip the trouble at the bud by destroying the plans of the hill people who frequently used to commit bloody raids upon the British subjects in Assam.

Discussing about the cause of the British penetration into the territories of the Nagas, Mackenzie writes: "The importance of opening up a direct communication between Assam and Manipur was at that time much insisted upon, and it was in the course of exploration directed to this end that we first came into conflict with the Nagas of these hills."[1] This compelled the government to dispatch survey parties to the Naga Hills, and confrontation began. The Nagas who did not like any sort of intervention in their affairs fought courageously with the British advance parties and caused big loss to the British. No doubt, they were subjugated, but their resistance and conflict could not be stopped with the result that the government came under compulsion to withdraw its forces from the Naga Hills and follow the policy of non-interference. This is evident from the statement of Lord Dalhousie, the then Governor-General. Expressing his dissent to the policy of interference, he wrote, "I dissent entirely from the policy of taking possession of their hills and establishing of our sovereignty over savage inhabitants. Our possession could bring no profit to us; and if would be as costly as it would be unproductive."[2] Thereafter, the policy of non-interference in the affairs of the hill tribes was followed.

However, the policy of non-interference could not prolong due to continuation of constant bloody raids upon the British subjects in the foothills of Assam. On the constant pressure exerted by the local British officers the government permitted them to precede towards the hill areas. In 1832, the British forces moved towards the territory of Cachar and by 1839, they annexed the whole Cachar to the British rule. This move brought the British "into contact with Angamis".[3] Lt. Gregory, the Officer-in-charge of North Cachar, reported to the government that "unless he was allowed to adopt more vigorous measures than what were permitted to his predecessors, he could not guarantee the safety of his sub-division".[4] The Lt. Governor Cecil Beadon, who believed in active and forward policy, expressed the apprehension that "in the course of a few years Assam would be divided among the Bhutiyas, Abores, Nagas, Garos, Mishmis and other wild tribes... ". He maintained, "If petty outrages were to be allowed by withdrawing the British from the frontier, they (British) would soon find themselves driven out of the Province."[5] Sir Cecil suggested the government that to save the situation the only way was "to reassert our authority over them (Nagas) and bring them under a system of administration suited to their circumstances and gradually to reclaim them from the habit of lawlessness to those of order and civilization".[6] The recommendations of the local British authorities were given due consideration by the government. As a result, the policy of extension of the British influence towards frontier areas began. More military posts were set up to watch the activities of the Nagas and suppress their rebellion. But the Nagas were fully determined to stop the British advance in their land.

Thereafter, no alternative was left for the government other than to follow the middle course of action whereby 'the policy of gradual extension of the British influence in the hills of the frontier was adopted. The Governor-General sought permission from the Secretary of State of India to shift the British headquarters from Chumukedima to Kohima. The permission was soon granted. Thus, the policy of interference in the affairs of the hill people once more began and a new administrative zone was created in 1866 for the Angami areas. The Nagas observing the British new policy of interference increased their hostile activities against the British. Thereafter, the government soon shifted the headquarters from Chumukedima to Kohima following the move to dispatch a number of survey parties to the Naga Hills and survey the areas including the areas of the Lothas and the Aos.

Naga Warriors and British Forces: Face to Face

All these activities of the British government invoked the Nagas and they began to oppose the British advance. The number of the Naga's raids over the plains area including the tea gardens increased to a great extent. The British posts were attacked and the survey parties were harassed. From 1874 to 1876, they plundered not less than six villages, destroyed wholly or partially the villages, which were friendly to the British. They killed 334 persons. The Nagas even killed the Deputy Commissioner of Chumukedima when he was engaged in survey work at Pangti, a Lotha Naga village. By 1877, the hostile activities of the Nagas increased to such an extent that it compelled the government to take more decisive and stern action. The Secretary of State of India, observing the reports of his officers of Assam, who demanded direct action, permitted them to penetrate into the interior and suppress Naga rebelions. In March 1879, despite stiff and tough resistance offered by the Nagas, Kohima was made the virtual district headquarters of the Naga Hills. Such move of the government made it ample clear that the government was fully determined to annex the Naga territories to the British rule. Both Wokha and Kohima were brought under the British control.

The Naga people who preferred independence and non-interference applied all the efforts to resist the British advance. Specially the Angami people waged a big war against the British, which is known as the *Khonoma battle*. The Naga warriors, who had gathered from different villages with a full determination to fight last battle with the British forces, fought bravely and harmed the British troops a lot. However, they could not win over the mighty British force and no way was left for the Naga warriors other than to bow down to the British.

The defeat of the Khonoma battle marked the end of serious troubles and hostility in the Naga Hills. The government, thereafter, became more and more tough and rough towards the Nagas. The battle strengthened the determination of the government to nip the trouble at the bud by bringing all the Nagas under the British control. Hence, the government fortified its position in the Naga Hills. People witnessed construction of more approachable roads and bridges in the areas of the Nagas. A new district was created calling it as The Naga Hills District comprising the areas from Burail on the south to Nowgong on the north. An exhaustive memorandum on the future administration of the Naga areas was prepared.[7] The memorandum talked of establishing fixed boundary in the Naga Hills area and impose permanent British rule over the Nagas. The government accepted the proposal and the Naga Hills district witnessed "the progressive establishment of peace and good order and quiet submission of the Nagas to our rule".[8]

Subjugation of Naga Tribes and Annexation of their Land

Thus by 1908, the British became the sovereign master of both the Kohima and the Mokokchung areas including Wokha. The tribes who were living in Tuensang area were also subjugated to complete the process of British colonization.[9] By 1922, the entire Tuensang area passed into the hands of the British. Thereafter, the eastern frontier of north-east became safe and secured. The government applied the efforts to bring the tribes under the British control that were living in west of Pataki and in the Hukwang Valley of Burma. These tribes were known as Singpho, Khamti, Miri, Abore etc., who are now in Arunachal Pradesh.

Before the beginning of the First World War the British government had established effective control over the hill territories of North East Frontier. Almost all the major tribes living in the frontier either willingly or unwillingly accepted the British suzerainty. The government sent numerous expeditions and survey parties to complete the process of colonization. The story of colonization of North East is full of confrontation between the war-like tribes and the British troops resulting in murder, arrest, plunder, loot and burning of the houses. The British did not like to create a buffer zone by granting them independence. Hence, it took all the risks and troubles to achieve the objective. The gallant, zealous, enthusiastic and adventurous British officers who had been posted to the frontier areas left no stone unturned to defeat the tribes and subjugate them. They performed their responsibility even at the cost of their lives. Even the snowy ranges of the Himalaya could not deter them from completing their mission. They did it all in the interest of the British Empire.

A critical study of confrontation of the Nagas with the British forces brings the fact to the light that the Naga warriors of Kohima and Mokokchung, surrendered to the British, no doubt, but after a tough fight. This is evident from the statement of James Jonstone who had himself taken part in the Khonoma battle. He writes, "The Nagas met us with heavy fire and showers of spears and stones. One of the spears struck Ridgeway and he was badly wounded in the left shoulder by a fire shot."[10] He further writes, "Though the British succeeded in defeating the Nagas, they (the British) suffered a great loss. Three British officers were killed, four wounded and forty-four rank and file were either killed or injured."[11]

Consolidation of British Rule

Under the New district the tribes like Lotha and Angami were brought under the direct British control. Thereafter, successful efforts were applied to subjugate the tribes living in the areas of Mokokchung and Tuensang. Several survey parties under the heavy military escorts entered these areas to survey the land and the people. The Ao, Phom, Konyak tribes offered resistance, no doubt, but the resistance could hardly stop the British advance. By 1908, Mokokchung was granted the status of sub-divisions of the Naga Hills district. The entire hill areas between the Dikhu and Sarai rivers comprising Borjan, Wackchung, Wanchang and Liangkha were annexed and put under the newly created Mokokchung sub-division. Thus, by 1908, the British became the sovereign master of both the Kohima and the Mokokchung areas including Wokha. The tribes who were living in Tuensang area were also subjugated to complete the process of British colonization.[12] By 1922, the entire Tuensang area passed into the hands of the British. Thereafter, the eastern frontier of north-east became safe and secured. The government applied the efforts to bring the tribes under the British control who were living in west of Pataki and in the Hukwang Valley of Burma. These tribes were known as Singpho, Khamti, Miri, Abore, etc.

Thus the British annexed the independent Naga villages to the British India and extended their control over more and more areas. In 1881, the government declared the Naga Hills as a district of British India under the province of Assam.

Thereafter, the government soon adopted the policy of friendship towards the Nagas and applied all the possible efforts to pacify them and make them understand that their progress and prosperity were interlinked with the British administration. The British administrative officers could now go about the hills unattended. They toured even distant villages and asserted their authority by establishing friendly contacts with the village headmen to whom the government had authorized to decide disputes according to the Naga customary laws.

The government appointed paid interpreters who were called *Dubhasis* (who could speak two languages) from amongst the senior villagers who were loyal to the British rule. The assignment, which was given to the *Dubhasis* was to assist the Deputy Commissioner to administer the district. According to Milan Ganguli, "These *Dubhasis* who knew Assamese or Manipuri or English and could translate local dialects into those languages, wearing their official uniform of a red flannel waistcoat and a red blanket in addition to their tribal costume, played an appreciable role in enhancing the British interest in the areas" and bringing the Nagas closer to the British authorities.[13]

The objectives behind establishing friendly relations with the Nagas was "the advancement of the commerce of the frontier" and to settle "any obstruction to a trade that the agents of Marwaris may bring" to the notice of the government. Barpujari, confirming the objective, writes: "To serve the interests, which were extensions of revenues and police jurisdiction and the speculation of European speculators beyond the boarder areas, Peace mission followed one after another to conciliate the tribes." Such policy of the government remained heartening because "even the valiant Angami chiefs entered into agreement acknowledging the authority of the government, agreeing to pay tributes and assuring to abstain from internecine feuds".[14] In return the government opened a slate depot at Dimapur. The efforts continued to befriend the Nagas by visiting their lands and making agreements with them. The Nagas according to the treaty agreed not to molest their neighbours and abstain from plundering, excursions and cutting of heads of the people. It is said that the Angami accepted the suzerainty of the British authority and allowed them to settle their internal disputes also.[15]

British Administrative Pattern For North-East India

Having full control over Assam including the hill territories, the British government divided Assam into two categories—purely plains area and hill area. The plains area was put under direct control of the British administration. Before the arrival of the British in the territories of the hill people, the tribes living there were in prolonged isolation and separation. They had a little idea about the outer world except their own. Their contacts with the Assamese living nearby boarder areas were confined only to the commercial relations. Each tribe maintained their own system of administration based on the customary laws and traditional. practices. They all preferred isolation and non-interference. Hence while determining the pattern of administration for the hill tribes the government always kept in mind their traditional practices. That is why the pattern of administration adopted by the British government for the hill people was quite dissimilar to that of the people of the plains area.

The creation of the post of Chief Commissioner in Assam in 1874 was a great landmark in the history of political administration in North-East India. In fact, this was the beginning of making Assam a province. Before the creation of the post of Chief Commissioner in Assam, the whole territories of Assam were treated as the administrative part of Bengal. After the annexation of the hill tribes to the British rule, the responsibility of the Lt. Governor of Bengal increased to such an extent that it demanded reconsideration of administrative policy of the government. Now the Lt. Governor was not in a position to provide effective administration to the people who came under his control. Hence, with a view to lightening his responsibility and giving Assam an independent administrative status, Assam was separated from Bengal in 1874, with the instruction that the system of administration of Assam would be simple and inexpensive, and the Secretary would not have the full complement of departments as staff as normally entertained by a Chief Secretary.[16]

Col. H.K. Keating was appointed as the first Chief Commissioner of Assam. The British government delegated to the Chief Commissioner all powers, which were vested in the Lt. Governor of Bengal by the direct operation of an Act of Governor-General-in-Council, which also conferred the same powers on the Chief Commissioner of Oudh, the Central Provinces and the British Burma. In other districts of Assam including the Shurma Valley and hill districts, the Chief Commissioner continued to perform himself the duties of a Commissioner who used to act as the Chief Executive Officer.[17]

According to Mackenzie "on this frontier (North-eastern) the policy has been from the beginning not a policy of 'coercion' and 'contemptuous devastation' as it has been sometimes erroneously described, but a firm and kind policy of defense and conciliation".[18] It is true, the government occupied these areas keeping in view the strategic significance of the areas for safety and security of the British Empire in India. The government wanted to maintain friendly relations with the hill tribes. That is why it did not want to disturb the traditional set-up of the hill tribes. What the government did for administrative adjustment for the hill people was promulgation of certain Acts and Regulations, which provided summary legislation and little administrative interference in their local affairs. It was this administrative policy of the British government, which is being preferred even by the government of India today. The hill tribes of North East India are still enjoying maximum autonomies approved by the Constitution of India.

The Inner Line Regulation, 1873, which empowered the Lt. Governor of Assam to earmark the Inner Line, was brought into effect with the marked objective to please the Hill tribes and put them in confinement. According to the provisions of the Inner Line Regulation no British subject could go beyond a certain frontier that was drawn along the foothills of the North eastern and south-eastern boarder of the Brahmputra Valley. If any one wanted to cross the Line, he/she had to obtain gate-pass from the government officials not below the rank of a magistrate. The territories which came under the Inner Line were treated as the special areas and government made separate administrative provisions for them. The Regulation empowered the Governor to make summary legislation and also the power to frame rules for the tribal peoples according to the needs and circumstances.[19]

The district of Nagaland was constituted in 1861 and it was made over to the charge of the newly Chief Commissioner of Assam in 1874. First, the government was in favour of bringing only strategic areas of the Nagas under the British rule, but considering the reports of its officers, it changed the mind and brought entire territories of the Nagas under the district.

A study of the government's correspondence reveals the truth that it were the local British officers who recommended the higher government to incorporate all Naga tribes to the British rule. For instance, the Chief Commissioner of Assam wrote the government that "We shall have no real peace until we have absorbed the whole hill areas between this and the Chindwin."[20] The letter, which was sent to the Secretary of State in England stated that "The Naga Hills district was in frontier area and the officers of this state control the tribes just across the frontier, the line of control should be extended."[21] The government accepted the recommendation with the result that the whole Naga areas came under the British rule.

In 1898, the province of Assam was created separating the whole of North-East India and put under it. The Chief Commissioner still remained the chief administrative officer of newly created province. In 1905, the period of Lord Curzon witnessed some major administrative changes made in Assam. Lord Curzon combined the eastern districts of Bengal with Assam and constituted a new Province, which was called as the Province of Eastern Bengal and Assam. However, such administrative provision could not last and in 1912 one more major change was brought in the administrative pattern of Assam by restoring it to its former position. Assam became a Governor's province only in 1921 in accordance with the provisions of the Government of India Act, 1919.

During the administration of the Chief Commissioner in Assam, the Chief Commissioner assumed enormous administrative powers. The government of India "delegated to the Chief Commissioner all powers, which were vested with the Lt. Governor of Bengal by the direct operation of an Act of Governor-General-in-Council, which also conferred the same powers on the Chief Commissioner of Oudh, the Central Provinces and the British Burma". Each district was provided with a Deputy Commissioner supported with Additional Deputy Commissioner and Extra Assistant Commissioner. It is to be noted that such administrative system, in the beginning, was applicable to the plains districts of Assam, not the hill districts. In the hill districts and in certain frontier tracts such as the North Cachar Subdivision, the Mikir Hills Tract in Nowgong, and the Dibrugrah Frontier Tract in Lakhimpur, some differences were made in judicial and financial administration. In these areas the high court possessed no jurisdiction except over European British subjects. The hill districts were formerly under the operation of the Deregulation District Act XXII of 1869, which was repealed by the Scheduled District Act XIV of 1874. Subsequently, the Frontier Tracts Regulation II of 1980 was passed. This empowered the Deputy Commissioner with previous sanction of the Governor-General-in-Council to direct that any enactment in force in any Frontier Tracts "shall cease to be in force therein and this Regulation (with the additional power of extension conferred by Regulation III of 1884) has been brought into force in all the hill districts and Frontier Tracts referred to above".[22]

The Chief Commissioner himself was the chief appellate authority in civil and criminal cases. The Deputy Commissioner exercised the combined powers of District and Session judges and magistrate of the district. The Assistant Commissioner and the Extra

Assistant Commissioner enjoyed the powers of magistrates and *munsifs*. In the hill areas the judicial administration in all petty civil and criminal cases was carried on by the village tribunals, presided over by the village headman who was chosen from among the village people themselves. The procedure of the village tribunals was free from legal technicalities.[23]

So far the revenue administration was concerned, in the beginning, the hill districts were kept away from any kind of taxes except house tax. But in the Garo Hills and a small area in the Jaintia Hills and the Naga Hills there were tracts where land revenue was imposed. The Mauzadars were the agencies to collect the taxes or revenues. The house tax in the hill districts such as the Garo Hills, the Jaintia Hills and the Naga Hills was collected and paid by the village headmen who "like Mauzadars of the Assam Valley" are remunerated by a commission. "These officers are called Lashkars and Lakmas in the Garo Hills, Dollis and Sardars in the Jaintia Hills and Khasi Hills, Lumbardars in the Naga Hills, and Mauzadars in North Cachar Hills."[24]

So far the police administration was concerned, in each of the plains district there was an officer who was called District Superintendent or an Assistant Superintendent of Police. These officers formed part of the Bengal staff of police officers. In the report of the Assam government it is recorded that in addition to these officers whose work was to superintend the prevention and detection of crime, there was a small staff consisting of one civil and three military police officers, who under the designation of Commandants of Military Police controlled the division of the Assam police force, which performs semi-military duties in manning the frontier outposts. This division of force "besides being subject to Act V of 1961, is under a special Regulation (the Assam Military Police Regulation, 1890), which makes provision for the enforcement of due discipline, and assimilate generally the terms of service to those prevailing in the native army".[25]

Creation of Naga Hills District

The district of the Naga Hills was formulated as early as in 1861 but it was "made over to the charge of the newly appointed

Chief Commissioner of Assam in 1874.[26] The formation of a full-fledged district of the Naga Hills was an important land mark in the history of the relations of the Nagas with the British. It has already been discussed that the downfall of the Nagas at the battle of Khonoma, had enabled the British to bring whole of the Naga territories under the British control. In 1879, Charles Elliot, the Chief Commissioner of Assam, prepared an exhaustive memorandum on the future administration of the Naga Hills. He proposed the laying down of a permanent boundary and division of the district for the convenience of the administration without giving any heed to the location of the tribes with the result that those new administrative boundaries divided the tribes. There were several Naga tribes who were left in Manipur, Cachar and Myanmar. The legacy of such fault of administrative division of the government has created a big problem in the north-eastern states even today. The Nagas have been constantly putting pressure upon the government of India to integrate all the Naga tribes under a single administrative pattern of Nagaland government.

Elliot favoured the imposition of house tax, appointment of village headman and the opening of dispensaries, village schools and other possible facilities for the well-being of the Nagas to win over their hearts and obtain cooperation.[27] He also directed the British officers and his assistants to maintain direct contact with the Nagas by visiting their respective villages.[28] Elliot's proposal and direction reveal the truth that he was in favour of bringing the western and central portions of the Naga Hills as settled district in the new province of Assam. The proposal of Elliot was approved by the government with the result that the portions earmarked were put under the Naga Hills district including the Angami and Lotha areas.

It has already been discussed that the British government in due course annexed the areas occupied by the Nagas, which were yet beyond the control of the government on certain excuses. The British officers wanted that all these Naga villages must be brought under the British rule keeping in view the administrative convenience and broader interests of the government. As a result, the Deputy Commissioner of the Naga Hills district started correspondence with the government in this regard.[29] Davis, the

Deputy Commissioner, wrote to the government, "If the control area be not extended to include the whole Sema tribe, then the rule prohibiting the Deputy Commissioner from crossing the border without formal permission should be relaxed, as it is very necessary that he should be able to settle cases brought by people within the control area against people living outside it." He further wrote: "The prohibition rule has... led to a deplorable amount of bloodshed and numerous murderous outrages just across our frontier, which would not have occurred if the policy of the pre-Yichumi (Sumi) days had been followed of recent years."[30]

The government accepted the proposal of Davis with the result that the boundary line of the Naga hills district was extended, which affected a long strip of country from Yeim in the north along the line of the Tizu, which became its junction with the Hipu, the boundary of the administered area down to Shohemi on the south.[31] Thereafter, Major Cole, who had been the Deputy Commissioner of the Naga Hills district, suggested the government in 1907, "The only sensible thing to do was to accept as inevitable the ultimate absorption of all unadministered territory between India and Burma (Myanmar); if our advances in this direction to be gradual, they should be at any rate be constant and sooner the thing was faced the better."[32]

Davis, the then Deputy Commissioner of the Naga Hills district, was of the view that there would be no real peace "until we have absorbed the whole hill areas between this (British occupied area) and the Chindwin". Hence he suggested the government to do the absorbing 'gradually and economically'. The government of India, realizing the significance of the suggestions of its officers, recommended the case to the Secretary of the State in London, but the latter declined to open new frontier and to go to such an extent. However, the British officials sitting in Assam and the Hills did not loose the courage and hope. They went on pressurizing the government in this regard.

The government of Bengal and Assam were of the view that until the whole of the Naga areas were not included in the British territory, it was impossible to maintain law and order there. So they continued their efforts to pressurize the government in this regard. The proposal was once more made to "include the whole country lying between Dikhu and the Safrai rivers".[35] In 1908, again a proposal was made in which "the inclusion of an extended area covering the whole of that part of the sub-division (Mokokchung) now lying between the Dikhu and its present north-east and south boundaries including such places as Borjan, Wakching, Wanching and Lonkhim was recommended".[34] The government, thereafter, took up the initiative to consolidate the British rule over each and every Naga village. The process continued till the process of colonization of the Naga Hills was fully completed.

Declaration of Hill Districts as Excluded Area

By the second decade of the 20th century, the government succeeded in establishing its rule over most of the parts of the North-eastern frontier. The government very cautiously and effectively dealt with the tribes while imposing the British administration over them. Several new posts were opened and some new important roads were constructed to link these tribes and develop trade and commercial relations. The officers posted to the areas were strictly instructed to maintain good relations with the hill people and ensure that their sentiment and emotions were not affected. That is why the hill people—either of the Naga Hills or Lushai Hills or of frontier tracts—they all began to appreciate the British rule and willingly extended the hands of friendship with the British accepting their suzerainty.

By 1919, administrative changes were made in the Naga Hills district under the Government of India Act 1919 on the basis of recommendation of the Montague-Chelmsford Report, which had recommended some more reforms in the hill areas. It was suggested that the typically backward tracts of Assam should be excluded from the jurisdiction of the reformed control. It meant the legislative council was to be debarred from having any legislative authority either to enact "legislation or to make a resolution for the area declared excluded". Legislation for such areas was to be effected entirely by means of Regulations. Robert Reid and Barnes had strongly recommended for the exclusion of the frontier areas from the said scheme. The Function Committee, too, wanted to divide the hill areas into two categories—the wholly excluded areas and the partially excluded areas. It further mentioned that the areas wholly excluded should be under the control of the Governor and the legislation for this area should be effected through Regulation only. Regarding the partially excluded area it was said that it would be administered by the Governor-General-in-Council. All these suggestions were incorporated in the Act of 1919.

In January 1921, the Governor-General-in-Council declared that the administration of these areas would be directed by the Governor-General-in-Council and the Governor would make any modification in the administration of the tracts and districts. No minister was made responsible for the administration of the Backward Tracts and Districts. Thus, it is obvious that the British government declared the hill districts and frontier tracts as Backward Tracts. Thereafter, the government of India under the authority of the aforesaid Act passed the Government of India (Excluded and Partially Excluded) Order, 1936, which declared and specified the Excluded and partially excluded areas of the Province of Assam. The Part-I of the Schedule to the Order consisted of the Excluded Areas and Part-II contained the Partially Excluded Areas. The North-East Frontier consisting of the Sadidya, Balipara and the Lakhimpur Tracts was brought under the Part-I. As a result, the administration of these Tracts remained out of the purview of the Central and the state legislatures. The Governor of Assam as a representative of the Government of India assumed full responsibility to administer the areas with the help of the political officers and the Deputy Commissioners. The Excluded Areas consisted of the areas, which were mostly backward and there was no possibility at all to practise advanced form of administration. That is why neither any minister nor the legislature was given any authority to administer these areas. In the case of the partially excluded areas where people were not as backward as that of the former, the legislative assembly was not debarred from discussing their matters. It was given authority to discuss the tribal matters with the prior permission of the Governor. Moreover, it totally depended upon the Governor of Assam whether he liked to implement any legislative Act in the Partially Excluded Areas. The

Governor was given the discretionary power to decide whether provincial Act should be applied or not, with certain modifications in the Act in the tribal belt of the Partially Excluded Areas.

Before the independence of India, the Indian Independent Act, 1947, passed by the British parliament provided that all parts of the province of Assam should be governed as nearly as might be in accordance with the Government of India Act, 1935, the Order-in-Council and other Instruments made there-under. As a result, the special responsibility of the Governor disappeared. Hence from 15th august 1947, the administration of the Excluded and Partially Excluded Areas was entrusted to the government of India. The Indian Provincial Constitution Order, 1947, provided that "The Governor-General shall by order make such provisions as appears to him necessary or expedient for making commissions or additions to, and adoption and modifications of, the Government of India Act, 1935 in the application to the separate new provisions." Thus, the independent government of India got full authority to make any political or administrative or territorial adjustments in the territories of the North Eastern frontiers.

Proposal to Exclude Naga Hills from rest of the Country

No doubt, the tribal people of North East India had not much contact with the people of the plains. It is also a fact that their cultures, behaviours, dialects, and faiths totally differed from that of the plains people of India. By their nature the tribal people did not like any outside interference in their local affairs. The provisions what the British government made for them to exclude them from the main stream of administration, should be appreciated in the sense that those protected them from undue interference. But it is also true that the British did not want that the national freedom movement, which was going against the British rule in the country, might influence the hill people and provide them opportunity to participate in freedom struggle creating troubles for the government. There was someone who wanted to separate the hill people of North-East India from the rest of the country.

The Christian missionaries were actively engaged in these areas to cultivate the English culture and assimilate the people in that culture. They were trying their level best to convert the tribal people into Christianity. The hill people preferred separation because it was in their nature. Moreover, their prolonged isolation had made them sensitive and suspicious towards the Indians. Some of the British officers showing undue sympathy towards these people, instigated them against the plains people. The purpose of promulgating the Inner Line Regulation and prohibiting the plains people from free entry into the hill areas was a sinister design of the British administrators to keep the hill people away from any influence of the plains.

J.C. Johari has rightly observed: "The British masters designed their intriguing policy of saving the hill people scattered over Tirap and Tuensang Divisions of the North-East Frontier Agency (NEFA), who had been living in their tribal isolation with little contact with the outside word, from the growing impact of the freedom movement under the Congress leadership by means of seeking their gradual but steady proselytisation as the best way to make them the loyal members of their misconceived 'Crown colony.'[35] It was Robert Reid, the Governor of Assam, who had proposed the plan of Crown Colony comprising the Naga Hills, North-East Frontier Tracts and Chittagong Hill Tract of East Bengal. However, the Labour government of England did not accept such ruinous proposal of Robert Reid specialy at the time when it had to vacate India.

Secondly, the British officers living in the hills misguided the hill people telling them that they would not be liked by Indian Hindus and Muslims because the tribal Christians took beef and pork while the Hindus disliked beef and Muslims pork. Robert Reid, the then Governor of Assam, went to that extent saying: "We have no right to allow this great body of non-Indian animistic and Christians to be drawn into the struggle between the Hindus and Muslims which is now and will be in future, with ever-increasing intensity, the dominating factor of politics in India proper."[36]

Thus, all these mischifs of the British officials regarding the status and political future of the hill people of North-East India misguided them and they began to feel that they were separate people and they had nothing to do with the rest of India. Their apprehension that they would be treated badly by both the Hindus and Muslims of independent India, made them more suspicious and skeptical towards India. Their attitude towards India and the Indians became unfriendly. This idea was rooted in their mind that they must have separate political status of their own if they wanted to live freely and independently. That is why when the Simon Commission came to India with the purpose to study the existing administrative patterns and suggest modifications for future political as well as administrative changes, the issue of the hill of the North-East India also came on the forefront. The Naga people began to demand a separate political status. They submitted memorandum demanding separate political status for them.

Impact of the British Rule on the Nagas

With the advent of the British rule and spread of Christianity in Nagaland, the significance of the village organizations including Putu Menden began to decline. Though the British administrators did a little interference in the local affairs of the Nagas, the new set of rules and administration, which were imposed on the Nagas by the British, attracted the Nagas towards them broadening their mind. Moreover, the Christianity made a deep dent in the Naga society and tried its level best to erode the customary practices of the Nagas making them more and more responsive to the new set of social organizations and religious faith. The new religion (Christianity) asked the Naga believers to part with all their old culture and follow the new European or American culture in almost all aspects of life. The missionaries "condemned our (Nagas') old culture as most sinful, godless and useless".[37]

The arrival of the British and the introduction of the British administration in the Naga Hills created immense impact on the life of the Nagas in all aspects. The Nagas, who came in close contact with the British way of life and living, became apt in changing their traditional way of life. The close association of the Naga people with the white people tempted the former to follow English way of life including their habits and style. The new generation of the Nagas became more and more prone to British customs. Changes took place in the ordinary dresses of the Nagas.

To wear half-pants, long pants, petticoats etc., became a fashion among the Nagas and they began to show aversion towards their traditional garments except during the period of festivals and ceremonies. The conservative Nagas became worried about gradual disappearance of their cultural life. Modern education taught them how to maintain new way of life and new economy made them able to maintain modern living standard. Introduction of new political structure and laws, the setting up of new administrative headquarters in towns, a new economic system and new fiscal practices provided speed for modernization in the Naga Hills. Administrators, military and police personnel, technicians, bureaucrats, businessmen, engineers, contractors, workers etc., further gave impetus to the growth of modernization and helped enough to change the traditional life of the Nagas. In the words of B.P. Singh, "Familiarization of these tribes with new ideals, coupled with the subsequent independence and democratization of the polity have taken them into the modern world, with all its strengths and dangers."[38]

Prior to the colonial administration and establishment of institutional schools, written form of any script was unknown to the Naga people. If they had any education, it was all informal. The introduction of colonial education introduced the their new generation with new values, no doubt, but at the cost of disruption of the indigenous system of learning and redirected them to the new pattern of modern education much more inclined towards secularism. According to Elwin, the introduction of modern education had substantial influence on the socio-cultural life of the Nagas. New syllabus taught in the schools set up by the government and the missionary people broadened the mental make-up and vision of the Naga people. The educated Nagas began to understand the differences as well as usefulness between traditionality and modernity. The social system, in which they had been living since time immemorial, became useless to the Naga people under the light of new social system. They wanted to go for a new lifestyle which they were now accustomed to. Their old habits and faith began to change fast.

With the advance of trade and commerce, their needs increased. To serve the increased needs the Naga people developed close contact with the plains people while doing business. Traditional style of the Nagas began to disappear. The newly constructed administrative establishments, houses and bungalows made the affluent Nagas enchanted towards new style of life supported with modern material facilities. The industrial products and textile clothes changed their choices. Moreover, the Naga society witnessed first time differences between the rural and urban life. The growth of towns attracted the villagers to shift towards urban areas for better life based on modern facilities. Such moves helped urbanization. Small towns or business centers appeared with new varieties of things. Marketing developed on the land of the Nagas. These were the things, which they had never seen. They wanted to use the materials which could give them more comfort and pleasure. Changes took place in architecture, arts, designs and house construction.

The primitive technology of food production, dyeing, weaving and construction of houses also began to change. The Naga people keeping aside the local loom-made cloth began to prefer factory produced cloth. They began to discard those things and goods which were directly produced from the soil and replaced them with factory made goods. The wooden and bamboo cups and plates and other utensils were replaced by manufactured goods made from aluminum. Mentioning about changing cultural pattern of the Ao Naga, J.P. Mills writes, "Nowadays the breaking down of old customs under the influence of the American Baptist Mission and the establishment of the Fuller Technical school at Kohima, have led to the starting of a considerable number of small smithies in the Ao country."[39]

Under the administrative patterns mentioned above, the hill territories of North-East India grew up. In due course, some sub-divisional headquarters were set up. The government appointed *Gauburahs* and *Dobhasis* (the persons having the knowledge of English and local tongues) to have links with villages. The government adopted friendly relations with the Nagas and tried to reach them. The Naga people who had opposed the British advance in their land, over time, became staunch supporters as well as appreciators of the British people and their rule. They took the British and their rule as blessings in disguise.

Their association with the British officers became very much close. The *Gauburahs, Dobhasis,* teachers, low rank Naga government servants and educated Naga people were the first who came in close contact with the British officials and the western Christian missionaries. The pastors of the churches also came in close contact with the British. They all got maximum support and sympathy from the government. The mild and friendly behaviour of the British government and its officers with the Nagas created fertile ground and favourable circumstance for the British to go nearer. Their (Nagas') praise for the British had no bound. They forgot all bitterness and enmity towards the British and the British rule. They began to appreciate the government. The Christian missionaries, too, played vital role to bring the Nagas near to the British. Thus the relations with the British and the Nagas became friendly and smooth.

An analytical study of the relations of the hill people with the British government brings out the fact that the arrival of the British and Christian missionaries in the land of the Nagas and their efforts to indoctrinate the Naga people with new faith and new style of life created immense impact upon the people. It marked a turning point in the Nagas' socio-economic, political, religious and educational history. The subjugation of the various Naga tribes and integration of their territories to the British rule resulted in unification of the various disintegrated Naga tribes on the one hand, and learning of a new socio-politico and prestigious order supported with well organized bureaucracy caused major changes not only in attitudinal and behavioural pattern of the Naga life but also in their social structure. The confinement of the ancient Naga people with their small world and their prolonged isolation from the rest of the world was for the first time fully broken by the British rulers who ventured to break through the hitherto forbidden land of the war-like tribes.

In Nagaland the British officers left everlasting impact upon the Naga people. The close association of the Naga people with the British sharpened their mind and broadened their approach. The consolidation of various scattered Naga tribes under the single pattern of administration served as a better device to integrate these people. The parochial approach of the Nagas began to disappear. First time, they came in contact with the Europeans. They had little knowledge about outside world except some portions of Assam. Before the arrival of the British in Nagaland, there was no system of education except the Morong where oral teaching regarding the practical life was given among the youths by the Naga elders. The British government along with the missionaries opened some primary schools in some of the areas, but not with intention to impart general education among the Nagas, but to produce the clerical staff to assist the British administration. In conformity with this fact, Aoso Yonuo wrote that the government introduced western system of education to bring the Nagas in touch with modern civilization and "to use educated class as a link between the ruler and the ruled."[40] Moreover, progress of education till 1908 was not encouraging. In 1903-04, there were one secondary, 22 primary and 2 special schools in the Naga Hills district. More than two-thirds of the students were only in the primary schools. The number of the students in the schools in 1890-91, 1900-01 and 1903-04 was 297, 319 and 647 respectively, which was very much less compared with the population of the district. According to 1901 census report, the literacy of the Naga Hills district was only 1.03%. The medium of instruction was English and the students directly or indirectly were related to the Christian missionaries. The missionaries played a vital role in spreading education and new culture among the Nagas, who were beguiled to denounce their old cultural values and ethos. Since there is a separate chapter on the role of education in changing the Naga society, it is enough here to say that new education which came in Nagaland along with the British and Western Baptist Christian missionaries played a vital role in transforming the traditional Naga society.

In the pursuit of establishing good relations with the Naga people and to give them "good advice for the peaceful settlement of any dispute that might have come up and sometimes, distributing presents just to keep the Nagas in good spirit", the government appointed Gauburahs and Dubhasis by prescribing certain monthly salaries for them. The government also followed the policy of non-interference in their customary laws and traditional behaviour with the purpose to please the Nagas. However, the British government and the missionary people applied certain methods, which gradually created bad impact upon their cultural and social values.

The Naga people who had been accustomed to the habit of 'head-hunting war, first time realized its menace and its futility after coming in contact with the white people only. They knew that what they were following with pride and valour was nothing but their barbarity only. Under the impact of new education and modern view they realized that this was a black spot on the ancient culture of the Naga people. So they totally abstained from such wild and dangerous habits. Moreover, under the realisation that all the Naga tribes bear the same origin and belong to the same race, the different tribes who had been bitter enemy of each other, came close and became sympathetic to each other. This was all due to broadening of their parochial approach under the regime of the British. While participating in the First and Second World Wars many of the Nagas had got the opportunity to visit several nations in Asia and Europe where they met and interacted with different people. That broadened their mind and enabled them to understand the real meaning of life.

Thus, it is obvious that the arrival of the British and spread of Christianity in the land of the Nagas ushered in a new era where the Naga people got acquainted with new things, which they had never known. No doubt, the impact of westernization destroyed some good ancient values of the Naga people, but what they got was greater than what they lost. With the arrival of the British in their land their understanding really changed. They realized the futility and meaninglessness of wild faith as well as wild behaviours. They got the opportunity to join with the advanced people.

The educational institutions began to produce a class of educated Nagas who obtained the concept to differentiate the past and present values of the Nagas. Education, in fact, liquidated all the outdated taboos to advance their career in various branches of learning. The Ao people who first came in close contact with the British and understood the value of new life took all the troubles to educate their children even sending them out of the Naga Hills for higher studies. With the changing opinion and attitude, realisation came to these people that the devotion to education was the only way to get rid of backwardness. It was a new institutionalized educational system which paved the way for close association of the Nagas with the western people, opening a new chapter in the history of the Naga people. Education and their contacts with the Europeans sharpened their parochial attitude and broadened their way of thinking. The world with which the Nagas were introduced was far greater than the world in which they had been living for centuries. They began to understand the meaning of civilization. They became ready to take all the troubles to join their hands with new civilization. The rules and administration provided by the British government brought various Naga tribes under a single pattern of administration where their common political consciousness grew.

Changing Political Consciousness

The British rule and administration in the Nagaland made the Nagas to keep united under a single pattern of administrative set-up. No scope for disintegration was left out at all. The tribes who had been living separately maintaining their respective identities, began to feel that they were one and they all belonged to the same blood. Their parochial attitude and chauvinistic heroism began to disappear that led to the growth of their unity. Time came soon when the Naga people came in close contact with each other extending the hand of brotherhood and friendship. New idea for a larger Naga Hills substituted the traditional political concept of tiny sovereign village state. The authority of chieftains or village headmen declined. The Village Council and the Council of Elders remained in existence, no doubt, but with little significance.

The close association of the Naga intellectuals with the British officials made them aware about their future political status. Some of the British officials being more sympathetic to the cause of the Nagas began to instigate them against the mainstream of the Indian nationalism. And that made them worried about the future political status of the Nagas after the departure of the British from India. By the thirties of the 20th century several Nagas had received higher education and by that time they had learnt more about the world. Hence a national feeling emerged among them and they began to work for the unity of the Nagas. The Naga Club, which came into being in 1915 with the main objectives of "promotion of understanding, development of fraternal feeling and unity among the Nagas", began to serve as the first political platform for the educated Nagas. Piketo Sema has rightly remarked that the Naga Club "provided the needed social and political foundation to the Naga tribes and was symbolic of the emerging or rather incipient sense of solidarity among the Nagas".[41]

The Naga Club assumed the shape of Naga National Council (NNC) and became instrumental in formulating the Naga political policies and organizing the people to raise the voice in favour of their formulated policies related to the future political status of the Naga people after the departure of the British from India. The leaders of the NNC had direct patronage of the British officials who helped them enough to sharpen their political consciousness. It was C.R. Powsey, the Deputy Commissioner of the Naga Hills, who had helped the Naga intellectuals to constitute the NNC and work for the Nagas' unity and strength. The leaders of the NNC who belonged to almost all the Naga tribes, had submitted the memorandum before the Simon Commission in 1929, expressing the feeling that the Nagas had "much fear of introduction of foreign laws and customs to suppress over own customary laws". Hence, the Naga intellectuals demanded "safeguards" from the government.[42] The memorandum submitted by the NNC to the Simon Commission explicitly stated that the Naga Hills should be withdrawn from the reform scheme and moreover be kept directly under the British government and the Nagas should be permitted to determine their political future when the British left the Naga Hills.

As the years rolled down the Naga unity and strength was strengthened. Their political consciousness developed to a consideration extent. They had understood what nationalism was. Hence during the time of the British departure from India the Naga intellectuals became more and more active to plead the cause of the Nagas' future political status. The NNC being the only symbol of the their unity became more active to fight for the cause of the

Naga political future. On June 19, 1946, it passed resolutions at Wokha stating that "The NNC stands for the solidarity of all the Naga tribes including those of the unadministered areas." It further stated: "The Naga Hills should be continuously included in an autonomous Assam in a free India, with local autonomy and due safeguards for the interests of the Nagas and the Naga tribes should have a separate electorate".[43]

The activities of the NNC showed that the Naga leaders had become matured. Their vision had been broadened. By then they had become more farsighted. They wanted their political identity independent of others' direct or indirect influence. It is evident from the statement of the declaration of the NNC, which *inter alia* said:

> "The NNC stands for the unification of all Naga tribes and their freedom... Our country is connected with India, connected in many ways. We should continue that connection... We shall enjoy home rule in our country, but on broader issues reconnected with India. We must fight for it, we must get it, keep on watching."[45]

Thus, it is very much obvious that the British rule for the Nagas proved a blessings in disguise. The Nagas who opposed the British advance in their land by tooth and nail, became the followers of not only the British people but also their living style and way of life. By mid 20th Century they had totally changed. New generation of the Nagas got enchanted with the charm of western civilization. English as a language was given due place in the Naga Hills.

The British people did a lot to bring the Nagas at the threshold of modernity by changing their attitude and behaviours. It is true that it were the British who integrated the scattered and disunited Naga tribes and taught them the lesson of unity and strength. But it is also true that the British government who occupied the land of the Nagas did nothing notable for economic development of the poor and backward Naga tribes. The British came to the land of the Nagas and established their rule over these semi-civilized people not to make them advance, but to control their perpetual habits of raids and make the north-eastern frontiers safe and secured.

The economic life of the early Nagas was based on cultivation and husbandry. They produced food materials, no doubt, but they had no alternative to earn money. They lacked professionalism other than cultivation. Economic development is the essential part of modernity. The Nagas found themselves at the threshold of modernity, but without proper means to avail the modern facilities. The British government made no plan for their economic development. There was no budget allocation for the development of the village and villagers, except that some of the villages were linked with *kacha* roads. No system was developed to grant loan to villagers or establish departments related to development of rural areas, agriculture, irrigation, soil conservation, industries, etc. The British government hardly took the trouble to establish higher educational institutions supported with financial aids. Besides there were no proper medical facilities.

The economic conditions of the Nagas who availed the opportunity to serve the British government, prospered, no doubt, but that too with limitation. Most of the youths remained unemployed because no avenues for employment were opened. The economic conditions of the villagers did hardly get any change. They could not avail the opportunity to arrange education for their children due to their poor economic conditions. They were not able to send their wards to the towns for education. No doubt, social, economic and political consciousness of the Naga people changed, but not to the villagers living in remote areas. Even the light of education could not reach the remote villages. Hence to the people living in the far flung villages social and economic changes could have no impact. They still followed traditional way of living.

Different disintegrated Naga tribes came closer with the feeling that they are one and they must live together, no doubt, but this feeling was confined to the educated Naga leaders. Tribalism in the name of superiority of tribes still remained embedded in feeling and attitude of the general Nagas. Thoughts for Nagas' unity began at the political platform. The more politically conscious and educated Naga leaders joined their hands to bring the people together, but the task was not so easy. Each tribe had a history of its own and every one of the tribe was very much proud of their past history. They all wanted to preserve their separate identities. The old bitterness and enmity among the tribes had still left scars in the heart and mind of the people. There were tribes who had been far behind in the pace of civilization and development. The advanced tribes wanted to maintain their superiority over the backwards. Hence it was a Herculean task to unite the Nagas and to teach them the meaning of nationalism and prepare them to follow the call of unity given by their leaders. Even among the leaders the feeling of superiority and inferiority continued. However, it is heartening to note that the process of Naga unity at least began under the care and control of the Nagas who were worried about their future political status giving not much thought to economic development.

The days of the British departure were approaching and the Naga leaders were growing more impatient. They were determined to have their independent political identity while the government of India was not ready at all to grant the Nagas to fulfill their political wish with the result that the future course of political activities in the Naga Hills, which followed soon after the British departure, proved injurious to both the government of India and the Naga people as a whole. This fact has been discussed in a separate chapter.

In conclusion it may be said that the arrival of the British in the Naga Hills and their close contact with the Naga people changed the social, cultural, economic, political and religious history of the state to a considerable extent. It paved the way for modernization and urbanization of the Naga society and enabled the Naga people to stand together and fight for a better common cause. It changed their old habits and behaviours. The Nagas felt much obliged and indebted to the British for their contribution to the growth of the Naga society. The Naga tribes such as Ao, Angami, Lotha, Sema, Rengma, Chakhesang, who were first to come in close contact with the British and establish friendly and cordial relations with them, availed better opportunity for development and prosperity. Later on, the tribes like Chang, Konayak, Phom, Sangtam, Yimchunger, Khiamnungan, Chakhesang and Rengma also came in contact with the British. Hence they remained behind in the pace of their development. Today, Aos among other tribes of the Naga are more advanced in all aspects of life. It is all because the Ao people were first to understand the benefits of the British arrival in their land and they tried their level best to take the maximum benefits from the government.

References

1. Mackenzie, *History of the Relations of the Government with the Hill Tribes of North East Frontier of Bengal,* (Calcutta,), 1984, p. 102.
2. Quoted in Alemchiba, *A Brief Historical Account of Nagaland* (Kohima), 1972, p. 58.
3. Mackenzie, A., *History of the Relations of the Government with the Hill Tribes of North East Frontier of Bengal, op. cit.,* 1984, pp. 100-02.
4. Elwin, V., *The Nagas in the Nineteenth Century,* Bombay, 1969, p. 166.
5. *Ibid.*
6. *Bengal Judicial Proceedings,* April, 1866, No. 240.
7. *Foreign Political Proceeding,* January 1882, No.135.
8. *The Accounts of the Province of Assam,* 1903, p. 77.
9. Robert Reid, *History of Frontier Areas Bordering on Assam,* Shillong, 1942, pp. 100-01.
10. Jonstone James, *My Experience in Manipur and Naga Hills,* London, 1896, p.172.
11. *Ibid.*
12. Robert Reid, *History of Frontier Areas Bordering on Assam,* Shillong, 1942, pp. 100-01.
13. Ganguli, M., *A Pilgrimage to the Nagas,* Oxford & IBH Publishing Company New Delhi, 1984, p. 14.
14. Barpujari, H.K., *Problem of the Hill Tribes,* "Preface".
15. Butler, John, *Travel and Adventure in the Province of Assam,* London, 1855, pp. 39-40.

16. Datta Ray, *Assam Secretariat- 1874-1947*, Calcutta, 1977, p. 1.
17. "Report of the Assam Government, *Physical and Political Geography of the people of Assam*, 1987, p. 99.
18. Mackenzie, A., *The North East Frontier of India*, Delhi, 1981, p. 55.
19. *Ibid.* p. 209.
20. Robert Reid, *History of Frontier Areas Bordering on Assam, op. cit.,* 1942, pp. 130-33.
21. *Ibid.* p. 139.
22. "Report of the Assam Government," *Physical and Political Geography of the people of Assam*, 1987, p. 102.
23. *Ibid.* pp. 102-03.
24. *Ibid.* pp. 105-06.
25. *Ibid.* p. 106.
26. Mackenzie, A., *The North East Frontier of India*, Delhi, 1981, p. 124.
27. *Ibid.*
28. *Ibid.*
29. "Robert Reid, *History of Frontier Areas Bordering on Assam, op. cit.*, 1942, pp. 130-33.
30. Datta Ray, *Assam Secretariat, op. cit.,* pp. 41-56.
31. *Ibid.*
32. "Report of the Assam Government," *Physical and Political Geography of the people of Assam*, 1987, p. 139.
33. *Eastern Bengal and Assam Secretariat, Political*, June 1908, pp. 322-34.
34. *Ibid.*
35. Johari, J.C. "Creation of Nagaland State: Triumph of Ebullient Infra-Nationalism", *Indian Journal of Political Science Association,* Vol. XXXVI, No.1, January-March, 1975, pp. 13-14.
36. Quoted in Rao, V.V. *A Century of Tribal Politics in North East India-1874-1974*, New Delhi, 1976, p. 151.

37. Bendangnagshi, *Glimpses of Naga History*, Sarighat Guwahati, 1976, pp. 18-19.
38. Singh, B.P., *Problem of change: a study of North East India*, Oxford University Press, 1997, p. 51.
39. Mills, J.P. *The Ao Nagas*, Oxford University Press, London, 1973, pp. 97-98.
40. Asoso Yonuo, *The Rising Nagas*, Vivek Publishing House, New Delhi, 1974, p.110.
41. Sema, Piketo *British Policy and Administration- 1882-1947*, New Delhi, 1972, p. 142.
42. *The Naga Nation*, Vol. 1, No.5, Kohima, April 1946, pp. 5-6.
43. Cited in Asoso Yonuo, *The Rising Nagas*, Vivek Publishing House, New Delhi, 1974, p. 89.
44. *The Naga Nation*, Vol. 1, No.5, Kohima, April 1946, pp. 5-6.

***

3

Role of Christian Missionaries

The Western Christian missionaries landed in India along with the colonial masters who had arrived here with the marked intention to establish trade and commercial relations. The East India Company was permitted by the Mughal rulers to do the business, but the Company applying the tactics of 'divide and rule' succeeded in establishing its political suzerainty over the whole of India.

The Baptist missionary people from America lost no time to reach India with the sole objective to implant the tree of Christianity specially in the pockets where no religious light had yet reached. No doubt, Hinduism and Islam were the dominant religions of the country and major portions of the population were under these two religions in India, but there were still some pockets where the light of the institutionalized religion had not reached. This encouraged the Baptist missionaries to serve the purpose. They were fully determined to complete the mission by carrying on the movement for spreading Christianity in India at any cost. They did hardly care for difficulties and problems, which were awaiting them on their way to achieve the task. They possessed missionary zeal in the name of the Almighty, which supplied them energy and enthusiasm to work for the mission. What they needed was political support to achieve the target. Hence, wherever the western people established colonial rule, the missionaries followed them and carried on their work.

North-East India was yet virgin areas for spread of new faith specially among the hill people. Neither Hindu preachers nor Buddhist monks dared to penetrate into the mountainous parts of the areas and contact the war-like hill people. Mughal rulers were not allowed by the Ahoms to occupy the valley of the Brahmaputra. Though the Ahoms, occupying the Valley of Brahmaputra, had adopted Hinduism as their religion, they, too, never tried to bring the hill people under the influence of their religion. Perhaps they treated the hill people differently. Moreover, the natural obstacles and their hatred towards the barbarous hill tribes remained the barrier between the Hindus of the plains and the hill people.

This chapter discusses about the arrival of the Christian missionaries in North-East India and their venture to penetrate into the hills of Nagaland and sow the seed of Christianity, which prospered as a big Christian tree spreading its branches to the areas occupied by the hill tribes. The chapter also analyses the role of Christian missionaries in transforming the Naga society by establishing cordial relations with the Nagas and opening new schools in the Naga Hills.

Missionaries in North-East India

The western missionaries arrived in North-East India soon after the British put their foot in the Valley of Brahmaputra. They made Sibsagar their main centre from where they continued their activities. Establishment of the British rule in the plains and hills of Assam made the task of the missionaries very easy to baptize the hill people who were yet animists by faith. But they had to face tough resistance of the Nagas while spreading new faith among them. With courage and enthusiasm the missionaries did their work so wisely that they succeeded in completing their mission despite tough resistance and opposition from the tribal people. As a result, the whole of the Hill areas of Assam including the frontiers came under the influence of Christianity and most of the hill inhabitants became Christians because the missionaries were neither worried about the toughness of the hills and mountains nor afraid of their lives while contacting the war-like hill tribes in North-East India. The natural obstacles did not deter the Christian missionaries who from the forties of the19th century had begun to arrive in Assam to take up missionary work and from there "ventured into the wilds of the frontier hills to civilize the rude tribes through the spread of Christianity".[1]

The nineteenth century was the century of missionary zeal and expansion of churches in Asia. In that pursuit the American Baptist Christian missionaries arrived at Calcutta and from there they travelled to different parts of the frontier and applied their best efforts to baptize the hill people even at the risk of their lives. According to the Missionary Magazine report, from September 1845, Sibsagar was one of the most central and important positions for missionary activities in Assam. It was that central place where the devoted missionaries began their work to bring the whole of North-eastern frontier areas under the influence of Christianity. Nidhi Medhi was the first Assamese convert baptized at Jaipur by Dr. Bronson in 1841. Thereafter, the missionary people became busy with "translating, printing, teaching and preaching both in and around Sibsagar".[2] However, the course was not an easy one as anticipated. A serious trouble appeared before the missionaries and the converts in Assam because people did not allow the new converts to reside in the society. A rumour was spread that the stay of the converts in the society would bring more trouble for the people as a whole. As a result, it became the responsibility of the Mission to provide them shelter and profession both. This is evident from the report of the Missionary Magazine. The Report stated: "In 1853, a problem arose which is till a serious question affecting the prosperity of this Mission. The total or partial dependence of the native converts on the mission for temporal support is regarded as an evil ......The necessity of furnishing employment to all the native Christians as means of support is a serious burden and the plan itself is not adapted to promote that personal independence and strength of character".[3]

Anyway, the efforts of the missionaries continued to follow their mission despite the problems, that erupted on their way.

With the arrival of Dr. Clark at Sibsagar in 1868, the progress of missionary work multiplied because he was a man of farsightedness and everlasting courage and enthusiasm. He soon observed that the work of missionaries was very slow and confined only to the plains of Assam. He noted: "It is certainly painful for us at Sibsagar to be unable to lift our eyes without seeing these hills and thinking of the men on them who have no knowledge of Christ." In 1876, Dr. Clark turned over the Assamese work and went to the hills of the frontier.

Baptization of the Nagas

In the early days of the American Baptist mission at Sibsagar, the first Naga who was baptized on 12 September 1847 was a Konyak, namely, Hube. The Second Naga called as Lungsang Francis, an Ao from Merangkong village, was baptized on 7 September 1851 at Sisbsagar. After conversion, when they returned to their homes and tried to influence others for Christianity, the villagers opposed the spread of Christianity on the ground that it could create confusion in the minds of the Naga people. As a result Lungsang was attacked by the villagers and killed on the spot. The incident was so serious that the missionary people dared not enter the Naga Hills and carry on their work till 1871.

In1870, Subongmeren Ao while visiting Sisbsagar came in contact with Dr. Clark, the Missionary-in-charge of mission and printing press. He was baptized in October 1871 by Clark and became the first contact person who created the fertile ground for future evangelization of the Naga Hills. Thereafter, Godhula, a Baptist Assamese and devotee of Dr. Clark, who had the zeal and devotion to the work of the Mission, reached the Naga Hills with the mission to do what he could in acquiring the vernacular of some of the few Nagas. Godhula at the instruction of Clark moved for the Naga Hills and stayed there for a few days in the village Dekahaimong. During his second visit to the Naga Hills he returned to Sibsagar with some Nagas (nine in number), who were baptized. On their return home a small chapel was built in the village separately because they were not allowed to live with other people. In 1872, Clark himself "marched through the foothills following narrow jungle paths until he reached Molungyimsen (now Molung) on 18 December 1872 and baptized fifteen more Nagas there".[4] It was the first time that some Nagas were baptized on their own land despite the opposition of the villagers. In the words of Philip: "Thereafter the field was ripe and ready for harvest.... People were on the move and God stirred their minds and individuals were converted. Groups of people were coming forward for baptism and public witnessing".[5]

As the years rolled down, both Clark and Godhula became pioneers of Christian Mission in Nagaland. Molung became the first village to uphold Christianity in 1876 when Clark established the first Church on 24 October 1876. While having contact with those Ao Nagas who used to visit plains of Assam either for trade or to take shelter during the period of epidemics, Godhula had learnt the dialect of the Ao people. It was this learning which helped him enough to establish good relations with the Ao people at Molung. He, along with his wife, took the trouble and visited the Ao area as many as six times to get acquainted with the people and understand their nature.

Godhula was a sober and well behaved gentleman. It was he who succeeded in bringing the Aos near to the Christian Mission and made them understand about the goodness of Christianity. Godhula "made good use of the Ao language and some Ao songs, which fascinated the people. The songs and the prayers he said were to a God called Jehovah and for the progress of the people. The village elders realized that Godhula meant no harm, and so he was set free perhaps to make social contact without any restriction."[6] When the process of baptization of the Nagas on their own land was on, the Nagas were fighting with the British forces. Hence when Godhula entered the Naga Hills, the Naga people, in the beginning, took him as the spy of the East India Company. However, Godhula's behaviour towards the village people was so good that he was recognized as well-wisher of the Nagas. This fact has been substantiated by Clark himself who while appreciating his service to the Mission wrote that the people "became convinced that he was not a government spy; and then there was entire freedom of conversation and a very great desire to hear the gospel. He was then shown every favour and honour, which they could bestow.... When he left, men, women and children shed tears."[7] Godhula knew that there was no other way to win over the Naga people other than extending the language of love and sympathy to them. Such was the love and care of Godhula for the Nagas, which enabled them to live among war-like tribes without any harm. However, there were some people who did not like Godhula's activities related to Christianity. Since many of the people were not in favour of adopting the new faith, Godhula got threat and warning from them. Hence Clark allowed him to leave the place and return to Assam. That is why he could not continue his service for long in the Naga Hills.

Another cause of leaving the Naga Hills for Godhula was that during the seventies of the 18th century, head-hunting war in the Naga Hills was at the climax. There was not even a single day when at least one or two heads were not hunted. At this very critical juncture Godhula had visited almost all the Ao villages and persuaded many Aos to accept Christianity. His activities made the conservative Ao people angry. Hence he was warned. It is said that seeing the headless and limbless bodies "Godhula and his friend Homburg got frightened and left the village at once to Sibsagar. Henceforth, Godhula was reluctant to go to the Hills".[8]

After the return of Godhula from the Naga Hills, entire responsibility to spread Christianity in the Hills came upon Clark and his wife. They created wonderful history in spreading Christianity among the Nagas. Clark was an American and he had arrived in India with a missionary zeal to serve those people who were yet deprived of the light of God. At that time for entrance into the Naga Hills permission from the government was a must. Dr Clark was not permitted to enter into deep interior of the Hills, but his zeal was so great that neither the threat of the Nagas nor inconvenience of the land deterred him to stop his missionary service. Hence without the government's permission and without caring for his life, he not only entered the Naga Hills but also lived with the Naga people despite their opposition and protest for long years. He did remarkable service to the Mission. It was Clark who tried his best to provide fertile ground for the growth of Christianity in the Naga Hills.

The first church on the territory of the Ao Naga was established in 1876 by Clark despite tough opposition of the villagers, but polite and mild behaviour of Clark settled the issue amicably. He separated the Christian group of the Nagas from the non-Christian group. Thereafter, Molung became the first centre of Christian activities in the Naga Hills. A time came when many Nagas joined the movement of Clark and accepted Christianity giving up their long practised religious faith. Thus, the efforts and labour of Clark and his wife yielded the desired results.

Religion is not a Sectoral Monopoly

A critical study of growth of Christianity in Nagaland reveals the fact that the Christian missionaries faced not only topographical inconveniences and troubles in the hill areas but also encountered tough resistance of the indigenous people who were not ready to abandon the religious faith, which they had been carrying from time immemorial. Christianity was the product of the sermons and preaching of Jesus Christ where there is no room for any traditional faith of the tribal society. Moreover, the banner of Christianity, in the 19th century, was held by the Americans and Europeans who had their own civilization. They wanted to spread not only Christianity but their western culture and civilization also. The western people were very much proud of their culture and civilization. To them other cultures and civilizations of the world were inferior to that of theirs. That is why they hated all the religions or civilizations except Christianity.

One of the features of western civilization was that it was based on racial discrimination. There was no room for adjustment of cultural tenets of other societies. Hence they condemned the religions and religious faiths of other societies, which were beyond the purview of Christianity. It is true that the Nagas of the 19th century were not much civilized, but they were not barbarous also. The pattern of traditions and social norms as well as religious faith what the Ao people carried at that time was not much inferior or harmful except a few wild habits like head-hunting war. The western missionaries thought that the religious faiths, culture and civilization of the Nagas were worthless. Hence the Christianity asked the new Naga believers to part with all their old culture as well as habits and follow the new European or American culture in almost all aspects of the life. Bendangangshi also writes that the Missionary people "condemned our old culture as most sinful, Godless and useless".[9] Panger Imchen is also of the view: "In trying to establish the Church of Christ among the Ao, there was lamentable destruction to valuable ancient traditions, customs and moral values".[10]

One of the worst features of the preachers of a particular religion has been to condemn the religious values and cultural ethos of other religions. They think that their religion is the best of all and other religions are full of evils and ignorance. That is why religious conflicts in the world have been a dominant feature from the beginning of the human civilization. According to Oxford English dictionary, a religion "is a particular system of faith and worship" and the "recognition on the part of man of some destiny unseen power as having control of his destiny". Again, a religion is "a general mental and moral attitude resulting from this belief... devotion to some principles, strict fidelity or faithfulness; conscientiousness, pious affection or attachment".[11] Absolute faith in an absolute power is the base of a religion. Each religion has its base, which itself is based on faith. That faith is an absolute power which demands "obedience, reverence and worship". It deserves obedience because of its prevalent universal order and justice, which it implies to uphold the creation. It commands reverence because it is loyal, benevolent and lovely to all. It is the subject of worship due to its divinity, complaisance, purity and piety. Moreover, a religion affects human conduct and behaviour to make the people generous, noble, complaisant, pure, kind and benevolent. That is why the preachers of a religion call upon the followers to be devoid of all sorts of deceits, violent acts and their evils.

It has been observed that both Christian and Muslim religions have been propounded by prophets or messengers of God and propagated by their disciples and followers with a view to expanding religious scope and influencing others to join the established religious sects. Such a religion becomes sectarian in its character and under such religious systems the religion becomes creed or dogma, the primary aim of which is to dominate other religions. Once a religion is given a sectoral form and institutionalized dogmatic character, it becomes the property of the institution which wants to establish religious hold and bring the whole world under its control and influence. Jhingru has rightly observed that "the religion institutionalized becomes interested in maintaining its hold on the populous and social institutions, and develops a rigid creed, a set of rituals and laws, which are declared as binding upon all its followers".[12]

A religion does not recognize a community or a group. It is universal, uniformal, comprehensive and applicable to all in the similar degree of goodness. Religion in the real sense is the highest spiritual knowledge which "cannot be bought nor can it be acquired from books." In real sense a religion is a way to God as well as man's relations with his fellow-beings. According to Swami Vivekananda, religion cannot be found anywhere except in the core of the human heart. It is not monopolistic domination of particular religious community. Rather it is "a system of belief, practice and philosophical values concerned with definition of the sacred, the comprehension of the life and salvation from the problem of human existence". Again, "Religious traditions are the results of man's attempt to capture and enshrine his philosophical and spiritual insights so that they are available to the individuals as well as he faces life and its stresses, confusion and complexities".[13]

No doubt, a religion is a "social phenomena because it necessarily stresses fellowship in the development, teaching and participation of religious insights and knowledge. However, it cannot be monopolized by a group. A religion, which claims its superiority over other religions or religious faiths, is, in fact, not a true religion but a sectoral creed in the guise of religious character.

The aforementioned comments about the sectoral or monopolistic religions are not against the spirit and character of Christianity, but against the missionaries who while spreading Christianity in the world looked down upon other religions and condemned them. While spreading Christianity among the Nagas or other hill tribes of the frontier of the North-East, their primary aim had been to destroy the existing tribal religious norms and impose upon them a new set of faith and values under the banner of Christianity. That is why they tried their level best to establish supremacy of Christianity over the Nagas by condemning their religious and social patterns, which they had been following for long.

Blessings of the Government to the Missionaries

History bears the testimony that wherever the western colonial masters established their rule, the western missionaries followed them and worked hard for the spread of Christianity under the patronage and protection of the colonial masters. The people either traditional or modern, who have their own religious faith as well as religious rituals, never prefer to adopt religions and cultures of others. Truth is that the sectoral or institutionalized religious organisatisons have been engaged in spreading and imposing their faith upon the weaker, poor and isolated people all over the world. The Christian missionaries have been found far ahead to persuade the people to accept Christianity as a religion and western civilization as a way of life.

In the case of the Nagas, the Company Government helped these missionaries enough to achieve their mission and give strong foundation of Christian faith among the tribals even at the cost of destroying their good cultural values. P.T. Philip sharing the same opinion has expressed the view that it was not the missionary but the British Political agent in Assam who initiated missionary work in Assam. Major Jenkins, Commissioner General of Assam, was much more interested in missionary work among the tribals of Assam. The British government officials serving in Bengal and Assam not only provided the missionaries protection and shelter but also encouraged them to work for missionary mission.

Panger has rightly remarked that "In the eyes of the Gospel any culture or society, both modern and ancient, are seen as, under darkness or under the devil's government, and any unchristianzed country is termed unsaved, unreached and devoid of the knowledge of the Truth. While doing such things the British government helped them enough."[14] A general survey of the works of missionaries all over the world reveals the truth that the missionaries thought that no religion was better than Christianity. They found shortcomings in Hinduism, Islam, Sikhism, Buddhism, etc. In other words they were not ready at all to accept the truth that all religions have equal value and all speak of the godly truth and work for humanity as a whole. They thought that it was the Christianity, which had understood the meaning of God and developed love for humanity. It was all because they lacked the real knowledge of other religions, which existed even before the appearance of Christianity and spoke better truth than it had. Under such type of understanding if they condemned the Naga's religious facts, then there is no surprise.

Conflicts between Missionaries and Natives

It is true that when the western missionaries entered the land of the Nagas, there were some evils and inhuman practices among them. They were indulged in head-hunting war-fare and inter-village feuds. They also believed in existence of ghosts and evil souls. They had many superstitious beliefs and performed certain superstitious acts also. Despite all these they possessed many social and cultural values, which are still helpful to reconstitute the better Naga society. The western missionaries overlooked all these realities because they wanted to set the values, which they contained. When Dr Clark set up a new village (Dekahaimong) on the mountain top about three miles west of Molungyimsen for the Nagas who had adopted Christianity, it created more doubt and suspicion in the mind of the common Nagas. The new faith asked the converts to stop the sacrifice of animals or cattle. Thereafter, the villagers suffered from some sort of epidemics. They thought that it all happened due to the arrival of Christianity and avoidance of their old ceremonial sacrifices. Consequently "a threat came from the old village to exterminate the new village and to take possession of the white man's head as well".[15]

It appears that there were two great factors, which created allergy in the Nagas against Christianity. Whether Christianity was good or bad they hardly knew in the beginning. The Nagas were animists and they thought that there were several gods, and those gods when unpleased might cause big harm to the people. Hence to please such gods they used to sacrifice animals. The missionaries asked them to stop such practice. The Nagas were not ready at all to drop down their long practised customary ceremony. Those who stopped such practice at the initiative of the missionaries also suffered from epidemics of natural calamities. They took it as a curse of the unpleased god. As a result, they thought it better to please their assumed gods by sacrificing animals. Secondly, the people were very much suspicious of the British in their land. Several battles had been fought against the British. Hence any white man who was seen in their land, they took him as the British spy. As a result, they never allowed them to muddle with their affairs and live with them. That is why they forced Godhula to leave their land and warned Dr Clark to face any eventuality in case he lived in the land of the Ao Naga. On the other hand, the missionaries thought that these people were backward, uncivilized and cruel. Hence they were under the impression that when light spreads amongst them, every thing would come down automatically. So they continued their efforts even at the cost of their lives.

The efforts and courage of the missionaries began to yield desired fruits in course of time. Mrs. Clark, who followed her husband to assist him in his pious mission, was of the view that "Adherents of the old, cruel faith were quick to see that the gospel of peace and love would rapidly empty their (Ao's) skull houses and put to rout most of the old customs handed down from forefathers... . The Missionary's presence and his teaching had spread like wild-fire from mountain peak to mountain peak."[16] On the other hand, the fast spreading Christianity made the Naga people more and more upset. The hostility of the Nagas towards the missionary people went on increasing day by day. No doubt, the Nagas who had accepted the new faith sided with the missionaries, but at the cost of sharp division of the villagers. This is evident from the statement of Mrs. Clark who wrote: "There was a division in the village councils; repeated efforts were made by the opponents of Christianity to inveigle their village into war with other villages... . To intimidate the missionary, a war party of young men ambushed one whole week for human heads, which they intended to throw down before him (Clark) as a symbolical of what might expect himself in case he did not retreat to the plains".[17]

The opponents made attacks upon the newly established Christian village, Molung. Clark had several narrow escapes. Mr. Clark writes, "Before the English protection came, it was emphatically the divine arm upon which the missionaries daily trusted." Such affairs continued till the British Indian government fully controlled the situation in 1885. Thereafter, Clark and his followers were found very busy in Molung "pushing evangelistic work, managing, receiving frequent visitors from other villages, caring for the converts from pang of darkness, pagan superstition and customs making them so difficult to cast off entirely the patience, the anxious solitude".[18]

With the legal permission of the government and also with the support of Mr. Clark, Mrs. Clark, along with Rev and Mrs. Perring, in 1892, and Rev. and Mrs. Haggard, in 1893, missionary works continued despite the opposition of the traditional Nagas.The Commissioner of Assam, Col. Hopkinton, had already permitted the missionaries to spread Christianity among the Nagas with the condition that there should not be "conflict with British imperial dominion in British Indian empire".[19] They took the life risk to complete the mission with the object "to spread the teaching of the Christian religion among the Naga people" and to bring them "to the enlightenment of knowledge through education".[20]

Dr. M.M. Clark, The Founder of Christianity in Nagaland

Dr Clark was a true devotee of God. He had patience and foresight both. He had entered the Naga Hills with strong determination to rescue the Nagas and bring them to the light. Hence nothing could deter him. He knew how to win over the people. He also knew how to pacify the semi-civilized people. He had moral courage and unflinching faith in God and His blessing. Describing his miid character and benevolence, Aoso Yonuo writes:

"He smiled at the Naga men, women and children, spoke meekly to them, treated them tenderly, cured the sick, prayed for them and distributed them the leaflets, pamphlets of Christ wherever he went and whomsoever he met... . He established schools, entrusted to the care of the teacher living in village, taught in a primary school for two hours, quite apart from his preaching engagement".[21]

Clark took himself as a messenger of God to baptize maximum Nagas and spread Christianity among them. He took the trouble to learn unwritten language of the Aos, compiled a large vocabulary, translated some portion of the scripture of the Bible, composed Christian hymns in Ao language and produced Christian literature. The efforts of Reverend Clark and his associates, indeed, gave strong foundation of Christianity in Nagaland specially among the Ao Nagas.

As the years rolled down, Christianity prospered year after year. In the words of Panger Imchen, "Things began to change with mass conversions resulting in confusion, division and disunity. Everything began to move towards the light of gospel, which resulted in both a positive as well as destructive effect on their old culture." No doubt, Dr Clark must be given credit to get Christianity flourish in the land of the Nagas, but it was the government behind him and other missionaries who received all required support and protection from the government while working in Nagaland. Panger has rightly observed: "It would be one-sided view if all the changes and progress are attributed to Christian missionaries. The major role of change was played by the British rulers at the most crucial period of its beginning."[22] Agreeing to the same view F.S. Downs wrote, "This new order ushered in a period of tremendous change. The main agent of change was the government itself. Christianity provided the means whereby the people of the region were able to accommodate themselves to the new world brought in by the British."[23]

No doubt, the British rulers helped the missionaries to spread Christianity in Nagaland but there were sharp differences between the missionaries and the government officials as far as their motives were concerned. While the missionaries were committed for total change of culture, the government officials were in favour of retaining all essential elements of the old culture including their clothes and hair-styles. Moreover, the government extended the grants-in-aid to missionary schools and scholarship to students to a great extent on the condition that the students must remain unchanged in their dress and cultural behaviour.[24] The Christian missionaries hardly cared for the instruction given by the government to maintain old culture of the Nagas to avoid tussles. This is evident from the letter of J.P. Mills, the Sub-divisional Officer of Mokokchung, to the Mission Secretary, Impure, which inter alia said:

"Those non-Christians do not want to go to Christian schools because there they are taught of things, which their parents did not wish. They are forced to sleep in the Christian hostels over against their wish to sleep in Arichu. Their parents want them to be under the rules of Arichu".[25] However, contrary to such allegation Mr. Kijung, the former Executive Secretary, Ao Church Council, said that the school children with their parents wanted to sleep in the hostels rather than in the Arichu.[26]

In the beginning, the Ao people who were much more traditional in their approach and stubborn in their behaviour, opposed the Christian way of life, no doubt, but the goodness of Christianity in comparison to their native values was so great that it attracted more and more people with the result that the number of the followers multiplied year after year. The missionary people continued their efforts to convince the Nagas that Christianity was for their betterment not for any harm. The progress of Christianity in the Naga Hills continued slowly but steadily. The people witnessed coming of new churches and new schools in their land.

Mrs. Clark took the trouble to open a girls school. The converts were asked to teach in the school and tell the students gospels and Bible's stories. Dr. Cark took the trouble to visit the Naga villages and settle the blood-feuds and advise the people to live in peace and goodwill with their neighbours. He also urged the government to extend its authority to the villages which had been rejected by the government due to their infertility.

For Mr. and Mrs. Clark and their followers the work was not easy. Describing the troubles and inconvenience plus life risk involved in the missionary works in the Naga Hills, Revenburg has written that "Our second year at Molung has passed. During the year, we passed through much risk by which our lives were jeopardized; but through all God was better than our foolish ways. It has been the time of severe trial to our Churches' members. The horror of savage war-fare at outdoor required all the fortitude we all possessed to remain at outposts.[27]

No doubt, the school was set up at Molung, but the presence of the students was very thin. Perhaps the interest of the people in sending their children to the school was not yet developed. This is evident from the statement of Revenburg who wrote. "The spiritual life at the time was not high; only a few coverts were reported. The school was not very successful... . These savages very naturally do not appreciate the value of school".[28]

Impure as the main Centre of Christian Activities

When the number of missionaries at Molung increased and joined the hands of Dr Clark, the progress of the missionary work improved. The need was felt to shift the venue to accommodate the new comers and work without much interference. Due to increasing hostility towards the Mission centre Molung was considered not sufficient to accommodate new comers. Hence Impure was chosen as the new site in 1894. The place was forty miles away from Molung and fifteen miles from Mokokchung. This newly selected place was more suitable and central place for the furtherance of the gospel among the Aos and neighbouring tribes. Thus, Impure became the main centre of the Christian Missionaries' activities. In the words of Philip "Impure, as a Christian centre, began to show its light to the Ao tribe and to over half of dozen other tribes. The Church started growing."[29] Gospel spread from there to different directions among other Naga tribes such as Lotha, Angami, Sema, Konyak, Yimchunger, Chang, Sangtam and Khiamnungan.

Impure began to flourish day and night. It was only from this centre, which was under the charge of Dr Haggard and his wife, Mr. and Mrs. Clark and others set a crusade for spreading the gospel. It also became the centre of education and medical services in the Naga Hills. The medical treatments attracted the people more. Opinion of the Nagas about the missionaries began to change. They realized that the missionary people were their friends, not foes. The behaviour of doctors as well as missionaries was very much sound and sympathetic towards the patients. In the absence of medical treatment many Nagas used to be the victims of various types of diseases. They had no alternative other than some sorts of herbal treatment to cure the diseases. The medical centre at Impure appeared as a centre of health relief to the Naga people. Hence it was natural to have inclination towards the missionaries.

Thus the missionaries got ample opportunity to extend their friendship with the Nagas and take them in good faith for spreading the faith of Christianity. This encouraged them. They established more schools and medical centers. They also set up new churches in villages. The movements of the missionary people towards the villages increased. They established close contact with the Nagas and made them understand the futility of their wild and dirty habits such as head-hunting wars, blood-feuds with the neighbours, drinking rice bear, system of bachelor dormitories, superstitions, religious and ceremonial sacrifices and having hatred towards others. They were taught the significance of peace and the ways how to maintain peace. In the words of Asoso Yonuo, "The Nagas were exhorted to become Christians, by leaving all these unproductive concepts and practices for the happiness of souls, love and services taught by Jesus Christ".[30]

Once the pace for development of Christianity in the Naga Hills was set perfectly at Impure, it continued flourishing all over the Hills. With the advance of the British rule in the interior of the Naga Hills and imposition of the British rule over the people, the buildings of churches and gospel of God increased without any stop. Now Dr Clark arrived at Ungma, one of the biggest Ao villages. From there he moved towards another Ao village, namely, Longkhum. These two Ao villages were not only highly populated but also most conscious. Both the villages came under the spell of Christianity due to soft and mild behaviour of Clark.

Growing Faith of the Nagas Towards Christianity

Dr Clark knew that the Christianity in the Naga Hills could hardly flourish without assistance of the government. Hence he tried to change the mind of the Aos towards the British government and develop helping attitude for the government officials in the land of the Nagas. This is evident from the words he spoke to the Naga people while coming in their close contact. He said, "With their method of warfare and with arms being used by them they could not compete with the British in the battlefield."[31] The impact of such words upon the Naga people was so great that they, instead of waging war against the British, accepted their sovereignty. Their wrath against the British began to diminish day by day and forgetting enmity towards the British people they began to extend their hand of friendship with the government. Clark had convinced the Ao Nagas that if they wanted to develop, they would have to come close to the government. The Ao people accepting the good counsel of Clark became the friends of the British government and came nearer to the British officials. Thus, Clark did a commendable service not only to the British government but also to the Naga people.

The Faith in Christianity began to develop among the Nagas as well as the Aos. The number of converts surprisingly multiplied. They began to welcome the move of conferences of missionaries. They also started taking part in prayers conducted in the churches. This fact is evident from the report of Dr Clark, which *inter alia* stated, "We found revival had been in progress at Molung for several weeks. The Lord has visited His people at Molung. There was a similar revival in 1885."[32] Haggard confirming the same truth reported, "The holy spirit is moving upon the hearts of the people, souls are being saved, and backsliders are reclaimed".[33]

Clark left the Naga Hills in 1893, but the seed of Christianity, which he had put in the soil of the Nagas, began to grow up into a charming tree. By the year 1897, the missionaries who were actively engaged in the missionary work, left no stone unturned to nurture the Christianity planted by Clark and his wife. The people of Ungma and Longkhum had come under the charm of Christianity. According to the report of Perrine, by 1897, the whole village had turned to Christ and asked for preacher whom they supported, loved, cherished and evidently obeyed. The preacher who was sent was described as an old and faithful saint."[34] The year 1898 was marked as the year of 'reaping and rejoicing'. Four new churches were organized making a total of six self-supporting churches. The number of Baptized Nagas began to increase. In the year 1885 Mission stations had been established at Kohima and Wokha. These stations also became active to indoctrinate more Nagas with the new faith.

Changing Faith and Behaviour of the Indigenous Nagas

The impact of Christianity on the Naga people became obvious by the end of the nineteenth century. The Nagas who were so proud of their traditional culture and social values began to either forget or neglect them. Their inclination towards Mission centers and their love for Christianity developed to a considerable extent. Discussing about the impact of Christianity upon the Ao people, Panger Imchen writes, "The changes and progress made by the gospel to Ao is tremendous on individual, social and religious levels. They found that their old faith was not the ultimate goal in the search for truth. The gospel ... was the base for progress and enlightenment. Their minds were transformed to a newer and richer life ... they never wanted to go back to their former way of life".[35] Iralu, a retired Naga medical officer, writes, "If Christianity had not come to Nagaland, things would be entirely different. Life, individually and collectively, would be different".[36] Mr. Iralu is very much correct in his observation. Christianity gave the Nagas a new life, a new faith and a new civilization related to the western society, but at the cost of their cultural values and social norms.

With the acceptance of Christianity in the Naga villages, the fear of raids, mass killings, distrust and constant restlessness faded away and a new humanity was established. Missionaries not only preached the Nagas religion, but also taught them hygiene, temperance from heavy drink and chewing betelnut. The new faith brought more clean life, a more meaningful and longevity to life. Medicines, brought by the British people and distributed among the villagers, controlled the drastic diseases. Inter-village feuds came down. In the words of Panger "enmity was replaced by peace and goodwill. Head-hunters were converted into soul searcher." According to Sunep, "The new religion offered them enough food to satisfy their religious bent of mind".[37]

TABLE- I
BAPTISM AT MOLUNG IN THE EARLY PERIOD
(Year-wise)

1878	1880	1881	1882	1883	1885	1886
7 persons	5 persons	2 persons	9 persons	6 persons	24 persons	2 persons

Missionary activities at Molung began in 1876 with the arrival of Dr Clark. The table clearly indicates that in the beginning the process of baptism was very slow. Till 1886 except 1885, very few persons turned up to adopt new faith. It is all because the period was passing through tough resistance against the Christianity. Rather it was the period of enmity. The Ao people opposed the spread of Christianity by tooth and nail at the time. However, the number of converts went on increasing in the coming years.

TABLE- II
NUMBER OF CHURCHES AND BAPTISM AT IMPURE MISSION CENTRE

Year	Number of churches	Membership	Baptized
1901	9	368	68
1902	11	399	76
1903	9	467	94
1904	9	551	39

Table II indicates that the number of churches at Mission Centre, Impure, increased from 9 to 11 in 1902, but it again declined. The reason of decline was weakness of maintenance and shortage of funds. However, the number of membership of the churches was on increase year-wise, but variation is found in the number of baptized people. Sometimes the membership increased and sometimes it decreased. It was all because the people had not yet fully submitted to the Mission.

TABLE L- III

SCHOOL STATISTICS AT IMPURE MISSION CENTRE

Year	Number of schools	Average monthly enrolment	Average daily attendance	Cost of maintenance
1901	1 station school	35	29.25	Rs. 1343/-
	9 village school	134.7	91	Rs. 684/-
1902	1 station school	48.8	41.1	Rs. 1649/-
	9 village school	120.1	Nil	Rs. 527/-
1903	1 station school	59.8	99.6	Rs. 423/-
	18 village school	199.9	99.6	Rs. 823.10
1904	2 station school	77.4	50.2	Rs. 1650/-
	19 village school	198.9	–	Rs. 1158/-

Sources: Source Material of History of Christianity, compiled by C. Walu Walling, Literature department, Baptist Arogo Mungdang, Impure, 2001, pp. 73-378.

The statistics shown in the above mentioned tables indicates that at the Mission centre the number of the schools remained maximum two, while the number of the village schools went on increasing year-wise. Secondly, the expenditure on the school at the Mission centre was greater than that of the village schools. One more notable difference is that the average percentage of attendance in the village schools is far lower than that of the Mission school. It shows that the schools at the Mission centre were nicely managed while little attention was paid to the village schools. However, the students were available in both types of the school, which means the Naga people had understood the significance of education by 1904-05.

Missionary and Institutionalised Education

By 1904-05, bible schools were set up with a view to imparting training to the church leaders for preaching. Membership of the bible schools multiplied year after year. The annual conference of the Mission was attended by a good number of converts. A large number of converts came from the schools established by the Mission. Schools were the evangelizing agencies and the teachers also served as evangelists and pastors for the villages, which had established churches. The Mission schools presented Jesus Christ as the source of true knowledge. According to the report of Clark, "Through the schools the gospel is made to reach the mountaineers more rapidly and permanently than by another means".[38] Dr Clark was very much correct in his observation. Education, in fact, served two purposes together. Firstly, it attracted the Nagas towards the activities of the missionaries, and secondly, it made the task of the missionaries easy to prepare the brigade of preachers and pastors. The task, which was performed by the outsiders, was now done by the natives themselves.

In 1904, English was introduced as the second medium of teaching in the schools. Before that the only language of instruction was Assamese. By the year 1905, there were 24 schools and 420 pupils. In the same year, about twenty more new villages upheld the Christian faith in Ao territories. The church membership grew to 685 with 195 baptisms in that particular year. Impure Mission Centre continued its activities with trusted and committed missionaries like E.G. Miller, Mr. and Mrs. Longwell, Dr and Mrs. R.R. Barkley and Mr. and Mrs. Smith who had joined the Centre in 1912. As a result, by 1913, Christianity made headway in almost all villages of the Ao area. The annual association was attended by 1300 Naga Christians in the same year.

Growth of Churches and Revival Services

The number of churches and also the converts increased in the Naga Hills by the year 1913. The interests of the Naga people developed in schools and churches, no doubt, but the whole of the Naga population was not swayed by the influence of Christianity.

The tussle and opposition were still on. A great many people yet disliked the growth of Christianity at the cost of their old culture and traditions. The missionaries did not like that the new converts should take part in old religious and cultural ceremonies. What they demanded from the new converts was a complete dedication to the new faith. Hence, the land for the growth of Christianity was not yet fully fertile. The reaction was so sharp that "In most Ao villages, Christians were persecuted and threatened with expulsion from the village, from clan inheritance and restricted from cultivation of their common lands".[39] The villages, which were yet out of the influence of Christianity, remained stubborn in their old ways. Horam writes: "Forbidding dancing and drinking of even the mildest rice bear led to many villages splitting up into two." Alemchiba, too, writes that "they (missionaries) felt (that) every ceremony should be abolished... . The tendency was to abolish abruptly the old things and substitute individualism for the strong community feeling... the result was a conflict not necessarily a conflict of arms but of culture".[40] Anyway, the missionaries continued their works despite resistance and opposition of the traditional Nagas.

The revival service became an effective means to attract more and more people to new faith and new way of life. Group conversion multiplied the number of the converts and churches both. By 1920, the number of churches grew to 46 with 3838 members. Bible classes attracted more non-Christian people from different villages. The annual conference became a type of festival. In 1922, the Church celebrated the 50th anniversary of Dr Clark's arrival in the Naga Hills. It is said that the ceremony was attended by 3000 Christians. By 1929, the translation of the New Testament was completed. Secondary school lessons and textbooks for the schools were prepared and printed. By 1930, the church became almost entirely self-supporting under the able leadership.

It is said that Missionary Churches of the Ao did a remarkable service to the growth of Christianity in the entire Naga Hills. According to 33rd Missionary Conference Report, with the assistance and conviction of the Ao Christians the work was extended to the border tribes like Sangtam, Chang, Phom, Konyak and Yimchunger. The Ao people, in fact, became the source of encouragement and pioneering of the tribes mentioned above for becoming Christians.[41] Thereafter, despite some opposition and protest, "Churches grew stronger and stronger. Membership multiplied year by year. The estimated membership for 1941 was 13,776".[42] All churches were nicely organized with special funds and trained pastors. The year 1947 became the jubilee year of the Ao Baptist Association; 11295 delegates from 58 churches attended the service. By the year 1947, the membership of the churches in the Ao areas alone, rose to 15734 and in 1949, it was 20593. Baptism among the Aos and other border tribes reportedly increased to 2548 in 1950 and 2750 in 1951.

Factors Responsible for the Growth of Christianity among the Nagas

A very pertinent question may be raised here as to why did the opposition of the Nagas who wanted to maintain their own traditional culture and religion went on declining and the number of the new converts and new churches went on increasing. The answer is not far to seek. Firstly, it was the mild and sympathetic behaviour of the western Baptist missionaries who remained close and served the Naga villagers despite their misbehaviour and enmity towards the missionaries. Secondly, a time came when the Ao people recognized them and realized their mistakes. It appears that the Nagas were not much opposed to the Christianity, but they opposed the missionary's condemnation of their old culture and religious faiths. The missionary people realizing this fact did not object much to the Nagas social and cultural practices and withdrew the view to destroy their old culture and traditions except their wild habits. Moreover, the Naga people found many things new and useful in the new religion, which their ancient religion did not possess. This attracted them towards Christianity. Observing the same view Panger writes that "when the gospel was introduced to the Ao, it was accepted outright by the people as they seemed to have been tired of their unhappy religion and the time was ripe for the coming of the Light".[43] Thirdly, in the beginning, the Mission Centre bore entire expenditure on the maintenance of churches and helping the new converts financially in various aspects of life. The economic conditions of the Nagas were pathetic and lamentable. The charity and financial assistance served them as a boon during the days of crisis. The policy of the missionary people "has been to establish churches generally with financial help from the Mission, and then withdraw mission support as the churches became able to carry their own burden".[44] It was the economic assistance given to the Nagas by the Mission Centers, which brought them very much near to the Christianity even at the cost of destruction of their old culture.

Fourthly, the British government that had already consolidated its rule over the Nagas assisted the missionaries by various means such as controlling the adamant and cruel Nagas, giving protection to the missionaries, taking the educated Nagas in good faith and making them understand the significance of Christianity and its relevance to the modern world. In the words of Mar Ponger, "One of the main reasons for the growth of church in India was not the conversion of the few people here and there... but mass movements towards Christianity." Fifthly, but not the least, education spread by the mission and government schools produced the educated or literate Nagas, who began to understand the futility of wild habits and customs of their people. In fact, these people helped the missionaries not only to spread Christianity by assuming the responsibility of preachers and pastors, but also expanded the way of Christianity by convincing their own people about the benefits of Christianity.

Before the British left India, Christianity in North-East specially among the tribals was a reality. Almost all the villages in Nagaland had come under the banner of churches. Each church was well organized and manned by Naga pastors. Various church associations were formed, which began to play remarkable roles not only to spread Christianity but also to enrich it. The Holy Spirit awakening sweeps over the entire tribal churches in several stages resulted in the revival of the whole villages. Gospel preaching became more vigorous. As a result "Membership swelled up and indigenous leadership was developed... . There was mass awakening among Lotha, Angami, Sema and Tangkhul tribes by 1946. The

Christian community grew to half the total population in the Lotha tribe as a result of awakening".[45] During sixties of the 20th century a strong mass awakening was started to cover all Naga tribes. This move increased the number of churches all over Nagaland. In the words of V.K. Nuh, "Thatched curb buildings were extended for several times in...to accommodate the overcrowding of membership in the churches on account of mass-rush".[46]

The Angami Baptist Association (ABA) was formed in 1912 with a mission school at Kohima. Through this mission enlightenment reached to all tribes living in Kohima area. In the beginning, the progress of mission work was slow as it happened in Mokokchung area. But situation totally changed as the years rolled down. Number of converts increased who worked hard for the growth of Christianity in Kohima sub-division. The Baptist Church Associations were established in other areas of Nagaland. In 1926, the people of Wokha witnessed the coming of an Association comprising devoted workers. In Lotha area notable growth of Christianity began from the year 1926 when the number of baptized Christians increased. In 1933, the number of converts increased to 1265. There were 35 churches and 1789 members at the end of the year 1936. In 1941, the number of churches rose to 46 with 2000 members. The missionaries of Impure and Kohima used to attend to the urgent needs of the Lotha churches from time to time. Bible classes were held twice or thrice in a year. Today, there are nearly 80 churches in the villages and towns of Wokha district.

The Sema Baptist Association was set up in 1922. It is said that "without the work of a missionary or the preaching of a native evangelist, people (Semas) became Christians and organized themselves into churches".[47] It all happened after a sick lady was cured by prayer. Thereafter, a movement of the people began, which did all remarkable work to develop faith in Christianity in the Sema area. By the year 1933, the membership of the churches in the Sema area increased to 40 in 55 villages. In 1938, a mission school was set up at Aizuto. The mission school under the headmastership of Mokden Ao began to function smoothly. By the end of 1957, there were 194 churches and a total membership of 181,628 persons with a Christian community of 40,562. By

1971, the number of Sema churches increased to 269 with 9 in the town areas. The Bible conferences, Christian Endeavour Sunday School, special leadership in training and Christian Home Conference gave remarkable push to the growth of Christianity in Sema area.

The tribes who were yet out of the influence of Christianity, got attracted towards it and joined the movement. The people of the Chakhesang area witnessed Baptist Church Association in only 1949. In the land of the Kuki the Church Association was formed in 1926 while the people of Rengma and Zeliangrong found the Baptist Church Association in 1943 and 1953 respectively. Thereafter, Christianity appeared in other backward tribes like Chang, Sangtam, Yimchunger, Konyak, Phom and Khiamnungan. In the words of P.T. Philip, "When the Nagas received the light from the world of God, they did not want to keep it under bushel. They wanted to pass on the light ... from hill to hill, village to village and tribe to tribe."[48] The Naga evangelists assumed full responsibility to evangelize the villagers.

The East India Company's government, in the beginning, did not like to interfere with social habits, religious beliefs and practices of the native people because the interference would go against the company's commercial interests. That is why the British government, before 1793, refused to allow any missionary to set up their permanent station in India. It was the Danish government, which for the first time offered the missionaries protection and privileges and set up primary press to publish scriptures in Indian languages. Thereafter, the western missionaries began to arrive in India and start their activities, which resulted in clashes and disputes between the missionaries and the Hindus. No doubt, Lord Minto put restriction on the publications and printing of the missionary literature, but later on he, too, became liberal to missionaries. By 1818, Serampur became the centre of main activities of the missionaries, which started vernacular schools. The purpose was to train the students and send them for missionary work to their fellow Indians. Alexander Duff, the famous missionary who reached Calcutta in 1830, maintained that "high English education without religion was a blind suicidal policy".[49] Calcutta became not only the headquarters of the British government but also the main centre of Christian missionaries. It was Calcutta from where the missionaries spread all over north-eastern region of the country. So far the case of Nagaland is concerned, soon after establishment of the British rule over the Nagas, the activities of the western missionaries began and continued till the entire area came under the direct influence of Christianity and people accepted it as their main religion.

The Move of Traditional Naga Society Towards Modernity

Before a detail discussion is made about the role of Christianity in modernizing the Naga traditional society it would be convenient to have a cursory view over the meaning of modernization and traditionality. A traditional society is a society, whose social, cultural, religious and ethical values are rooted in customary beliefs and practices. It carries traditional values based on customs and conventions. On the other hand, modernity is an attraction towards new values and new social structure based on scientific research and progress. Its base is rationality, not blind faith or customary beliefs. Traditionality as well as tribalism believe in *status quo* while modernity is revolutionary, which demands quick changes. Traditional society is rustic by its nature and rural by structure while modernity is modern in its approach and urban in its structure. Moreover, modernization as a form of cultural reforms is basically universalistic. Modern social values are 'pan-humanistic', 'trans-ethnic' and 'non-ideological'. It symbolizes rational attitudes towards new social values and their evaluation from universalistic and not particularistic viewpoint as it generally happens with the traditional society. Root of modernity is in scientific world-view and it has deeper and positive associations with levels of diffusion of scientific knowledge, technical skill and technical resources. On the other hand, the traditional social values specially in tribal societies are particularistic and typical.

According to Yogendra Singh: "Modernization as a form of cultural responses involves attributes which are basically universalistic and evolutionary.... Modernization in this respect should be treated as a kind of cultural universal... a level at which the institutionalization of a higher order of culture is possible".[50] Modernity is not an exclusive possession of any one ethnic or cultural group, but it belongs to the humanity as a whole. According to Max Weber, emphasis on formal rationality, experiment, codification, verification and rational utilitarian orientation in behaviour and thought are some of the unique substantive questions of western cultural tradition, which come under the category of modern society. Scientific, technological and industrial revolutions have played a big role in transforming the old society or making them modern. Components of modernity are science, technology, urbanization, industrialization, rapid mass communication, new education, new political order and economic system.

A modern society has been identified as a society characterized by the application of technology, by extensive social inter-dependence, by urbanization, literacy, social mobility and secularization.[51] In the case of India modernization took place, no doubt, but it was the copy of westernization. In fact modernization is rooted in westernization, which means application of modern attitude prevailing in western countries.

In the case of hill people in India specially in the north-eastern part, Christianity appeared among the hill people as a new light and helped them enough in changing their old styles in various aspects of life. It helped the semi-civilized people to become civilized by controlling their wild behaviour and learning new ways of life. It moulded the Naga people towards humanism keeping away barbarianism. It helped the people to stop perpetual killings in internal feuds and village warfare. Christianity also forbade people from abusive habits like drinking and smoking. It was the Christianity, which ended the dirtiest and the bloodiest practice of head-hunting war. Christianity broadened the mind of the Nagas to think religion from a broader perspective and understand religion in its universal perspective. The education started by the missionaries enabled the Naga youths to know the world and understand the environment systematically and scientifically. Their knowledge about the nature and the world expanded. They learnt that humanism and brotherhood are also integral parts of religion.

Such thinking of the Nagas not only stopped violence in Nagaland but also paved the way for the growth of permanent peace and prosperity of the people of the state. Their behaviour became sublime and polite towards other people. Their faith in the Almighty became firm and permanent. Christianity in Nagaland, in fact, contributed a lot to change traditional, social, religious, cultural and ethical values of the Naga people. Their traditional world almost disappeared and a new world, which appeared before them was far greater and better than what they had. A time came when they all became grateful to the missionaries who changed their traditional attitudes and behaviour taking great pain and life risk. They still remember such missionaries who dedicated their lives to the cause of the Nagas despite their opposition and resistance. For instance, Dr Clark and his wife are immortal among the Naga people. The pair is always remembered for the services what they did for the Naga people. That is why the village Ungma has installed the statue of Mr. and Mrs. Clark in their sweet memory.

The tradition-bound behaviour of the ancient Nagas, devoid of reason and metaphysics, carried various ill practices based on simple faiths. It was new Christian faith, which was based on highly developed religious philosophy, brought an end to the evil practices of the Naga people "by teaching them as to how to live together in peace, love and tolerance with one another as good neighbours.... Christianity was an inward machinery, which brought modernization, western ways of life, education, the renaissance of Nagaism and unity among Nagas".[52] According to Terhuja: "If one responsible dynamic factor were to be singled out for an overall change in the life of the Nagas, it would undoubtedly be the introduction of Christianity among them".[53]

Before the arrival of the British and Christian missionaries in the Naga Hills the Nagas suffered from various diseases due to lack of proper medical facilities and treatment. They all were illiterate. There was neither school nor any educational system. People were ignorant of the language, script and syllabus. It was the missionaries who took enough trouble to establish schools and introduce new pattern of education based on syllabus. They provided trained teachers also. They persuaded the young Nagas to join schools and learn new things. The word modernization was alien to them. Sangyu has rightly observed, "Among the various operative forces, which penetrated the North East region with the British entrance, ecclesiology has played a very important role in the entire process of the modernization of the Angamis".[54] Through various biblical conferences, prayers and annual conferences the Christian missionaries taught the Naga people to look into the advances of the world in science, technology, education and asked them to overcome traditional prejudices. They also made them understand the futility and meaninglessness of the wild faith and wild behaviour.

Thus Christianity was a process which created everlasting impact on the Nagas and their traditional and vague animistic beliefs began to erode gradually. They began to incline towards the concept of one God, and Christ being the only son of God. Their faith in old rituals began to disappear and Christianity "ushered in a transformation from animistic tradition based on superstitious practices to a more orderly society where the guiding principle was no longer that of natural human urges but based rather on the laws of God and love for one's fellow man".[55] The schools, which were established by the missionaries, began to produce not only teachers but the students who got the wisdom to differentiate their past and future and choose to advance their career in various branches of learning.[56] Education and religion liquidated all the outdated taboos... and trained them in the new path of progress. With the help of education realisation came to them that full devotion to education was the only way of development and such educational facilities were possible only with association of the missionaries.[57]

There may not be two opinions about the fact that the British rulers and the Christian missionaries helped the Naga people to cast off their traditional attitude towards truth and give up wild behaviour. It is also true that they moulded the Nagâ people towards the way of modernity, but only in thinking. Their main emphasis was to convert the animist Nagas to the faith of Christianity and used them as a tool to spread Christianity to the pockets where no religious preaching had reached. If secularism is the indispensable component of modernity, the Nagas were yet far behind. Their mental horizon was yet limited to the world of tribalism due to lack of proper secularized higher education. There was no industrialization and urbanization during the British regime in the Naga Hills with the result that social mobilization remained static. The rustic people sunk into deep down of poverty could hardly think of new life and new values. The flow of the outsiders was very much restricted. As a result, there was no chance of exposure of the Nagas to other peoples. The Nagas were still in the shackle of isolation and separation. In such situation it was not possible for them to develop their mental make-up to the universal level. The Naga society was still particularistic, not universalistic. Some changes took place in their social, religious and political institutions, but not on universalistic pattern. The villages were still governed by customary laws and practices. The feeling of modernization took place, no doubt, but not among the masses, but among those who managed to be near to the British administration and missionaries. There were many who could not feel what modernization was. They knew about new things, but they had no resources to enjoy these things. Hence they were bound to follow the old living style. Under such facts it may be said that it is wrong to assume that the missionaries played the role to modernize the Naga society.

The western Christian missionaries left Nagaland in 1955 when their work was almost over. They would have prolonged their stay in Nagaland, but the appearance of Naga freedom movement and battle between the Indian armed forces and the Naga militants, perhaps, was the vital cause, which forced the missionaries to leave the place. Thereafter, the Naga pastors and church associations assumed the responsibility to manage the churches and continue gospel services. After independence most of the schools were taken over by the government and secular education was provided. However, the state still has several schools of high standard, which are run by the Christian organizations.

Christianity and loss of the Nagas

It is true that the western Christian missionaries did a lot for the Naga people, and made efforts to transform their society from traditionalism to modernity, but there is a reverse aspect of Christianity in Nagaland. The western missionary's character was orthodox and dogmatic. They were not ready at all to adjust with other frame of social, cultural and religious behaviours. That is why they insisted, from the beginning, to substitute the old Naga culture and social values for those of their own. They wanted to impose upon the Nagas a restrictive behaviour. Smith has rightly observed: "There is grave danger that Christianity, as presented to these people, comes to the little more than the adoption of another set of taboos... Under the old system the Nagas had to refrain from working in the field on certain days... they must refrain from work on the Christian Sabbath".[58] Elvin also remarked: "The activities of the Baptist Mission among the Nagas have demoralized the people, destroying tribal solidarity and forbidden the joys and feasting, the decoration and romance of communal life".[59]

No doubt, the ancient Naga people had no institutionalised education. But it does not mean that they did not possess any set of goodness. The cultural values what they possessed are still relevant in the Naga society. The early Nagas were honest, simple and straight-forward and their wants were limited, because they were satisfied with what they had. Their community life was full of joys, which they shared together. Their Morong was the best institution, which used to impart practical teaching to the youngsters. They maintained strict discipline in the family and villages. They did hardly allow indulging their sons and daughters in dirty practices. The social system and cultural values specially among the Aos were so nice that these are appreciated even today by the conscious and reasonable Nagas. The spread of Christianity and imposition of new civilization badly affected ancient Nagas' social, religious and cultural values. They were asked and rather forced to do away with all their traditional cultural values only because these values had no similarity with the values, which were imposed upon them by the missionaries. The simple and innocent people could hardly distinguish the goodness between these two sets of cultures. They simply accepted the new culture and civilization because they were asked that the culture which they had held was injurious and useless.

On the other hand, the missionaries who were predetermined to impose western culture upon "an un-modern or unenlightened country" were not ready at all to see the goodness of ancient Naga culture and provide room for that in the newly imposed culture. Christianity came to the Naga people "dressed in western garb, ... both in thought and practice, in its social, moral and political aspects".[60] It is true that early missionary people had no intention to destroy the beauty of ancient Naga culture. For instance, Dr Clark appreciated the goodness of Aos' village governing system. The village was divided into Christian and non-Christian groups after formation of the new Christian village at Molung. Clark, when he came to know that formation of a new Christian village had divided the villagers, he repented. This is evident from his statement, which *inter alia* said, "This religion should not disturb the village government system. Had I known it before, I would never have built a new village (Molungyimsen)".[61] In another letter Clark further regretted his mistake for separation of the village in two rival groups—Christian and non-Christian. The letter read, "To build a new village with the believers separate from non-believers will not be fair to the Gospel. What I have done may have been a mistake".[62]

After departure of Clark from the Naga Hills, the missionaries who assumed the responsibility to spread Christianity among the Nagas, did hardly care and honour for ancient Nagas' cultural and social attributes. Christianity and western civilization are responsible for dividing the Naga society into two classes—the well-maintained class having complete association with the western style of living and the class though Christian, yet underdeveloped. Those Aos who thought the white people as 'angelic and heavenly', blindly follow their religion, way of life and style. Even after the departure of the white people from Nagaland, the Aos who were much closed to them hardly forget the days that they had passed with them. They called the days 'smart days with white men in schools, church centers and in their bungalows'. Panger has rightly remarked that "the old folk always have a proud story about the British days... the moral impact of the west is still strongly felt. Those who live with the whites prove to be more disciplined than the younger generation in all aspects of life".[63]

While analyzing the contributions of the western missionaries to the Naga people in the 16th Ao Theological Conference in 1980, the following view was expressed:

"Missionaries did many good things for the Aos. But they did some bad things also. They created destruction in social and cultural life of the Aos... . They failed to differentiate the socio-cultural aspect and religious aspect of the life and culture of the Aos. Along with the worship of Satan they buried our culture because the Ao Christians regarded Ao culture as a sin. They (missionaries) tried to impact Christianity in American culture. This is the first wound that disintegrates our culture. The Aos are suffering from this wound till today without finding a healing balm".[64]

Thus it is very much obvious that the western missionaries while replacing the ancient Nagas' faith with the new faith of Christianity, did all to bring about total change in the ancient culture of the people. This is another fact that the ancient Naga culture was so deep and so good that it was not possible for them to erode it totally. There were some people who ever remained proud of their ancient cultural and social as well as political values. They accepted Christianity, no doubt, but not at the cost of total destruction of their ancestral values, which were passed from generation to generation. It should be remembered that the culture and traditions are rooted in the blood and heart of the people. No alien power or elements can uproot entire traditions and customs if they have real values. The Nagas' ancient culture and social values were valuable. That is why the ancient traditional wisdom and social practices including religious festival and ceremonies are as fresh today as it were in the beginning. It is heartening to note that, today, the Nagas as a whole are very much aware of their past cultural values. They are applying all the efforts to revive and preserve them. The Nagas are rich in their old cultural and social values which are inter-related. There is an urgent need to encourage them to continue with the values what their ancestors possessed centuries back.

References

1. Asoso, Yonuo, *The Rising Nagas,* Vivek Publishing House, New Delhi, 1974, p. 110
2. Walu, C Walling. *All is light,* Source material on History of Christianity Literature, Department of Baptist Argo, Impure, Mokokchung, 2001, p. 3.
3. *Ibid.*
4. Philips, P.T., *The Growth of Baptist Church in Nagaland,* Guwahati, 1982, p.53.
5. *Ibid.*
6. Bendangnagshi, *History of Christianity in Nagaland—1872-1972,* Shalen Ministry Publication, Natural Printing Press, Bangkok, 2004, p.70.
7. "Clark's Letters, *BMM,* December 1871, pp. 125ff.
8. *Olem KilepLashir Mungchen,* Molungimsen Baptist Church, 1976, p. 23.
9. Bendangnagshi, *Glimpses of Naga History,* Saraighat Offset Press, Guwahati, 1993, pp. 78-79.
10. Panger Imchen, *Ancient Ao Nagas Religion and Culture,* Har-Anand Publications, New Delhi, 1993, p. 148.
11. *Oxford English Dictionary* (2nd edition), R.W. Burchfield (Ed),New York, 1991, pp. 566-69.
12. Jhingru, S., "Religional Communalism", in B. Bidwai, *Religion and Communalism,* New Delhi, p. 76.
13. *Encyclopedia Dictionary of Society,* B.B. Sharma (Ed), Vol. 4, New Delhi, 1992, p. 786.
14. Imchen Panger, *Ancient Ao Nagas Religion and Culture, op. cit.,* 1993, p. 148.
15. Philips, P.T., *The Growth of Baptist Church in Nagaland. op. cit.,* 1982, p. 55.
16. Clark M.M. (Mrs.), *A Corner in India,* Christian Literature Centre, Guwahati, 1978, pp. 15-18.
17. *Ibid.*
18. *Ibid.* p. 141.

19. Yonuo, Asoso, *The Rising Nagas, op. cit.*, 1974, p.115.
20. Ganguli, M., *A Pilgrimage to the Nagas*, Oxford & IMH Publishing Company, New Delhi, 1984, p. 77.
21. Yonuo, Asoso, *The Rising Nagas, op. cit.*, 1974, pp. 115-16.
22. Imchen, Panger, *Ancient Ao Nagas Religion and Culture, op. cit.*, 1993, p.153.
23. Downs, F.S., *Christianity in North East India*, Christian Literature Centre, Guwahati, 1984, p. 196.
24. *Ibid.* p. 154.
25. "A Letter of J.P. Mills, SDO, dated 10th June 1892, to Impure Mission Centre," Mokokchung.
26. Kinjung, Ao, Nokinkekter Monchen, *Abode of Warriors*, Christian Literature Centre, Guwahati, 1941, p. 109.
27. Narola, Revenburg (Ed), *The Star of the Naga Hills*, Judson Press, Philadelphia, 1941, p. 265.
28. *Ibid.*
29. Philips, P.T., *The Growth of Baptist Church in Nagaland, op. cit.*, 1982, p. 59.
30. Yonuo, Asoso, *The Rising Nagas, op. cit.*, 1974, pp. 116.
31. Bendangnagshi, *Glimpses of Naga History*, Guwahati, 1986, p.20.
32. Clarks, M.M., *A Corner in India*, (Annual Report), American Baptist Publication Society, Philadelphia, 1922, pp. 320-21.
33. *Ibid.* p. 323.
34. Cited in Philips, P.T., *The Growth of Baptist Church in Nagaland. op. cit.*, 1982, p. 69.
35. Imchen, Panger, *Ancient Ao Nagas Religion and Culture, op. cit.*, 1993, p. 154-55.
36. Cited in Philips, P.T., *The Growth of Baptist Church in Nagaland. op. cit.*, 1982, pp. 200-01.
37. E.T. Snep "A Glimpse at the Impact of Christianity on Naga Culture", published in *The Warrior*, vol. 4, No. 15, by the Directorate of Information, Publicity and Tourism, Government of Nagaland, Kohima, 1971.

38. M.M. Clark, *A Corner in India,* Report of the 8th Session Missionary Conference, *op. cit.,* 1904-1905, p. 58.
39. Imchen, Panger, *Ancient Ao Nagas Religion and Culture, op. cit.,* 1993, p.157.
40. Alemchiba, M., "Problems of Readjustment to the New situation with special reference to Naga Tribes", in *Highlander,* vol.4, No.1, March-April 1976, p. 3.
41. Downs, F.S., *The Mighty Work of God: A Brief History of the Council of Baptist Christians of North East India,* Christian Literature Centre, Guwahati, p. 113.
42. *Ibid.*
43. Imchen, Panger, *Ancient Ao Nagas Religion and Culture, op. cit.,* 1993, p.159.
44. Wallu, C. Walling, *All is Light,* (Source Material of Christianity), *op. cit.,* p.102.
45. V.K. Nuh, *Nagaland and Politics,* Vision Press, Kohima 1986, p. 62.
46. *Ibid.*
47. Sword, V.H., *Baptist in Assam,* Conference Press, Chicago, 1935, p. 115.
48. Philips, P.T. *The Growth of Baptist Church in Nagaland. op. cit.,* 1982, p. 127.
49. Panikar, K.M., *Asia and Western Dominions,* 2nd edition, George Allen & Unwin Ltd. London, 1954, p. 332.
50. Singh, Yogendra, *Modernization of Indian Tradition,* Rawat Publications, New Delhi, 1996, p. 61.
51. Sinai, I.R., *The Challenges of Modernization,* London Chatto and Windus, 1964, pp. 18-19.
52. Yonuo Asoso, *The Rising Nagas, op. cit.,* p. 120.
53. Terhuja, K., "The Christian Church among the Angami Nagas" in *Tribal Situation in India,* vol. 13, edited by K.S. Singh, Simila, 1972, p. 294.
54. Sangyu V., "A History of Nagas and Nagaland Dynamics of Oral Tradition in Village Formation", *Commonwealth Publications,* New Delhi, 1996, p. 115.

55. *Ibid.* pp. 117-18.
56. Puthenpurkal Joseph, Baptist Mission in Nagaland, Shillong, 1984, p. 121.
57. *Ibid.*
58. Smith, W.C., "Missionary Activities and Acculturation of Backward People". *Journal of Applied Sociology,* March-April, 1923, p. 185.
59. Elwin, V., "Aboriginals", *Oxford Pamphlets on Indian Affairs,* Bombay, 1944, p. 14.
60. Andi, Prani, "Theological Pioneering in India", *Religion and Society,* vol. XVII, No.1, March 1970, p. 76.
61. Cited in Imchen, Panger, *Ancient Ao Nagas Religion and Culture, op. cit.,* pp. 156-57.
62. Kinjung, L., Nokinketer Mongchen, *Abode of Warriors, op. cit.,* p.48.
63. Imchen, Panger, *Ancient Ao Nagas Religion and Culture, op. cit.,* 1983, pp. 161-62.
64. *Ibid,* p. 162.

***

4

Education and its Role

In an era of political unification of the various disintegrated Naga, tribes ushered the arrival of the British in the Naga Hills, alongwith the annexation of the Naga territories to the British rule and promulgation of the British special rules and regulations that sharpened their political consciousness. On the other hand, entrance of the western Baptist Christian missionaries in the land of the Nagas and their activities in the Naga Hills marked changes in social, religious and cultural life of the Naga people. While spreading the new faith among the animist Nagas and indoctrinating them with Christianity, the missionary people laid foundation of modern educational system, which opened a new chapter in the history of the Naga people. Though the main objective of the missionaries behind establishing schools in the Naga Hills was to prepare fertile ground for the growth of Christianity by producing native preachers and church pastors, in due course of time, education helped the Nagas to view the world from new angle and enabled them to get rid of their traditional wild behaviours. Education opened dimensions of new avenues in their life and helped them to come out of their parochial thinking. The preachers, who had made their entry into the Naga Hills along with the American Baptist Christian Missionaries, were mostly Assamese whose number was not sufficient. The missionary people needed trained and educated native preachers who could not only talk to the native people in their own language but also would succeed in persuading the animist Nagas to understand about the significance of Christianity. Under such need and realisation the missionaries took initiative to open schools in the Naga Hills.

The British government, needed educated Nagas who could assist the government in running the offices at least at the lower level. Hence, the government, too, encouraged and helped the missionaries to set up schools and impart education to the Nagas. As a result, in the beginning, the primary schools along with the Bible schools and training schools came into being. This chapter discusses and examines about the rise and growth of education in Nagaland during the British regime and analyses the impact of new education upon the life and thought of the Naga people. It also presents a short description about the growth of education in Nagaland after India's independence.

The ancient Naga people were cent per cent illiterate because there was no school nor they had the idea and capacity to send their children out of Nagaland for education. In real sense, they did not know anything about education. The only means to impart some sort of training and values to the younger generation was the Morong where the youngsters used to get together and hear sermons from their elders. In the beginning, the missionary people faced a lot of troubles and inconveniences to begin education in the Naga Hills since the tribal people lacked interest in education and the missionaries felt extreme difficulties to persuade the Nagas to join school and have education, because they were not friendly to them. Even the guardians were not ready to send their children to the schools established by the Christian Mission because of two reasons. Firstly, they had not yet recognized the missionaries and treated them as the spies of the British government. Secondly, they were all farmers and their compulsion was to work in the field from dawn to dusk alongwith whole family members. As they did not know the importance of education, they were not ready to send their children to schools at the cost of their field works. The girls had to perform domestic works besides field jobs.

The devoted missionaries, however, with their mild and sympathetic behaviours towards the Naga people changed the scenario and a day came when the Naga guardians began to realize the importance of education in life. The government, too, applied efforts to set some schools at primary levels while providing financial support. Thus, with the efforts of both the Christian missionaries and the British government, education, at the primary level first, began in the Naga Hills among the Ao people. Education in Nagaland actually began in full swing after India's independence. However, the missionary people and the British government must be appreciated for the efforts to give the foundation of institutional education in the Naga Hills and make the people interested in education.

Missioneries as Founders of Education

The devoted missionaries took all the troubles to give foundation of educational institutions in the Naga Hills. Though their main objective was to prepare fertile ground for the growth of Christianity and indoctrinate the animist Nagas with the new religion, the missionaries soon realized that the objective could not be achieved fully without providing modern education to the Nagas. Hence, they prepared the group of preachers from the land of the native to educate the people. First, the Bible schools and training schools were opened, but the problem, which came on the way, was to persuade the villagers to send their children to the schools. In the beginning, the government came ahead to provide financial assistance to the schools established by the missionaries.

In the words of Philips: "Probably, the Christian schools have been the most effective evangelistic in Nagaland. Whenever the missionaries went to Nagaland, they started schools at the station and nearby villages".[1] Bronson was the first pioneer to give the foundation of education in the Naga Hills. But real efforts to set up schools in the Naga Hills were applied by Mr. and Mrs. M.M. Clark. They not only set up schools but also provided syllabus for the teaching in the schools. Mr. Clark opened not less than eight missionary schools in different villages in the Ao area. He also persuaded Rev. King and Witter to start educational work among the Angamis and the Lothas respectively. Rev. King set a few primary schools in the Angami area while Witter took the initiative to open some schools in the Lotha areas. It was Rev. Desine who first started training school at Impure and then missionary school in the last part of the nineteenth century. The school set up at Impure, which was the strongest and earliest missionary station, aquired high reputation and attracted students from different places of the Naga Hills.

To start education among the semi-civilized people was not an easy task. Describing the difficulties what the missionaries faced in the Naga Hills while making the beginning of education there, Rev. Revenburg writes: "These savage (the Nagas) naturally do not appreciate the value of schools, and hence one difficulty is to overcome in making school work a success among them. One school I closed in April (1886) on account of fickleness of the teacher".[2] W.E. Witter also felt the same problem. He opened one school with three Naga students and he himself assumed the responsibility to teach them, but he soon experienced that it was not an easy task to teach the Nagas at that time. He noted down: "The school problem is a perplexing one. To get these savages to attend school, we must at least give them their rice... ."[3] Most of the parents disliked to send their children to schools even after taking rice. It was all because the parents did not want to spare them from the field work. The people did hardly understand the value and need of education. The only means of their livelihood was cultivation, which needed hard manual work. Hence they were reluctant to spare their children for the school. To them the field work was more important than attending schools. Dr Clark explaining the cause of not sending the children to the schools wrote that "So hard is the struggle for daily bread that the children must be pressed into work, whether on the field or for infants at home".[4] Though the working hour in the school was not more than one or two hours, the parents did not like to loose even that short period of time at the cost of cultivation or home work. Another cause for negligence of school was the lack of required curriculum in the school. The teachers taught mostly Bible and Gospels for which the Nagas had little interest at that time. However, the school ran with the students who were employed at the missionary stations. At certain places schools were closed down due to lack of required number of students.

Objectives Behind Introducing Education

While giving foundation of schools in the Naga Hills, the main objectives of the missionaries was "the proclamation of the gospel to the people of the village".[5] Since many villages had not yet adopted Christianity, the villagers were least interested in the teaching of gospels or hearing the stories of the Bible. Hence they did not attend schools despite persuasion and encouragement given to them by the missionary people. Moreover, the schools set up by the missionaries were not secular in nature and character. They declined to accept government's grants-in-aid because doing so they would have to make the school secular, which they did not like. Due to lack of proper financing the missionary schools suffered. They could not give the students proper stipends or scholarship. However, the missionary people did not give up their efforts in this regard because they knew that without spreading education it was impossible to spread Christianity among the Nagas. They continued the effort in the name of God. It is evident from the statement of Perrine, that said:

"It is my belief that Christ intended that all Christians should be some sorts of teachers and preachers... they should be receiving some sorts of training for Christ work ... . Our work is unique... what we want to do is simply prepare the Christians for the performance of the duties that must fall to them. Another thing what we desire to impress both our education system and otherwise, is that in the true sense... they must do the work not for us but for Master".[6]

With this faith and courage the number of schools began to increase and the villagers, too, began to pay attention to the value of education. With the advance of the years, the number of converts also increased.

Thus, it is very much obvious that the main objective behind teaching the Nagas was to prepare them for carrying out the jobs and responsibility of devoted Christians. With increasing number of schools the need was felt to set up high schools with the purpose "to take the best pupils of these village schools and give them a good training for teachers and preachers".[7] The fact is that the basic purpose of opening schools in the Naga Hills by the missionaries was to produce trained teachers and preachers who could proceed to the remote villages carrying the messages of the missionaries and induce the non-Christians to accept Christianity. To serve the purpose the missionaries set up training schools and enrolled the students and trained them to achieve the desired goal. In this regard Impure, the well-settled mission centre, became the first training centre for producing trained teachers and preachers from amongst the Naga people.

The Clarks: The Real Propounders of Education

The entrance of Dr. Clark into the Naga Hills, in fact, marked the real beginning of education in the Naga Hills district. He arrived in Nagaland in 1876 and set up a new village for Naga Christians, namely, *Molungyimsen* (Molung). It was this village where his wife Mary Mead Clark, started a formal school. Though, in the beginning, the school was mainly intended for women, it became the centre of education for both men and women. In 1883, a small printing press was also installed there. Molung village was shifted in 1894 to Impure with a purpose to facilitate the operation of mission activities. In 1895, a school with nine pupils was started with the marked intention to produce trained teachers, preachers, evangelists and pastors for churches. Later on, several devoted missionaries like Rev. and Mrs. S.A. Perrine and Dr and Mrs. F.P. Haggard joined the school as educational leaders and worked hard for the growth of education in the Naga Hills. In 1919, the school of Impure was designated as Impure Mission Training Idle School. By the time, several local teachers like Gwizao, Meru Zeliang, Pehielie Angami, Kumbho and Mayangnokcha Ao joined the educational system as teachers and played the viable role in this field.

By 1891, Ao grammar with vocabulary and illustrative sentences was prepared with hard labour of the American missionaries including Dr Clark. He devoted the labour to prepare Ao Naga English dictionary. In 1893, Ao Naga grammar with illustrative phrases was printed. The trained teachers were sent to different Naga villages with translations of various portions of the Holy Scriptures.

Years rolled down and the Naga people began to take more interest in education with the result that many of the schools became self-supporting with some financial aids of the government. Highlighting the fact Rev. Perrine writes: "The enthusiasm for education perceptibly increased during the year 1899. Indeed a revival in 'letters'—a sort of Naga Renaissance—was brought about (by Naga boys and girls). It would seem as if this alone would suffice to show the Naga people the value of education besides all our talk and religious interactions combined. This new interest aroused has given us no small encouragement".[9] It was this interest of the Naga people in education, which made the Impure School popular and full of students. In the words of Dowd: "The Impure School is intended to give a primary education to as many boys and girls as possible and to fit them to go out as teachers and preachers." He further writes, "Most of them (Nagas) come to us in absolute ignorance even of their letters, and began by learning to read their own language. They studied arithmetic, writing, spelling, physiology, hygiene, geography and history; at the same time special attention is given to the study of scriptures and practical Christian works".[10]

The education given till the end of the19th century in the Naga Hills covered, no doubt, some other subjects mentioned above, but emphasis was laid on religious teaching. The students both boys and girls wanted to attend the institutions for knowledge. They got the knowledge no doubt, but most of them were trained to serve the Christianity and gospel. Schools were yet non-secular. The Government, to establish the secular school, was yet reluctant with the result that education had fully come into the hands of the missionaries. Hence they prescribed the syllabus in the schools, which suited their objectives. According to R.B. Longwall: "The instruction, which was to follow was not to be of secular, but strictly of religious nature. The lessons were not in algebra, geometry and foreign languages, but in the observance of Christian mandates".[11]

Despite all these, Impure School became the centre of education in the Naga Hills district, though it lacked higher education. It was the only educational institution in the district for furnishing teachers to several Naga tribes. This school for many years remained as source of learning and supplying teachers (trained) to other villages, which were provided with some sort of schools. Mrs. and Mr. Clark were the pioneers to make Impure School an attractive centre of education.

More schools appeared in the Naga Hills in due course of time when the Naga people gradually were convinced that if they wanted development, it was education only, which could help them. In the beginning, the purpose of the school was not to impart secular education to the Naga people and integrate them with the mainstream of national education. Since many villages or majority of villages had not yet adopted Christianity, and the people were averse to the activities of the missionaries, they were least interested in the teaching of the gospels or hearing the teaching of the Bible. On the other hand, the mission stations were not sound economically to bear the burden of schools and support the students by giving them stipends or scholarships.

Since the objective was to spread Christianity, the missionary people did not give up their hope and tried their best to achieve their desired goal. They had unflinching faith in God and in His blessing. Rev. Perrine, who was in the Naga Hills, was a true devotee of Lord Christ. He believed that he was sent by God to impart Biblical sermons among the animist Nagas. God had chosen him to complete this pious task. He wanted that all those missionaries who were present in the Naga Hills must take some sort of training to preach Christianity. He did not like to spread secular education because it was not his purpose or aim. It is evident from his own statement, which said: "What we want to do is simply prepare the Christians for the performance of the duties that must fall to them.

Another thing what we desire to impress both our educational system and otherwise, is that in the truest sense...they (trained Christians) must do the work not for us but for Master."[12]

Thus, it is crystal clear that the main purpose of education was to produce native Christians to fulfill the task that was to spread Christianity among the animists. No doubt, the missionary people changed their style of teaching in the schools by introducing some more papers related to general study, but they hardly changed their objectives. When the number of schools increased in the villages, a need was felt to set up high schools or normal schools with the purpose "to take the best pupils of these village schools and give them a good training for teachers and preachers..."[13] The statement makes it clear that the basic purpose of setting up schools by the missionaries was to produce trained teachers and preachers who could go to the remote villages carrying the message of the missionaries and induce the non-Christians to accept Christianity. To serve the purpose the missionaries started 'training schools' and enrolled the students and trained them to achieve the desired goal. In that way Impure School assumed the full responsibility to serve the purpose.

In the first decade of the 20th century, the Impure school was taken by the government, but it was once more handed over to the Mission centre because of two factors—firstly, the inability of the government to manage the school and secondly, lack of effective control over it. But one of the realities was that the missionaries were not ready at all to give up their control over educational institution at Impure, which had become the most attractive centre for spreading Christianity and imparting religious education among the Nagas. Perrine, agreeing to the fact, wrote that "Through school gospel is made to reach the mountaineers more rapidly and permanently than by any other means".[14]

Government Initiative to Control Schools

There is not an iota of doubt that Impure School was taken back from the government's control, but the government had decided not to leave the schools entirely in the hands of the missionaries. Hence, it took over several schools in the villages and supplied definite curriculum suited to general education. The government, too, needed educated persons to assist it in handling the administration, but did not like that the Naga students should be totally deprived of general education. According to Philip, the Christian schools have been the most effective evangelistic in Nagaland. The missionaries went on with their mission in Nagaland, starting schools at stations (missionary) and nearby villages.[15] As the government was not in favour of allowing the missionaries to establish absolute monopoly over education in the Naga Hills, at the beginning of the 20th century it became alert and active in the field of education.

But due to half-hearted interest of the government in education, the missionaries' activities went on unabated. As a result, Impure remained the most attractive centre not only for good education but for Christian centre also. People from different tribes began to come to Impure to take part in religious activities. The missionaries had succeeded in establishing their hold and influence over the Nagas destroying their old traditional as well as customary behaviours and practices. Impure became the centre of attraction for new culture and new civilization. Hokishe Sema while participating in the 75th anniversary of Impure Mission Centre said, "It is an institution, which changed the entire course of our culture and customs. It lit the torch, which enlightened the darkness of Naga Hills and brought the rays of modern and new life to cut hemlocks and removed the grimness of social environment".[16]

The statement of Hokishe Sema in the praise of missionaries and their contribution to the betterment of the Naga people clearly shows that the missionaries had won over the heart and mind of the Nagas. There may not be a second thought about the fact that the Nagas, who were living in isolation and were devoid of all sorts of new life and modern civilization, obtained the light. The missionaries must be credited for opening and widening the path of universal knowledge among the Nagas by establishing schools and imparting sermons. They should also be appreciated for the courage and patience, which they had to mould the semi-civilized Naga people towards new civilization and new life. But it all happened at the cost of destruction of values of the ancient Nagas which were being carried from generation to generation. The civilization and the culture in which the Nagas landed with the help of the missionaries yielded numerous problems also.

The products of the schools began to take little interests in their traditional activities. They were not ready at all to go back to the traditional life and use traditional garments or dress. They became proud of new civilization and new style of life. The girls and boys who attended the missionary schools were not ready to assist their parents either in the fields or in the house-hold affairs. The changes which were taking place among the Nagas at the cost of their age-old customs and traditions, were disliked even by some of the British officials who were Christians but averse to the activities of the missionaries. For instance, Hutton, one of the British officials in the Naga Hills, believed that missionaries were the "chief villains in bringing unwelcome and dilapidating changes".[17] J.P. Mills, too, noted that the American Baptist Mission was "carrying certain amount of education among girls", but "this does not meet with the approval of the conservatives", who "regarded it as useless and leading to idleness and immorality". Mills further wrote that the Ao girls who received training and education from the missionary schools "refused to demean themselves by working in the fields like their uneducated sisters, and preferred to sit in the village during the day doing nothing".[18] To quote Mills once more, "The girls who have had a Mission education find it hard to settle down to village life and reliable to go on the loose.... the consensus of opinion among respectable Aos undoubtedly is that there is grave risk of a Mission-trained girl getting above herself and so idle and immoral. And after all, the Ào is likely to know more of his womenfolk than any outsiders".[19]

Thus, it is very much obvious that the education served as a means to change the traditional concept of the educated Nagas and enabled them to know new things. It also helped them to understand the reality of the life and meet the challenges of the life without no reason. At the same time, it created a feeling among the educated Nagas that they were better than those who were yet uneducated or illiterate. They began to discriminate works.

Now manual works specially in the fields were looked down upon by the educated boys and girls. They declined to work in the fields or to look after the household affairs. This created reverse impact upon the guardians who began to refuse to send their wards to schools specially girls. The education of girls was seen as a waste of time and harmful to domestic labour. However, the missionaries putting much more emphasis on girl's education continued the efforts to persuade guardians for sending their girls to the schools.

It has already been stated that the missionaries had no faith in traditional society and they wanted to bring about total change in the traditional Naga society. However, it was not possible until the womenfolk would have been educated. Moreover, the educated Naga girls were found more responsive in comparison with the educated boys. There were British administrators like Hutton and Mills who believed that "the interests of the people were best served in a static society" while the missionaries "believed that the people were best served in a dynamic society".[20]

It is a universally acceptable fact that the Ao tribes in comparison to other Naga tribes have been far ahead in changing their traditional outlook and behavioural attitude only because the Aos were the first to recognize the significance of education. That is why they not only assisted the missionaries to set up schools in their areas but also willingly sent their children to schools for new education. The Ao people have been found moderate and liberal towards their women. They did not like to keep their women deprived of educational facilities. Moreover, in the Ao society the women had honourable place. They were treated as the mistresses of the house. Hence despite growing reluctance among the educated girls towards field works and household affairs, the Ao guardians did hardly restrict the girls from attending the schools with the result that both the males and females of the Aos got equal benefit of education.

The British Indian government began to take initiative for opening some schools in the Naga Hills only from the first decade of the 20th century. The study shows that the government was least interested in providing education to the Naga people. Hence, the assistance of the missionaries was indispensable for growth of education in Nagaland. The Naga people had twenty-two primary schools, one secondary school and two special schools by the years 1903-04. In 1873, Rev. G.D. King had already opened a school at Chumukedima, but the school could not run properly due to non-cooperation of the local people. The school was revived in 1889, but from 1895 it faced the trouble for shortage of teachers. The Deputy Commissioner of Assam, in 1903, assured all possible help to Regensburg and remained true to his promise with the result that the school at Chumukedima got the pace.

In 1941, a joint High School (presently known as Government High School, Kohima) was established by combined efforts of both the Mission and the government. Since the people of the Ao area were very much alert and conscious of the changes, which were taking place in the areas, they lost no time to avail the benefits of education. They welcomed the educational institutions in the Ao region and offered all the possible cooperation to both the missionaries and the government to establish new schools in their villages. Mokokchung, which was the sub-division of the Naga Hills district, had taken the shape of a town. A middle school was set up at Mokokchung in 1941. In 1943, a private High School was also set up, which was taken over by the government in 1948.

The Lotha people, too, were much alert and conscious to the changes taking place in the field of education in their region. They welcomed coming up of schools in their area but very late. According to Kiremwati, in the Lotha area "the beginning of education was beset with uncertainties". The Lotha people saw the first school in their area in 1885 when one Mission School was set up. However, the school was closed down due to departure of Rev. Witter from Wokha. It was only in 1925 when the government thought of opening a lower primary school at Okotso in 1941. Soon after that, a middle school was opened at Wokha by the government.

Education came very late in the Sema areas, too, The Sema people witnessed first Mission school in their areas in 1937 at Aizuto. So far the case of the Tuensang areas is concerned, the education came here very late because of its remoteness and backwardness of the people. Thus, it is obvious that the Aos, Angamis, Lothas and Semas are the people who first came in contact with modern education. Among these tribes, the Aos and Angamis were the first to get better opportunity for receiving modern education.

A general survey of growth of schools in Nagaland during the British region reflects the truth that the government had little interest in developing education in Nagaland. That is why the number of the schools set up by the government was very few. The British government was not a welfare government. It had occupied the Naga Hills not with the intention to develop the hill people, but to serve its own interest that was a safe and secured frontier. The government wanted some Nagas to be employed in the government jobs at lower level and for that primary education was enough. That is why the government did not take trouble to set up high schools or colleges even in the emerging towns. Moreover, the schools, which were set up by the missionary were found involved in imparting religious education, under the nose of the government, but it hardly controlled the missionary's activities and schools set up by them. Rather the government assisted the missionaries to carry on the system of education on their own line. The government hardly thought of taking over the Mission schools because it would have increased financial burden over the government, which it never liked. Moreover, the government was not in a mood to interfere in the affairs of the missionaries.

A General survey of Education and its Drawbacks during the British Period

The system of the educational institution, which began during the British period, was peculiar. Initially classes were regulated up to level II and the schools were known as the Lower Primary

Schools. Some schools were allowed to upgrade as Upper Primary School to run up to class IV. Only a few schools were later upgraded to run class up to VI and were called as Middle Schools. Before 1928, the Naga students had to go to Guwahati or Shillong for study beyond class VIII. It was only in 1938, that the government decided that beyond class VIII, education should be given to the Nagas in their own region. This provision gave the Naga students a great relief in the field of education on the one hand and enabled numerous students to continue studies on the other.

The earlier system of education in the Naga Hills was not only defective but difficult also. Describing the shortcomings of previous educational system of the Naga Hills, Kiremwati remarked that "The weakness of the then system and approach to education was due to the short term goals of producing persons to read the Bible and to work as clerks." He further writes: "The dual and mutual control by the church and the government, though of advantage to both, was not without problems resulting at times, even in closer of schools at places".[21] Kiremwati, who has been the founder Director of the Directorate of Higher and Technical Education of Nagaland, is the noted educationist of Nagaland. He has closely observed the system of education in Nagaland before India's independence. The remarks what he has passed are very much correct. The government and missionaries began education in Nagaland, no doubt, but their objective behind introducing education was parochial and motivated. To quote Kiremwati once more, "The short-sighted objectives and organizational dichotomy (of the British) generated instability and the system failed to lay a firm foundation of basic education".[22]

During 1940s, the Nagaland district, which was under the province of Assam got two high schools, one at Kohima and another at Mokokchung with full support of the government and with prescribed curriculum. Besides these, some more middle schools and primary schools were opened by the government in selected big villages. By this time Impure Central School had grown up as the biggest middle school in Assam for reading of Christianity. The policy of the government, in the beginning, had been to spread

Christianity and education both at a time to bring the Nagas under civilization.[23] With this point in view, the colonial educational policy was mainly directed to the extension of pecuniary grants to the Christian Missions in the Naga Hills.[24]

Till 1904, the British Indian government was reluctant to give required attention to the growth of education in the province of Assam. What the government did in this regard was simply an experiment in the field of education in North East India. At that time primary education in the whole province, in general, was in poor stage. Sixty per cent of the students in schools were classed as 'illiterate' as they were unable to read and write.[25] Since the government was not interested in doing welfare to the people, it allotted a little financial assistance to the schools with the result that neither the teachers were appropriate nor was the management efficient.[26]

An analytical study and close observation of the system of education during the British period and the reluctance of the government towards the education reveals the truth that in the Naga Hills district the government attributed slow progress of education and it largely depended on Mission schools for the education of the Naga tribes. There were only six primary schools in the Naga Hills district, which were maintained by the government. Besides that, there were sixteen mission schools, which received grants-in-aid from the government.[27] These (six) schools were located in Mokokchung, Wokha, Kohima, Jakhama and Choswozma. The Mission schools (sixteen in number) were located at Molung, Yangong, Srasomen, Womaken, Merankong, Akola, Asangma, Warmmung, Chungllyimsen, Chanki, Mamotong, Longkhum, Ungma, and Lungsang.

Mokokchung, occupied by the Ao tribe, was the first area where out of sixteen schools, maximum numbers of schools were set up. It is all because the missionaries landed first in the Ao area and made it their first abode. Secondly, the Ao people took no much time to understand the significance of education and cooperate with the missionaries and the government in setting up schools in their areas. Kohima stood number two in the field of education. The areas like Tuensang including Mon and Khiphere had not even single school. Neither the missionary, nor the government thought of taking pains to set up schools in that remote corner, which was occupied mostly by the people who were far away from the light of education and civilization. Even people of the area had little awareness about the significance of education during that period. A few families, who had the awareness, sent their children to Mokokchung and Kohima for education.

Growing Interest of the Government in Education

The British Indian government, in the beginning, did not want to annoy the missionaries by interfering in their affairs whether it was the education or gospel. But the education policy of the government changed by the beginning of 20th century. Question may be raised as to what factors compelled the government to make a shift in its educational policy. The answer is given here. The missionaries continued to bring development in the field of education, no doubt, but with the marked objective to spread Christianity, which the government disliked. The government also observed that the Mission schools were understaffed and often faced with a dearth of qualified teachers, which affected the growth of proper education. Thirdly, the local guardians were yet to reluctant to send their children to mission schools because the fear was constantly lurking in their mind that their children while getting education would be baptized. Hence in the circumstances, the government felt that it had "a moral obligation and responsibility towards their animist subjects...it realized that animist Nagas should not be deprived of modern education"[28]. In the words of Piketo: "In consideration of all these aspects, government modified its education policy in the district, and accordingly started taking over more and more village schools, which were in fact missions-venture schools".[29]

No doubt, the government took over several schools, but it does not mean that the Mission Centers were asked to stop its educational activities in the Naga Hills. The reality is that in Naga Hills the government took over the general village schools "leaving the missionaries in charge of the training schools which are to train teachers for the village schools." Moreover, the Christian missionaries "still continued to establish schools with the grants-in-aid (which) they received from the government".[30] There were many venture schools, run by the missionaries with government's grants-in-aid. In 1922, the number of government lower primary schools had risen to 42.[31]

By 1930s, the government once more decided to take over maximum schools of the Naga Hills district. The logic behind such step of the government was advanced that the missionaries had done appreciable jobs by establishing schools in the Naga Hills, but "solely with the object of Christianizing the children". "Some hill tribes have refused education because it brought Christianity with it, and it is unfair that they should be deprived of education because they are unwilling to abandon their tribal custom".[32]

With this logic the government went on taking over the school management from the Mission Centers. However, there were yet considerable number of schools under the management and control of the missionaries. In 1938, out of 167 educational institutions, 115 were government lower primary schools, 10 government-aided lower primary schools, 36 Mission-aided lower primary schools (up to Middle English standard), 2 Mission-aided upper primary standard and 1 government industrial school.[33] The government as per its policy declared decided to take over 10 schools annually for a period of five years. However, the government could not remain true to its declaration with the result that the number of the government schools could hardly increase. However, on such move, the Nagas who had not yet come under the influence of Christianity appreciated the move of the government. The number of the students in the schools increased. The curriculum prescribed by the government carried general education including arithmetic, geography, history, English and geometry. The efforts were also applied to provide the schools with well qualified teachers.

TABLE- I

GROWTH OF SCHOOLS IN THE NAGA HILLS DURING THE BRITISH PERIOD, 1882-1947

Year	Number of L.P. schools	Number of M.E. schools	Number of High schools	Number of Students Primary	Secondary	Total
(1)	(2)	(3)	(4)	(5)	(6)	(7)
1882-83	6	—	—	—	—	—
1883-84	6	—	—	107	—	107
1884-85	5	—	—	63	—	63
1885-86	11	—	—	—	—	—
1886-87	20	—	—	—	—	—
1887-88	10	—	—	199	—	199
1888-89	16	—	—	221	—	221
1889-90	15	—	—	256	—	256
1890-91	16	—	—	297	—	297
1891-92	17	—	—	332	—	332
1892-93	15	—	—	236	—	236
1893-94	17	—	—	299	—	299
1894-95	16	—	—	322	—	322
1895-96	14	—	—	330	—	330
1896-97	15	—	—	292	—	292
1897-98	17	1	—	371	—	371
1898-99	16	1	—	309	—	309
1899-00	13	1	—	211	—	211
1900-01	16	1	—	73	6	79
1900-02	16	1	—	80	5	85
1902-03	22	1	—	81	6	87
1903-04	22	1	—	—	—	—
1904-05	22	1	—	—	—	—
1905-06	—	1	—	—	—	—
1906-07	31	1	—	—	—	789

(Contd.)

(1)	(2)	(3)	(4)	(5)	(6)	(7)
1907-08	24	1	—	—	—	—
1908-09	21	1	—	—	—	—
1909-10	23	1	—	—	—	—
1910-11	24	1	—	—	—	—
1911-12	22	1	—	—	—	—
1912-13	26	1	—	385	—	385
1913-14	27	1	—	458	—	458
1914-15	27	1	—	525	—	525
1915-16	39	1	—	—	—	—
1916-17	35	1	—	659	92	751
1917-18	—	1	—	773	97	870
1918-19	32	1	—	815	106	921
1919-20	59	1	—	1279	123	1502
1920-21 1921-22	62 84	1 1	— —	1909 1051	111 106	2010 1157
1922-23	84	1	—	3209	110	3319
1923-24	85	1	—	2145	93	2238
1924-25	85	1	—	1868	92	1969
1925-26	88	1	—	2202	92	2314
1926-27	92	1	—	2401	79	2480
1927-28	107	1	—	2388	83	2471
1928-29	107	1	—	3132	92	3224
1929-30	124	1	—	3365	351	3716
1930-31	124	1	—	3677	611	4288
1931-32	149	1	—	3804	628	4432
1932-33	150	1	—	3835	602	4528
1933-34	145	1	—	3749	796	4545
1934-35	135	1	—	4261	958\9	5200
1935-36	141	1	—	4118	974	5092

(Contd.)

(1)	(2)	(3)	(4)	(5)	(6)	(7)
1936-37	141	1	—	4325	1120	5445
1937-38	141	1	1	3594	938	4532
1938-39	—	1	1	3912	997	4909
1939-40	—	1	1	—	—	—
1940-41	—	1	1	—	—	—
1941-42	—	1	1	—	—	
1942-43	—	1	1	—	—	—
1943-44	—	1	1	—	—	—
1944-45	—	1	1	—	—	—
1945-46	—	1	1	—	—	—
1946-47	161	3	1	—	—	
1947-48	—	—	—	—	—	17443

Source—Cited in *Piketo Sema, British Policy and Administration in Nagaland,* 1882-1947, pp. 81-83.

The table illustrated above lacks some statistics. However, it indicates that the growth of education in the Naga Hills began from the last decade of the 19th century. The schools, though a few in number, were set up, but the students were very few. Prior to 1897–98, the Naga Hills district had no middle school and the number of the primary schools was very much limited. The number of the high schools was nil before 1937–38. The district got only six secondary schools first time in 1900-01. It was only in 1947–48 when the number of high schools increased. The number of students both in the primary and secondary schools was limited. Up to 1921–22, there were not even two thousands students in total. Moreover, in the early period due to unavoidable circumstances the missionaries were compelled to close down some schools. At the time of India's independence the total number of students admitted in the schools of Naga Hills was 17,443, which is much less compared with the population of Naga Hills.

Thus, it is evident that the educational policy of the government was not sound. Curriculum was not proper and attractive. The textbooks used in schools were mostly translated by the missionaries. Even the number of translated books was limited. Language was another problem. The diversity of the tribal dialects posed considerable difficulties in determining the medium of instruction in schools. Each tribe had to use books translated or written in their own local dialects. As a result, the book written or translated into one tribal language could not be used by the students of other tribes. At the initial stage, the students were taught in their local vernaculars including Assamese and English. Out of three languages two were foreign languages for the Nagas, which created difficulty to students. Course was also difficult for the beginners. The Assamese language was dropped as medium of instruction, no doubt, but it was kept as compulsory paper. The Deputy Commissioner was at the head of educational system at that time. No new school could be opened without his permission. Describing the dwindling number of the schools and students, the Deputy Commissioner, in 1912, stated that the Nagas took little interest in education. Hence the government did not think of opening more number of schools specially in the higher section.[34] He also criticized the existent education system of the district. Another reason of the decline of enrolment in the schools, according to the government was the tough language burden. The government, keeping in view with the large number of drop-out of students and dwindling number of the schools, opened the industrial schools to provide technical education to those who could not carry on general education.

As a measure of encouragement, the government had provided scholarship to the Naga students, no doubt, but its scope was very much limited and the amount of money granted for it was small. In 1942, there were three primary scholarships of Rs. 3/-each and three Middle English scholarships of Rs. 10/- each. In 1946, there was a significant increase in the grant of scholarships. Now the total number of scholarships increased to 13.[35]

The basic intention of the government was to provide primary education to large villages and in emerging towns. There was no strong educational policy before the government. This is evident from the report of North East Frontier Agency of 1944, which noted: "Our present system is clearly gravely defective when applied to primitive tribes, for it tends to affect the individual rather than the community and, instead of making the individual more fitted for his community, to separate him from it and cause him to seek a living elsewhere, with the result that such good as he may have received is not ordinarily passed on by example to his fellow villagers."[36] The statement clearly indicates that the government had little interest in the higher education. The Government thought that either the Nagas were not fit for higher education or there was no need of higher education for them at that time because the highly educated Nagas had no scope for employment.

Hence higher education was not beneficial to the Nagas. As a result, the Naga boys and girls during the British regime remain deprived of the facilities of higher education. Only a few of them whose parents were capable of sending their children out of the Naga Hills for higher education, received it at their own efforts. Due to lack of higher educational institutions, the Nagas could not avail of the opportunity to have higher education. This is another fact that the preaching of gospels and lower level schooling "not only proselytized the Nagas, but also interrupted the flow of their indigenous culture as well".[37]

Impact of Education

Since Christianity and education went hand in hand in the Naga Hills that caused a shift of cultural loyalty from animism to Christianity, it changed the traditional outlook and living style of the Nagas.[38] As the students who were admitted in the schools had to give up folk songs, traditional dances, animal sacrifices and celebrations of various kinds of rituals, their love and attraction towards their own traditions and culture began to decline. The old dormitories were replaced with buildings of separate Christian youth's dormitories where songs of praises, prayer meetings and other spiritual values were encouraged.[39] Both Christianity and education slowly deprived the Nagas of their numerous traditional practices related to their daily life and living habits.[40]

Close contact of the Nagas with the American Baptist Mission brought about tremendous changes in social life of the Nagas. Dr Piketo has rightly remarked: "It was missionary, and not the administrator, who was the main harbinger of the change in belief and ways of life of the Nagas. The spread of the Gospel and the consequent conversion of the Nagas and the establishment of mission school made a major contribution to the furtherance of the gospel. Christian schools trained the Naga youths in the rudiments of modern education the main elements of which were reading, writing and arithmetic".[41] Down F. S. too, maintained that the schools, which were established with the primary purpose of communicating the Christian gospel, "were notably successful".[42] Elwin is of the view that the Christianity forced the converts to stop some old and heathen practices.[43] The gradual and progressive acceptance of Christianity and its mode of life caused a shift of cultural loyalty from animism to Christianity and changed the traditional outlook and living culture of the Nagas. The convert Nagas were encouraged to discoutinue folk songs, dances, sacrifices and celebration of various kinds of rituals and practices related to cultivation, construction of houses, founding of new villages, birth and death ceremonies, marriage system, etc. They were asked to abandon drinking, smoking and the old dormitory behaviours of the boys and girls. The old dormitories were replaced with new buildings of separate Christian youth dormitories for the furtherance of songs of praises, prayers meetings and other spiritual values.[44] A number of traditional practices related to their daily life and living habits were slowly removed from among the Naga Christians.[45]

It is true that the impact of Christianity during the period of the British rule in the Naga Hills was great, but it could not totally eradicate the Naga traditional habits and their customary laws. Both the groups of the Nagas, who had adopted Christianity as a religion, and the Nagas who, were yet non-Christians, practised their old habits and heathen festivals. Rather, practice of Christian way of life created confusion and tension among the Nagas for which, sometimes, the administration had to intervene. But such conflicts came down with the intervention of the government in the affairs. The Nagas were allowed to practise their old ceremonial habits and rituals. That is why the Nagas even today being the Christians follow their ancestral cultural, social and religious practices.

The Nagas are fast adopters of the new style of life. Their association with the white people tempted them to change their living style. Changes took place in the ordinary dresses of the Nagas. To bear half-pants, long pants, petticoats etc., became a fashion among the Naga people. They began to show aversion towards their traditional dresses except during the period of festivals and ceremonies. All these happenings made the conservative Nagas worried about their disappearing old cultural life.

Prior to the colonial administration and establishment of schools by the missionaries, written form of script was unknown to the Naga people. What they had in the name of education was informal education. The introduction of primary education disrupted the indigenous system of learning and redirected them to the new pattern of modern education. According to Elwin, the introduction of modern education created substantial impact on the socio-cultural life of the Nagas.[46] Clark also admitted that education and Christianity affected their (Nagas') religion, demeanor, customs and habits.[47]

A general survey and close observation of growth of education in Nagaland during the colonial period bring the facts to the light that the Christian missionaries introduced education among the Nagas and utilized it as a means to spread Christianity. In the words of Piketo, "The missionaries successfully used educational institutions as a nexus in public contact. Christian missionaries regarded education as one of the instruments of conversion."[48] Since the missionaries had to face tough resistance from the Naga villagers, they converted the schools into a prayer house and a place of propaganda for Christianity. To quote Piketo once more, "In mission schools, students organized Christian endeavour societies and conducted weekly meetings. These Christian youth organiasations actively propagated the gospel to the neighbouring villages".[49] The statement of Downs F. S. also confirms the truth that the basic purpose behind opening schools in the Naga Hills by the missionaries was to prepare the fertile ground for the growth of Christianity. He writes: "The main purpose of the school was evangelistic as the missionaries often stated in reply to those in America who objected to the educational activities".[50]

The primary schools managed and controlled by the Mission were used for evangelistic works, and the middle schools became the centre for production of church leaders. Both the Mission Schools set up at Impure and Kohima successfully helped the missionaries to achieve their desired objectives. The products of these schools helped them enough to spread Christianity among the Nagas in far flung areas. At Impure and Kohima Mission Centres there were provisions for the students with free food and lodging, clothing, soap, besides the distribution of paper boxes to enable pupils to keep their belongings. Such facilities attracted good number of students from different tribes.

A Critical Appraisal of the Impact of White People and their Society on the Nagas

So far the objective of the British Indian government behind introducing education at lower level is concerned, the study reflects the truth: "From the very beginning of their contact with the Nagas, the British officers perceived the necessity of introducing Christianity and education among the Naga tribes, for they considered education as the best agency for reclaiming the rugged Nagas to order and civilization".[51] It was this policy of the government towards education, which provided pecuniary grants to the Christian Mission in the Naga Hills. No doubt, a time came when the government made certain modification in its educational policy in the Naga Hills at the protest of the public leaders, but the modification remained confined to taking over some primary and middle schools from the missionaries and provide non-religious education. The government never thought of opening high or secondary schools among the Naga people. It is all because, the government was under the impression that the Nagas needed neither higher education nor there was any use for it to them because the scope of the services was limited and they could not go to other places for services. But the government overlooked the truth that education is meant not only for jobs or professions, but for knowledge also. It was the lame excuse of the government. Reality is that the government had little interest in providing educational facilities to the Nagas.

Any way, the foundation of education was given. Both the missionaries and the government must be appreciated for their efforts and troubles to introduce education among the people who knew nothing about modern institutional education. The missionaries may also be appreciated for the troubles, which they took to persuade the Naga people and made them interested in modern education. One should not forget that the time when the missionaries entered the Naga Hills, was quite unfavourable for the growth of education. To give education to the people who were not ready to recognize the missionaries and who were rather inimical to them, was a Herculean task. It was a Himalayan courage and everlasting tolerance of the missionaries, which enabled them to stay in the remote and undeveloped areas devoid of even minimum needs and spread education in the Naga Hills not in a few villages but in many of the villages, which were occupied by the semi-civilized and war-like tribes. Christianity and their education not only taught these people new universal values but also prohibited them from numerous evil practices, which they used to do out of their ignorance. The missionaries had the mission to spread Christianity among the animists, but it was not possible unless education would have been used as a tool.

An analytical study of the relations of the Nagas with the western people during the British period, and their impact upon the Naga people, compels one to come to the conclusion that their impact and influences resulted in two ways. Firstly, the Naga people as a whole got benefited in many ways. They learnt so many new things, which helped them to get rid of prolonged isolation, evil consequences of head-hunting wars, village feuds, internecine feuds, superstitious faiths and practices, etc. They got acquaintance with outside people. Introduction of schools brought modern education at their door. Spread of education sharpened their consciousness and enabled them to drop out harmful practices. Their strength increased due to solidarity of various Naga tribes who were inimical to each other. Establishment of medical centers protected them from falling easy prey to various complicated diseases. Non-availability of essential requirements of life had forced them to live with the minimum requirements and live a life of poverty. Availability of industrial goods helped them enough to change their primitive style of life. Growth of commerce and trade brought the required things at their door. Thus the arrival of the British and Western Christian missionaries in Nagaland served a big cause of social as well ass political transformation of the Naga society. The darkness among the Nagas disappeared and their ignorance eroded. They were enlightened. They found themselves on the threshold of changes. They were introduced with a new faith, a new world and a new society.

So far the negative or destructive impact of the British rule and Christian missionaries is concerned, the Naga people lost so many things. As it has been stated earlier, some of the Naga tribes were rich in their ancient cultural and social values. They possessed superior values like honesty, simplicity, straightforwardness, etc. Every Naga was a community-seeking man. To the ancient Nagas ethics and religion were the same. The premise of to the community was based on the idea that a community is custodian of individual's security and safety. Among the Aos everyone had full freedom to express his/her mind freely. They lacked the Machiavellian trait of politics, no doubt, but they had the ability and wisdom to rule themselves honouring the consent of the community members. Every Naga was self-sufficient and self-reliant. Their wants were limited and they were satisfied with what they had or what they could procure by doing labour. The concepts like exploitation, high social dignity, lust for power etc., were not known to the ancient Nagas. There was no feeling of being superior to others. They were much prone to the ethics—not to commit adultery, theft, robbery, stealing and telling lies. They possessed the qualities to work hard, respect elders, help needy persons, worship gods and live honestly. Though they were violent by nature, but not to friends and neighbours.

The indigenous people knew that the world was not only in form and matter, but sacred also. It had a creator, a ruler and a destroyer. They held the view that there was no difference between the secular world and religious world. In other words, they did not have double personality. To them the matter and spirit were reflection of the same power. They strongly believed that man was the creation of the Almighty who is all powerful and capable of doing any thing. God gives life, fortune and destiny. Such beliefs made them God-fearing beings.

All these qualities of the Naga people began to erode gradually with the rise of modern economic system and spread of modern education. The traditional outlook of the people changed, no doubt, but the consequences which appeared were dangerous. The social, political, religious and economic concepts changed at the cost of destruction of their old values. The Nagas now became apt, quick, and smart in adopting new values, new lifestyle and new fashion with pride. The new philosophy, the new thought and the new way of life dazzled the mind of the Nagas who made no delay in adopting them keeping aside their ancient cultural and social values. The new religion asked the Nagas to part with all their old culture and follow the new European or American culture in almost all respects of life. Like the missionaries the so-called educated Nagas began to condemn their own old culture as most sinful, godless and useless.[52] Such changes made the younger generation more adamant, unresponsive, non-committed and undisciplined.

Thus once the Naga people moved towards modernization under the influence of Christianity and modern education, they hardly looked back to their past cultural and social values. However, such changes could not spoil all the tenets of ancient Naga culture because of two factors. Firstly, the culture, which they adopted, was not the product of their own soil. Rather it was imposed upon them. Hence it had no relation with their heart. Secondly, the ancient Naga culture was so good and popular among the people that it was impossible for any alien force to destroy it completely. It was so deeply anchored into the heart and mind of its people that it could not be finished forever. Hence even today the Nagas, who are Christians by faith, are proud of their ancient cultural and social values. This is a fact that the emergence of new economic and political system in Nagaland resulted in transformation of Naga society into class-division. Individualism substituted collectivism. Lust and longing for material gains developed, which ultimately made the conscious and capable Naga to be wealth, dignity, status, and powerminded.

The external force that entered the Naga Hills consistently shaped the historical account of the modern Naga people. The rise of secularism and materialism gave severe blow to the ancient Naga's philosophy of religion and morality. To conclude with Elwin's remark, the activities of the Baptist mission among the Nagas "have demoralized the people, destroyed tribal solidarity and forbidden the joys and feasting, the decoration and romance of communal life".[53]

No doubt, the arrival of the British and the Christian missionaries in Nagaland and their activities destroyed Nagas' religious cultural and political values and systems. The Nagas' family norms, social ethics and cultural-religious values were also seriously disrupted in the name of modernization. At the same time one should not forget that both the British and the missionaries did a lot for the Naga people. "They broadened the parochial Naga's view and shaped a new society that became far better than the traditional society of the Nagas. Spread of Christianity opened the dynamics of Naga society that flourished in various directions as the years rolled down." The value of the gain what the Nagas obtained from the British and the western Christian missionaries, was, indeed, greater than that of what they had before the consolidation of the British rule and spread of Christianity in Nagaland.

Education After India's Independence and its Impact

No doubt, real pace of educational growth took place in Nagaland after independence and creation of Nagaland state under the Indian Union in December 1963. The educational ground prepared by the missionaries and the colonial government helped the Indian government as well as the government of Nagaland to develop modern higher education. Before independence the Naga people were not unknown to modern education. Their curiosity about education had been sharpened and they had fully recognized the significance of education and its role in a fast changing world. They had the mental foundation to receive higher education. What they lacked was not the interest in education but the facilities. That is why when the government established new schools and colleges in Nagaland, there was no problem of the dearth of students and their attendance in the educational institutions.

The first college, namely, the Fazl Ali College at Mokokchung, was established in 1959. The students were waiting for availing the opportunity for higher education. It was followed by opening of one science college at Kohima in 1961. Both the colleges were taken over by the government within a few years of their establishment. Thereafter, the government took over many schools and provided new syllabus and curriculum according to the needs of the time. The villages, which were yet deprived of the educational facilities, also had schools. By 1997, there were no towns and villages which had no school. It is, in fact, disheartening that the standard of these schools and colleges has gone down today.[54]

The tables mentioned above present the clear picture related to rapid growth in education. Today the state has not less than 45 affiliate colleges to the Nagaland University. The number of the students is growing remarkably year-wise. The Ministry of Education of the Government of Nagaland has assumed full responsibility to look after the schools and colleges and to manage the affairs. The Naga students are availing full opportunity to get different sorts of education in their own state. But it is deplorable that with the growth of educational institutions, the standard and value of education in Nagaland is going down.

TABLE-I

NUMBER OF EDUCATIONAL INSTITUTIONS

S/N	Institutions	2001-2002-			2002-2003			2003-2004		
		Govt.	Pvt.	Total	Govt.	Pvt.	Total	Govt.	Pvt.	Total
1.	Primary Schools	1309	190	1499	1311	190	1501	1318	190	1508
2.	Middle Schools	261	218	479	264	218	482	271	218	489
3.	High schools	123	198	321	121	200	321	125	206	331
4.	H/Secondary Schools	5	18	23	10	22	32	10	25	35
	Total	1698	624	2322	1706	630	2336	1724	639	2363

Source—*Statistical Handbook of Nagaland, 2004*, published by Directorate of Economics & Statistics, Government of Nagaland, Kohima.

TABLE-II

NUMBER OF STUDENTS IN EDUCATIONAL INSTITUTIONS

	2001-2002			**2002-2003**			**2003-2004**		
Types of Institutions	Boys	Girls	Total	Boys	Girls	Total	Boys	Girls	Total
Primary Schools	67454	63655	131109	69195	64536	133731	73960	69292	143252
Middle Schools	47003	45204	92207	47747	46293	94040	48509	47041	95550
High Schools	76582	68687	145269	78082	69544	147626	77390	68948	146338
H/Secondary Schools	21005	16957	37962	25196	20928	46124	26757	24159	50516
Total	212044	194503	406547	220220	201301	421521	226616	209440	436056

Source—*Statistical Handbook of Nagaland, 2004*, published by Directorate of Economics & Statistics, Government of Nagaland, Kohima.

Table-III

NUMBER OF TEACHERS IN INSTITUTIONS

		2001-2002-			2002-2003			2003-2004		
S/N	Types of Institutions	Man	Woman	Total	Man	Woman	Total	Man	Woman	Total
1	Primary Schools	4109	2843	6952	5188	3001	8189	4896	2578	2174
2	Middle Schools	2947	2082	5029	3076	2163	5239	3775	1590	5365
3.	High Schools	3297	2697	5994	3895	2333	6228	3962	2321	6283
4.	H/Secondary Schools	521	461	982	642	665	1307	752	767	1519
	Total	10874	8083	18957	12801	8162	20963	13385	7256	20641

Source—*Statistical Handbook of Nagaland, 2004*, published by Directorate of Economics & Statistics, Government of Nagaland, Kohima.

TABLE-IV

NUMBER OF HIGHER EDUCATIONAL INSTITUTIONS

		2001-2002-			2002-2003			2003-2004		
S/N	Types of Institutions	Govt.	Pvt.	Total	Govt.	Pvt.	Total	Govt.	Pvt.	Total
1.	University	1	-	1	1	-	1	1	-	1
2.	College, Gen	8	27	35	8	28	36	8	28	36
3.	College (Eng)	1	-	1	1	-	1	1	-	1
4.	College, Agri	1	-	1	1	-	1	1	-	1
5.	Polytechnics	2	-	2	2	-	2	2	-	2
6.	Law college	-	3	3	-	3	3	-	3	3
	Total	13	43	56	13	45	58	13	45	58

Source—*Statistical Handbook of Nagaland, 2004*, published by Directorate of Economics & Statistics, Government of Nagaland, Kohima.

TABLE-V

NUMBER OF STUDENTS IN HIGHER EDUCATION

S/N	Types of Institutions	2001-2002-			2002-2003			2003-2004		
		Boys	Girls	Total	Boys	Girls	Total	Boys	Girls	Total
1.	University	220	173	403	199	152	351	263	186	449
2.	College, Gen	11066	8030	19096	11215	7984	19199	11190	7724	18914
3.	College, Eng	55	21	76	46	29	75	46	34	80
4.	College, Agri	32	9	61	32	29	61	40	25	65
5.	Theology	692	608	1300	715	667	1382	784	695	1479
6.	Polytechnics	145	30	175	82	34	116	84	41	125
7.	Law College	299	75	374	179	61	240	234	80	314
	Total	12519	8966	21485	12468	8956	21424	12739	8449	21588

Source—*Statistical Handbook of Nagaland, 2004*, published by Directorate of Economics & Statistics, Government of Nagaland, Kohima.

TABLE-VI

NUMBER OF TEACHERS IN HIGHER EDUCATIONAL INSTITUTIONS

		2001-2002-			2002-2003			2003-2004		
S/N	Types of Institutions	Man	Woman	Total	Man	Woman	Total	Man	Woman	Total
1.	University	73	37	110	73	37	110	73	37	110
2.	College, Gen	521	268	789	514	256	770	511	274	785
3.	College, Eng	6	7	13	6	7	13	7	8	15
4.	College, Agri	33	6	39	33	6	39	33	6	39
5.	Theology	75	32	107	34	39	123	111	41	152
6.	Polytechnics	41	3	44	33	1	34	33	2	35
7.	Law college	13	4	17	13	3	16	11	4	15
	Total	762	357	1119	750	349	1105	763	360	1123

Source—*Statistical Handbook of Nagaland, 2004*, published by Directorate of Economics & Statistics, Government of Nagaland, Kohima.

Today, Nagaland is rich in education. The percentage of literacy is higher than any other hill states of North East India. Specially the Ao people are richer than any other Naga tribes in the field of education either at primary or higher level. The Ao tribe has given numerous officers, teachers, engineers, doctors, nurses, lawyers, etc. It has happened due to the close association with the missionaries and cordial relations with the British officers from whom they received inspiration for getting knowledge and wisdom. It has been observed that the most of the Ao families who are economically sound and mentally alert are ready to send their children for higher studies to any part of the country. The interest of the Ao students in education is highly appreciable. The education in the state of Nagaland began from the Ao area and it prospered all over the state beginning from the Mission Centre Impure, which itself is a part of the Ao region. It was the mild, soft and cooperative behaviours of the ancient Ao people, which attracted the missionaries to begin education from their areas. All these factors resulted in enriching the Ao people in the field of education. There are many old Ao Nagas who still remember the golden days of the British and the missionaries in their land and their mutual understanding about each other.

Today, education has brought about tremendous changes in the Naga society and in the concept of the Naga people. The university and colleges have produced thousands of Naga graduates and post-graduates who are shouldering the responsibility of the state administrative working at various levels in different departments of the government. Economic development of the state has opened wide variety of job opportunities in both rural and urban areas. Education has produced a number of politicians, administrators, engineers, doctors, teachers, administrative staff, police officers and personnel, contractors, businessmen, etc. All these developments are the result of education and of economic development of the state. The Naga society, which was classless, has moved fast towards class-consciousness. Since these facts have been discussed in the preceding chapter, here it is enough to say that the Naga society, which calls itself modern today, has gone under multifarious changes revolutionizing the mind and status of the Naga people. Modernization, as it generally happens, has produced a number of social evils widening the gap between the rich and the poor.

References

1. Philips, P.T. *The Growth of Baptist Churches in Nagaland,* 2nd edition, Christian Literary Centre, Guwahati, 1983, p. 53.
2. *73rd Annual Report, July 1887, Baptist Mission Movement, (BMM),* American Baptist Missionary Union, Boston, July, 1887, pp. 257-58.
3. *Ibid.*
4. *Ibid.* July 1884, p. 259.
5. *BMM,* July, 1884, p. 259.
6. *BMM,* 1896, pp. 320-22.
7. *BMM,* September, 1986, p. 371.
8. Philips, P.T., *The Growth of Baptist churches in Nagaland, op.cit.,* 1983, p. 175.
9. *BMM, A Report-*1899, *op. cit.,* p. 314.
10. *BMM,* January1905, pp. 19-20.
11. Longwal R.B., *A Report in BMM, op. cit.,* pp. 169-70.
12. *BMM,* 1896, pp. 320-22.
13. *BMM,* September 1886, p. 371.
14. Philips, P.T., *"The Growth of Baptist Churches in Nagaland," op. cit.,* p. 188.
15. *Ibid.*
16. *Cited in Ibid,* p. 188.
17. Hutton, J.H., *The Angami Nagas,* Oxford University Press London, 1911, pp. VI-VII.
18. Mills, J.P., *The Ao Nagas,* Oxford University Press, London, 1925, p. 214-15.
19. *Ibid.*
20. Fredric, S. Down, "The Christian Impression on the Status of Women in North-East India", *North-East Hills Publications,* Shillong, 1896, p.16.

21. Kiremwati, *"Education and the Nagas"*, Mokokchung Ao Baptist Church, Kohima, p. 18.
22. *Ibid.*
23. Foreign Department, *Political-A*, May 1840.
24. *Quinquennial Review of the Progress of Education in Assam*, 1912-1917, p. 99.
25. *Imperial Gazette of Assam*, 1906, pp. 71-72.
26. *Ibid.*
27. *Gazette of Naga Hills & Manipur*, Vol. IX, 1905, pp. 67-68.
28. *Quinquennial Review of the Progress of Education in Assam*, 1901-09, p. 108.
29. Piketo, Sema, *"British Policy and Administration in Nagaland"*, Scholars Publishing House, New Delhi, p. 79.
30. *Ibid.*
31. *Quinquennial Review of the Progress of Education in Assam*, 1917-22, p. 99.
32. *Ibid.* 1932-37, p. 63.
33. *Legislative Assembly Debates of Assam*, Vol. IV 1938, pp. 779-800.
34. *Report of the Progress of Education in Eastern Bengal and Assam*, Calcutta, p. 121.
35. *Quinquennial Review of the Progress of Education in Assam*, 1901-07, p. 118.
36. Home Department file No. 31/15/48, Public (Secret).
37. Piketo Sema, *op. cit.*, p. 86.
38. *Ibid.*
39. Clark, M.M., *A corner of India*, American Baptist Publishing Society, Philadelphia, p. 139.
40. Hamendorf, *The Naked Nagas*, Mathew & Co. London, 939, p. 268.
41. Piketo, Sema, *op. cit.* pp. 86-87.
42. Downs, F.S. "Christianity in North East India." *Natural Christian Council of Review*, vol. LXXXV, No. 9, September, 1965, Mysore Wesley Press, p. 14.

43. Elwin, V *The Nagas in the Nineteenth Century,* Oxford University Publications, Bombay 1969, p. 78.
44. Clark, M.M., *A Corner in India, op. cit.*, p. 139.
45. Haimendorf, *The Naked Nagas, op. cit.*, p. 268.
46. Elwin, V., *Nagaland Adviser Secretariat,* Shillong, 1969, p. 78.
47. Clark, M.M., *A Corner of India, op. cit.*, p.139.
48. Piketo, Sema, *op. cit.*, p. 74.
49. *Ibid.*
50. Downs, F.S, *Christianity in North East,* Guwahati, 1983, p. 95.
51. Foreign Department, *Pol. A,* May 1840, No 148.
52. Bendangnagshi, *Glimpses of Naga History,* Guwahati, 1983, pp. 18-19
53. Elwin, V., "The Aboriginals", published in the *Oxford Pamphlets on Indian Affairs,* Bombay, 1944, p. 14.
54. Kiremwati, *Education and the Nagas, op. cit.*, p.20.

***

5

Political Dimensions

Behind the peculiar and heart-rending history of Nagaland is its Political Evolution: Nagaland, the sixteenth constituent state of the Indian republic, was swayed by political evolution. Its journey from a district to state is full of turmoil, upheavals, violence and bloodshed. No state of North-East India shed as much blood as the Naga people did for the achievement of their own separate political identity and status. The people of Nagaland had to march through political turmoil and armed conflicts to achieve the status they have today. Unexpected loss of lives and properties resulting from the armed conflicts between the Naga freedom fighters and the Indian armed personnel is an unforgettable part of the Nagas' political history. At the same time huge amount of Naga blood has been shed due to factional fighting and killings among various armed Naga insurgent groups for establishing superiority over one another. The people are still in the grip of factional feuds and armed conflicts despite the fact that they have in general disliked such ominous frequent happenings of bloodshed. Political consciousness of the Nagas began expanding under the British rule. It resulted in formation of the Naga Club in 1918 comprising Headmen, Dobashis and government servants and having its branches at Kohima and Mokokchung. The basic objective of the Club was to look after the welfare of the Nagas by promoting the understanding and development of fraternal feeling and unity among the Nagas. It was, no doubt, an important platform to discuss the core affairs of the Naga society. In due course of time the Club assumed socio-political responsibility for the nascent Naga society on the plane of social welfare. In 1946, the nomenclature of the Naga Club was changed and it was called as Naga National Council (NNC), on which was thrust upon the responsibility of asserting the Nagas' right to self-determination. The NNC, symbolized as the climax of the Naga political consciousness, became instrumental to achieve the Nagas' right to self determination.

The people of Nagaland obtained a full-fledged state on 31st December 1963, but the cost, they had to pay for that, was beyond imaginaton. The Naga freedom movement, started soon after India's independence, reached to such a critical circumstance by 1955 that the leaders of the freedom fighters found themselves on the cross-road. It was this cross-road which divided the Naga leadership into two sections—the moderate and the extremist. The former wanted the solution of the Naga issue through peaceful means having negotiation with the government of India while the latter remained determined to the path of militancy as a means to achieve sovereign political status for the Nagas. The division resulted in inclination of the moderate Naga leaders towards the political leaders of India on one hand and on the other the continuation of armed struggle against the Government of India and a severe protest against the moderates.

The line followed by the moderates paved the way for the creation of Nagaland state under the Indian federal system, while the course of action followed by the extremists drew a battleline between the Government of India and the Naga militants. This chapter critically discusses and examines the growing political consciousness of the Naga people, its consequences and political future of the state and its people. It also analyses the political events which took place before and after the emergence of Nagaland state and their impact on the Naga people as a whole.

Efforts to Specify the Naga Issue

It has already been stated that the Naga people had some sort of political institutions and wisdom to govern the society even before the arrival of the British. There were various Naga tribes who used to govern their internal affairs according to the system of governance which was purely based on customary laws and traditional conventions. In the opinion of Asoso Yonuo, the political system the old Naga people had adopted and practised, was "perfectly a government, which least governs all and in which everyone follows his own conscience, which indicates not to interfere with the right of his fellows but to respect them for the return of the same kind of respect as to have a peaceful community where all human beings work to be equal in respect of the rights, opportunities, with complete disregard for inequality and ability, to good, just and free life".[1] With this fact in view Aoso Yonuo has observed that this system seems to envisage a society what a modern anarchist perennially lauds to establish on earth for healthy human society.

An analytical study of the relations of the hill people with the British government brings the fact to the light that the arrival of the British and Christian missionaries in the land of the Nagas and their activities towards the Naga marked a turning point in the Nagas' socio-economic, political, religious and educational history. The subjugation of the various Naga tribes and annexation of their territories to the British rule resulted in unification of tne various disintegrated Naga tribes on one hand, and learning of a new socio-politico and governance order supported with well organized bureaucracy caused major changes not only in attitudinal and behavioural pattern of the Naga life but also in their social structure. Confinement of the ancient Naga people to their small world and their prolonged isolation from the rest of the world was first time fully broken by the British rulers who ventured to get into the hitherto forbidden land of the war-like tribes.

The British officers sharpened the mind of the Nagas and broadened their approach. The consolidation of various scattered Naga tribes under the single pattern of administration served a better device to integrate these people. The parochial approach of the Nagas began to disappear. First time, they came in contact with the Europeans. They had little knowledge about the outside world except some parts of Assam. Before the arrival of the British in Nagaland, there was no system of education except the Morong where oral teaching regarding the practical life was given to the youths by the Naga elders. The British government along with the Missionaries opened some primary schools in some of the areas, and not with intention to impart general education among the Nagas, but to produce the clerical staff to assist the British administration.

The close association of the Naga intellectuals with the British officials made them aware about their future political status. Some of the British officials being more sympathetic to the cause of the Nagas began to instigate them against the mainstream of the Indian nationalism. That is why they became worried about future political status of the Nagas after the departure of the British from India. By thirties of the 20th century, several Nagas had received higher education. By that time they had learnt more about the world and its nation-states. Hence a national feeling emerged among them and they began to work for the unity of the Nagas. The Naga Club with the main objectives like "promotion of understanding, development of fraternal feeling and unity among the Nagas", began to serve as the first political platform for the educated Nagas. Piketo Sema has rightly remarked that the Naga Club "provided the needed social and political foundation to the Naga tribes and was symbolic of the emerging or rather incipient sense of solidarity among the Nagas".[2]

The Naga National Council (NNC) became instrumental in formulating the Naga political policies and organizing the people to raise the voice in favour of their formulated policies related to the future political status of the Naga people. The leaders of the NNC had direct patronage of the British officials who helped them enough to sharpen their political consciousness. It was C.R. Powsey, the Deputy Commissioner of the Naga Hills, who had helped the Naga intellectuals to constitute the NNC and work for the Nagas' unity and strength. The leaders of the Naga Club who represented various Naga tribes, had submitted the memorandum before the Simon Commission in 1929, expressing the feeling that the Nagas had "much fear of introduction of foreign laws and customs to suppress our own customary laws". Hence, the Naga intellectuals demanded "safeguards" from the government.[3] The memorandum submitted by the Naga Club to the Simon Commission explicitly stated that the Naga Hills should be withdrawn from the reform scheme and be kept directly under the British government and the Nagas should be permitted to determine their political future when the British left the Naga Hills. The Simon Commission recommended the government for special administrative regulations for the governance of the Naga people keeping them aloof from the mainstream.

Thereafter, the Nagas' unity and strength went on strengthening. Their political consciousness developed. Formation of the NNC having the support of the leaders of various Naga tribes boosted the morale of its leaders. Their desire to have independent political status for the Naga people became firm. At the time of the British departure from India the Naga intellectuals became more and more active to plead the cause of the Nagas' future political status. The NNC passed resolutions at Wokha on June 19, 1946, which stated that "The NNC stands for the solidarity of all the Nagas tribes including those of the unadministered areas". It further stated that "The Naga Hills should be continuously included in an autonomous Assam in a free India, with local autonomy and due safeguards for the interests of the Nagas and the Naga tribes should have a separate electorate".[4]

The memorandum submitted before the Simon Commission by the Naga Club shows that the Naga leaders had become matured enough to decide their future political course. Their vision had been broadened. They were more farsighted now. They felt that the Nagas were one and they must be allowed to live independently as they enjoyed independence before the arrival of the British. They wanted their political identity independent of other's direct or indirect influence. It is evident from the statement of the declaration of the NNC, which *inter alia* said:

> "The NNC stands for the unification of all Naga tribes and their freedom... . Our country is connected with India, connected in many ways. We should continue that connection... We shall enjoy home-rule in our country, but on broader issues reconnected with India. We must fight for it, we must get it, keep on watching."[5]

Thus, it is very much obvious that the traditional Nagas' views had totally changed by the mid of 20th century. They were worried about their future political status after the departure of the British. The days of the British departure were limited and the Naga leaders were growing more and more impatient. Under the hard determination the Naga leaders met several Indian political leaders including Mahatma Gandhi and strongly urged them to understand the problem of the Nagas and grant them independence. However, their entire efforts remained futile because the government of India was not ready at all to grant the Nagas their political wish with the result that the future course of political activities in the Naga Hills, which followed soon after the British departure, proved injurious to both the government of India and the Naga people as a whole.

The main cause of the Naga leaders' worries about their future political status was the silence of the British rulers during the time of their departure from India. It were the British officers who had encouraged the Naga people to go for their separate political status, but the British Labour government at London was not at all in a mood to take up the Naga issue and give a new dimension to the Indian politics. The Naga Hills was still a district under the provision of the 'Excluded Area'. The British Indian government did not like to make any change in the Naga Hills district. The Naga leaders submitted a memorandum before the British government on 20th February 1947 expressing their worries and demanded a separate political status for the Nagas. A part of the memorandum explicitly stated:

> "A constitution drawn by the people who have no knowledge of the Naga Hills and the Naga people will be quite unsuitable and unacceptable to the Naga people and thrown among forty crores of Indians, one million Nagas with their unique system will be wiped out of existence".[6]

However, the British government hardly paid any heed to the demand of the Naga people. It is a fact that the Naga people were scared of their future political status in free India. But it is also a fact that the Naga intelligentsia, who had established close associations with the local British officials, was misguided by them against the plains people of India. It was these officials who had suggested to the Naga leaders to convert the hill areas of Northeastern India into a 'Crown colony' or 'Trust Territory'. This is another act that the British Labour government under the leadership of Atlee was not ready to consider the Nagas' demand. Hence the British government transferred political power to the Indian political leaders on the midnight of 15th August 1947, but the political status of the Naga Hills district remained and it caused too much frustration to the Naga people as a whole. Thereafter, the Naga political leaders soon indulged in giving practical shape to the strategies, which they had thought of a little before India's independence.

Future Political Status

The Naga people on the eve of India's independence were not yet clear whether they wanted a sovereign political status or a separate political identity within India. In 1946, the Naga National Council (NNC), the only political organization of the Naga people, wanted the "solidarity of all the Naga tribes" and inclusion of Naga Hills "in an autonomous Assam in a free India, with local autonomy and due safeguards for the interests of the Nagas and the Naga tribes should have a separate electorate".[7] What the NNC demanded at the time was "a separate Naga country" and liked to "develop it according to genius and test of the Nagas" but "connected with India in matters of defense, finance, and foreign relations and whatever might be necessary for the benefits of the Nagas".[8] The stand of the NNC changed since 1947, and it began to put pressure for independence of the Nagas.[9]

The British Indian government left the Nagas' case unsolved with the result that the government of India inherited the Naga issue as a legacy of the British rule. The Indian leaders tried their level best to convince the Naga leaders that their safety and security would remain intact under the Indian federal system and they would be granted all internal autonomies as per their wish. But the Naga leaders were predetermined not to accept any thing less than sovereign political status. No doubt, an agreement known as the 'Hydery Agreement' was signed between the Naga leaders and the government of India regarding the political status of the Naga people in 1948 for ten years as the transitional period, but it could not be given practical shape due to differences between these two parties on the future status of the Naga Hills after expiry of the tenure of the Hydery Agreement.[10] The controversy could not be resolved with the result that the Hydery Agreement remained a futile historical document.

Course of Action Followed by the Nagas

Since the Indian political leaders were not in a mood to grant the Naga people even a separate political identity of their own, separating the Naga Hills from the province of Assam, the Naga people got disappointment, which ultimately resulted in a direct tussle between the Nagas and the government of India. Even against the wish of the Naga people, the Constituent Assembly of India on the suggestion of the Bardoloi Sub-Committee provided the Nagas 'Autonomous District Council' (ADC) under the Sixth Schedule of the Indian constitution.[11] The Constitution of India made relevant provisions in Article 244. The Autonomous District Council was to consist of 24 members of whom not less than three-fourths of the members were to be elected on the basis of universal adult franchise. Moreover, three seats in the Assam legislative assembly were also reserved for the Naga representatives. Part XVI of the Constitution (Articles 330 and 332) provided for the seats in the Lok Sabha and in the Rajya Sabha also. Thus, though the Nagas' demand for a sovereign political status was not conceded, some provisions were made for democratic processes for the Naga people in the Constitution of India. The government was under the impression that such autonomous provisions would satisfy the Naga leaders, but it was soon proved that such assumption of the Indian political leaders was not based on reality.

The provisions made in the Indian constitution for the Naga people were bound to fail because these were against the will of the Naga people as a whole. The Indian political leaders had neither understood the problem of the Nagas nor did they have the will to solve it. Hence the provisions made under the Sixth Schedule could not be given a trial due to boycott of the Naga people. Meanwhile, a dashing Naga leader, A.Z. Phizo appeared on the political scene of the Naga Hills and made no delay in capturing the Nagas' emotion and sentiment and converted them into their opposition against the government of India. Under the leadership of Phizo, who had been elected as the President of the NNC, the Naga electorate boycotted the elections for both the formation of the Autonomous District Council and Naga representatives for the Assam Legislative assembly. As a result, both the Assam Legislative Assembly and the Indian Parliament went without any Naga representatives till the second general election was held in 1957.

The understanding of the Indian political leaders that the creation of Autonomous District Council "would give the Naga a sense of participation in the administration and that they would gradually come within the mainstream of India were not based on a realistic assessment of the situation prevailing in the Naga Hills at that time".[12] The Naga leaders had responded negatively to the efforts of persuasions of the Indian leaders to accept the Indian constitution. That was enough hint for the government of India to understand the real situation, but the government could not view it seriously because the attention of the government at the time was badly engaged with the problem of Kashmir, entrance of the refugees and war between India and Pakistan. The country was passing through the phase of disintegration. The division of India had created a number of problems which sought immediate solution. Hence all the political leaders of the country were busy with resolving such challenges of the country. As a result the Naga issue could not be viewed properly.

Beginning of Naga Freedom Movement

The Naga society was matured enough to think of their future political life. They could not sit silently. A general understanding had been formed in the mind of Nagas that they had been underrated and deceived by Indian political leaders. They had been demanding a separate political identity for a long time. What was given to them was quite contrary to their will and expectation. Hence, it was natural for the Nagas to react against the constitutional provisions made for them. At this juncture, the question, which was vital for the Nagas and which perplexed their mind, was to decide their future course of action. Should the Naga people accept such provisions and continue their peaceful struggle for getting what they wanted or should they begin a protest movement against the government of India?

Phizo, the leader of the NNC, was a revolutionary leader. He believed in direct action even at the cost of blood. He had studied the mind of the Nagas. He had also worked hard to unite the Nagas belonging to different tribes and sub-tribes. The Naga people were fully convinced that they were independent and they must be independent at any cost. As a course of action in support of the demand of the NNC for an independent Nagaland, he conducted unilateral plebiscite all over the district of Naga Hills to know what the Naga people wanted—whether they liked to be in India or to have their own independent sovereign state. After full-fledged discussions they came to the conclusion that 99% of the Nagas were against merger with India.

On the other hand, the government of India paid no heed to the unilateral plebiscite conducted by the NNC. The government was not at all ready to give the Nagas more than what the constitution provided for them. Perhaps, the government was under the impression that a small group of the Nagas could hardly wage a war against the government. But the course, which was followed by the leaders of the NNC, was the path of confrontation. The leaders of the NNC asked the people to launch a non-cooperation movement against the government of India with a view to jeopardizing the government machinery in the Naga Hills. Since the non-cooperation movement did not bring the desired goal, the leaders of the NNC under the leadership of Phizo decided to resort to direct action taking up arms against the government. The leaders of the freedom fighters lost no time to contact the neighbouring countries to procure arms and ammunition as also their morale and material support. They managed to get military training for their recruits. The way for armed tussle was paved.

The leaders of the NNC had already declared Nagaland as an independent state and set up their own government on 14th August 1947, which was called as 'People's Sovereign Republic of free Nagaland'. The Naga government, equipped with arms and ammunitions and moral and material support from China and Pakistan, had the courage to wage a war against the government of India. The Naga freedom fighters, thereafter, adopted measures to ambush the army convoys, military posts and harass all those who were directly or indirectly associated with the government of India. They adopted the method of kidnapping, and torturing the government officials in the Naga Hills. Such actions of the Naga warriors provoked the government of India to put down the rebellion with iron hand.

So the government was determined not to let the Nagas go scot-free. To meet the situation and fight the Naga militancy it deployed security forces all over the Naga Hills. The government clamped section 144, which was supplanted later on by promulgating the Nagaland Disturbed Ordinance and Assam Maintenance of Public Order, which empowered the security personnel to deal with the Naga insurgents as they deemed necessary. Thereafter, the government of India applied all the suppressing measures with a view to curbing down the Naga rebellion.[13] The Indian armed troops carried on numerous operations against the Naga freedom fighters. Several of them were captured, harassed and even killed. No alternative was left for the Naga rebels except to go underground to save themselves from the direct action of the Indian security forces and carry on guerrilla warfare against the government of India.[14] They continued their guerilla war-fare from the underground. They ambushed the army convoys killing several armed personnel. In retaliation the security forces attacked not only the undergrounds' hideouts but also began to harass the innocent Naga villagers by burning their houses, granaries, etc. A number of innocent villagers were harassed, tortured and arrested on the basis of suspicion.

The security measures and inhuman acts of the Indian armed forces irritated the underground Nagas and created numerous problems for the general Naga people. The irritated Naga militants intensified their hostile activities. As a result, the whole of the Naga Hills was engulfed in total anarchy, complete disorder and confusion, etc.[15] A non-bailable arrest warrant was issued against Phizo who left India and reached England in 1956 for his safety.

Division in NNC and Emergence of Moderate Group

The Naga people had landed in very tough and rough situation due to freedom fighting. They had lost their peace and their sufferings knew no bounds. The Indian security forces viewed every Naga with suspicion and doubt. Phizo and his close associates were not yet ready to budge even an inch from their decided goal and determination.

The sudden departure of Phizo from the Naga Hills encouraged the moderate group, with a desire for peaceful solution of the Naga issue. They came on the forefront with demand to reconsider the stand of the NNC against the government. Despite heavy resistance and fight the Nagas' independence was not in the sight. Rather the struggle had brought more uncertainty and troubles to the Naga people. The moderate wing of the NNC, who had been against the use of violent force from the very beginning, realized that the Nagas had to change the mood to achieve the goal. Hence, they became vocal about peaceful method avoiding the path of insurgency and armed conflicts. However, the hard-core nationalists were still determined to continue the battle against the government of India with a view to achieve the goal.

Thereafter, in the words of Asoso Yonuo, "the open fighting broke out near Kohima between the rival factions of the NNC i.e., one who favoured Phizoism and those who opposed". The moderates under the leadership of T.N. Angami severing their relations with the militant group formed a Reformation Committee in February 1957, which became instrumental in arranging peace talks with the Indian leaders and creating a new political unit for the Nagas, namely, 'The Naga Hills Tuensang Area (NHTA)' in

1957, which ultimately resulted in creation of the Nagaland state under the Indian Republic.

The most attractive feature of the Reforming Committee was that while formulating its aims and objectives, it explicitly condemned and opposed the methods of violence. It also expressed its commitment to help restore peace, order and security in Nagaland and the resolution to win over those Nagas who were determined to fight with arms for the cause of the Nagas. The Committee declared:

"It stands by the Prime Minister's assurance that when peace is restored, administrative changes would be introduced in the Naga Hills in full consultation with the Naga people of all tribes.... It also claims for the Naga people the rightful share of India's independence and is convinced that the majority desire of the Nagas is for a separate administrative unit in keeping with the Naga tradition within the framework of the constitution of India".[16]

Thus the declaration of the Reforming Committee made it crystal clear that the NNC was a divided house and the Nagas, except extremists, wanted to join the mainstream of Indian nationalism, had they been granted separate administrative unit of their own. This also made clear that the moderate Nagas, who had realised the futility of armed struggle against the mighty power like India, were ready to accept the Indian constitution provided they were given internal autonomies.[17] It was not only the moderate Naga leaders who had realized the futility of the armed struggle against the government of India but even the Indian political leaders had also understood that the Nagas could not be subdued for ever. The challenges, which were posed to the government by the underground set-up, were enough for the government's leaders to realize that the Naga people could not be tagged on with Assam. That is why the then Prime Minister of India, Pt. Jawaharlal Nehru, had assured the Nagas to provide them with a separate status by changing the existing administrative procedure in the Naga Hills. The battle of the Nagas against the government of India at least forced the government to provide the Naga people with a sort of separate administrative unit.

The division in the NNC and emergence of the moderate group were the events, which brought about new dimension to the Naga politics. The society was divided on the issue of political future of the Nagas. The moderates preferred peace and progress. They liked independence, no doubt, but not at the cost of Naga blood and torment as well as of the Naga peace and prosperity. The extremists wanted to achieve freedom at any cost. Study shows that with the division of the NNC the Naga society, too, remained divided. The tussle and confrontation took place between moderate and extremists creating utter confusion in the minds of the general Nagas. However, the majority of the Naga people favoured the moderate group because to them peace was most essential.

The dissension in the NNC was a great set-back to the movement of national freedom. The Phizoists were not ready to tolerate silently such move of the moderates. They had already killed T. Shakharie, secretary of the NNC and one of the most veteran and foresighted Naga leaders, who had dare to dissociate from the path of militancy. The murder of Shakharie was committed as a sort of warning to other leaders of the NNC who were pleading for peaceful negotiation with the government of India. The extremists were of the view that such drastic action against their own leader would dampen the courage of other Naga leaders and they would drop their course of peaceful action, which they had planned, but the events, which followed after the murder of Shakharie, proved that the extremist Naga leaders were in illusion. The demand of the day was peace. Hence the loss of Shakharie was soon compensated by other dashing and peace loving Naga leaders who came forward openly to condemn the murder of Shakharie and also the violent path of the militants. The determination of the moderates to have negotiations with the government of India for solution of the Naga problem was strengthened and the leaders of the Reforming Committee continued their efforts to bring peace in Nagaland in the greater interest of the Naga people as a whole.

The Reforming Committee declaring that the "Majority demand of the Nagas is for a separate administrative unit keeping with the Naga tradition within the framework of the Indian constitution", sent a delegation of the Naga leaders to Pt. Jawaharlal Nehru, the then Prime Minister of India, who was expecting such move from the moderate Naga leaders. Now the ball was in the court of the Indian leaders. Naga freedom movement had been weakened. It was, in fact, an opportunity for the government of India to take the moderate Naga leaders in good faith. Hence, Pt. Nehru welcomed the delegation whole-heartedly in New Delhi. The talk with Pt. Nehru was fruitful. He assured the delegation of granting the Naga people a separate administrative unit with maximum autonomies provided peace and normalcy exist in the Naga Hills at the earliest possible.

Moderates to Negotiate Peace with India

During the mid fifties of the last century, the dissociation of the moderate Naga leaders from the path of militancy, their declaration to avoid violence and armed struggle, meeting of the Naga delegation with the Indian Prime Minister and commitment of the Baptist church leaders to work for peace, are the notable dimensions in the history of Naga politics. All these events opened a new chapter in the political history of Nagaland. These events also encouraged the growth of democratic processes in Nagaland on one hand, and paving the way for the suppression of the Naga freedom movement on the other. The Indian leaders were happy because the dissention of the NNC had given the government a favourable chance to apply the policy of divide and rule by appeasing the moderate Naga leaders. Asoso Yonuo has rightly observed that Pt. Nehru with a view to appeasing the moderate Nagas promised them not only special status but also of considering "any change except sovereign subject to the unity, integrity and security of the Indian Union."[18] Observing that the NNC was a divided house and a strong voice in favour of peace in Nagaland was emerging, Pt. Nehru adopted the policy of appeasement and applied the policy of peaceful administration, which was successful.

The course of events favoured the government of India and the moderate Naga leaders. What the existing circumstances needed was peace for trouble-free life. The Naga people were fed up with the continuous armed struggle where their life had become hell and progress was totally jeopardized. They had to face enormous troubles and inconveniences. The public opinion favoured the move of the moderate leaders. Hence, under such favourable circumstance the moderate Naga leaders with the help of the church leaders organized Naga People's Convention (NPC) in August 1957. Unexpected participation of the Naga delegations from different parts of the land in the NPC, proves the fact that the Naga people, in fact, wanted peaceful solution to the Naga issue. It boosted the morale of the moderate leaders. The delegates thoroughly discussed about the significance of peace in Nagaland and constituted a delegation with Imkongliba Ao as the chairman with a view to initiating peace talks with the Indian Prime Minister in New Delhi. The delegation reached New Delhi and opened peace dialogue with Pt. Nehru and other Union leaders on the 25th of September 1957.[19]

The historic convention of the NPC held on 22nd of August 1957, passed a resolution stating that "being deeply grieved by the killings and the widespread sufferings caused by burning of houses and granaries, the destruction of crops, grouping of villages, restriction of freedom of movement and speech, forced labour without payment, the resultant disease and hunger, we, a convention of the Naga people drawn from every tribe and area of the territories now known as the Naga Hills district of Assam and Tuensang Frontier Division, having met at Kohima on 22nd August 1957 in search of a solution to end the infinite sufferings and bloodshed, do hereby resolve as following:

"We maintain that the only answer to the Naga question is a satisfactory political settlement. In order to create the conditions necessary for a political settlement, the following immediate changes as an interim measure are essential. The present Naga Hills district of Assam and Tuensang Frontier Division of North East Frontier Agency (NEFA) along with the reserved forests, transferred out to the Naga Hills district after reform of 1921, should be constituted into a single administrative unit, under the External Affairs Ministry of the Government of India through the Governor of Assam acting as in his direction as the Agent of the President of India, speedy supension of hostilities and relief to sufferings.

"Appealing to the country-men in arms to give up the cult of violence, the convention asks for the prayer of all men of goodwill, both underground and overgrown and in government services for the achievement of a lasting and honourable peace".[20]

The resolution of the NPC passed at Kohima on 22nd of August 1957, made it clear that the Naga people wanted peace, suspension of hostile activities and peaceful negotiation. It also proposed the nature of separate administrative unit for the Naga people where unification of the various Naga tribes was a must. That is why it demanded transfer of Tuensang division from NEFA to the Naga Hills. It desired that the proposed administrative unit should be placed under the External Affair Ministry of India and the Governor of Assam should govern the Naga people as an Agent of the President of India. It shows that the Naga people did not want to be the administrative part of the province of Assam.

The NPC constituted a nine-man delegation headed by Imkongliba Ao to carry on political negotiation with the Central government of India. Since the government of India had already decided in principle to grant the Naga people a separate administrative unit, the delegation was received warmly by the Prime Minister in New Delhi. The negotiation began from 23rd of September and continued till 25th of September 1957 in a cordial and friendly atmosphere. The Government of India assured the Naga delegation that the government would soon do the needful to carve out a separate administrative unit for the Naga people within the constitution of India. On the other hand, the leader of the Naga delegation, Imkongliba, made it clear that the Naga people were quite averse to violence and bloodshed. Pt. Nehru being satisfied with the assurance of the Naga delegation for restoring peace in the Naga Hills said that an amendment to the constitution would be considered by the parliament in the next session in November and December1957. He also assured them that the government would grant amnesty to the rebels "in respect of all offences committed against the state in the past though amnesty would not cover future offences".[21]

To substantiate the assurance which Pt. Nehru gave to the Naga delegation, the Ministry of External Affairs of India issued a statement on 26th September 1957, which summarized the talks held between Pt. Nehru and the Naga delegation and also spelt out the scheme of future administration of the Naga Hills area. The statement issued by the External Affairs Ministry stated:

"The Naga Hills district and the Tuensang Frontier Division would be constituted into one administrative unit within the Indian Union directly under the President of India. This unit will be administered by the Governor of Assam on behalf of the President under the Ministry of External Affairs."

Creation of Naga Hills Tuensang Area (NHTA)

The move of the moderate Nagas towards the settlement of peace and future status of the Naga Hills was welcomed by the Naga people, no doubt, but it does not mean that entire Naga population was in favour of merging their territories with Indian once and for all. The underground set-up who have not given up the hope of liberating their land from India's occupation, disliked such move of the moderates. They thought that the government of India by applying the policy of divide and rule had succeeded in creating a division in the unity of the Naga people. No alternative was left for them other than to intensify their activities against both the government of India and also the Naga leaders who had promised to work with the government of India for the progress and prosperity of the Naga people. They began to hurl threats to such leaders by giving them warnings. They even went to the threatened extent to assassinate Mr. Imkongliba who had been instrumental in bringing the Naga people closer to the government of India. However, their threats did hardly create much impact upon the moderate Naga leaders to deviate from their decided course. On the other hand, the government of India did not like to make even the slightest delay to grant the Naga people a separate administrative unit. As a result, a Bill to make amendment in the Sixth Schedule of the Indian constitution was introduced in the Lok Sabha on November 20, 1957.

While introducing the Bill the then Home Minister, G.B. Pant, informed the House that the government of India had decided to grant the Naga people an independent status providing a separate administrative unit under the Indian Republic, keeping in view the persistent demand of the Naga people for a separate political unit. Justifying the arrangement for a separate administrative unit for the Nagas, the Home Minister said the Bill was the best solution in the given situation. He expressed the hope that the same arrangement would encourage the forces of peace and help others also to realize as to what was in the best interest of the Nagas. The Lok Sabha making no delay passed the Bill on the 28th of November 1957. Thereafter, President of India gave his assent to the Bill.

The Naga Hills Tuensang Area Act, 1957, created a new administrative unit known as the Naga Hills Tuensang Area (NHTA). The territory of the Tuensang area, which was hitherto under the NEFA, was transferred to the newly created unit, the Naga Hills Tuensang Area. The Naga Hills Tuensang Area Regulation (administration) was promulgated in November 1957, which provided a number of provisions for the administration of the NHTA. Section 3 of the Regulation provided that NHTA should be divided into three districts to be called Kohima, Mokokchung and Tuensang. Section 4 empowered the Governor of Assam to carry on the administration of NHTA as the Agent of the President of India.[22] Section 5 of the Regulation, further, provided that all the officers who were working in the Naga Hills area before formation of the NHTA would continue to exercise their respective powers and jurisdiction and to perform their respective duties in the same manner and to the same extent as before. Again, Section 6 made provision that all laws in force in the Naga Hills district or in the Tuensang Frontier division of NEFA immediately before the promulgation of this Act would continue in force in the districts of Kohima, Mokokchung and Tuensang until repealed or amended by a competent legislature or other competent authority.[23] The provision was also made that the property and assets within the district of Kohima and Mokokchung would henceforward vest in the Central Government, which meant the Government of Assam lost its jurisdiction over these properties and assets. It was further provided that "All rights, liabilities, obligation of the state government of Assam in relation to the district of Kohima and Mokokchung should be the rights, liabilities and obligation of the Central government.[24]

The creation of the NHTA was, in fact the first mile-stone in the emergence of legislative and democratic processes in Nagaland. The step the government of India took in this regard was late, no doubt, but it may be called as a wise step. It not only eased the tense situation of Nagaland but also won over the heart of many Nagas. In the opinion of the editor of the *New York Times*, too, "It was "a realistic approach" and the step as such was a "wise one." *The Manchester Guardian*, too, remarked that the Prime minister's offer to the Nagas was like a "statesman effort".[25]

Creation of NHTA was the outcome of the prevailing disturbed situation of the Naga Hills. The unit was created keeping in view the demand of the moderates, no doubt, but at the same time it was done to suppress the Naga rebellion. But to save the life and properties of the Nagas and protect the peace, the step of the moderates must be appreciated. It was their wisdom and farsightedness which enabled them to have political link with India having their own separate political unit under the constitution of India. It was natural that the move was against the will and interest of the such Nagas who were ready to accept nothing other than independent sovereign status. Hence the underground leaders continued their efforts to achieve the goal, though their strength had already been subdued.

Preparation for Full-Fledged Statehood

The creation of NHTA was not the final goal of the moderate Naga leaders. Their ultimate aim was to achieve a full-fledged state. Creation of NHTA was only a half-way journey. The Naga leaders had enough wisdom how to achieve their desired goal. Hence, the second Naga People Convention, which was held in May 1958, with a view to chalk out future programme and find a device to bring the underground Nagas in the mainstream of India, set up a Select Committee and a Liaison Committee, which constituted a

Drafting Committee with a view to preparing a plan for the political settlement of the Naga issue. The committee formulated a sixteen-point proposals, which essentially subscribed to the establishment of Nagaland State within the Indian Union. The third Naga People Convention, which met at Mokokchung in October 1959, finally adopted the sixteen-point proposals "to form the basis of negotiation with the government of India for the final political settlement".

The proposal envisaged the formation of a new state to be known as Nagaland within the Indian Union. For the transitional period an interim government of the Naga people was to be formed, which would prepare the ground for the formation of new state. A Council of Ministers responsible to the Naga Legislative Assembly was also proposed, which would assist and advise the Governor. Special provision was demanded for the people of Tuensang area keeping in view their backwardness.[26] The proposal also talked of inclusion of contiguous Naga areas with Nagaland, formation of a separate Naga regiment in the Indian army and continuation of the Inner Line Regulation, 1974.

Thus, the sixteen-point proposals formed the basis of the proposed Nagaland state. Despite the protest of the underground Nagas a fifteen-man Naga delegation headed by Imkongliba Ao reached Delhi and met Pt. Nehru on 26th July, 1960, and submitted the sixteen-point proposals with a request to grant the Naga people a full-fledged state of their own under the Indian Union. Pt. Nehru who had become too much sympathetic to the cause of the moderate Nagas readily agreed to consider the demand of the Naga delegation despite the opposite views of the Home Minister and the Reorganization Committee of States of India. The Reorganization Committee was of the view that the separation of the Naga Hills from Assam "will add to the cost of the administration and coordination of the policy and programme between the state of Assam and the hill areas on the one hand, and between the hills districts themselves on the other. It will become more difficult".[26]

Advent of Interim Body: A *de-facto* Legslature

It appears that Pt. Nehru was predetermined to grant the Naga people the full-fledged state. He thought that such step would prove the policy to kill two birds with one stone. Creation of Nagaland state would enable the Nagas to practise the democratic processes and at the same time it would weaken the strength of the underground Nagas. He was correct in his observation. Pt. Nehru was under the realisation that the basic cause of the Naga's militancy was their assimilation with Assam. Hence once the Naga people achieved the status of statehood, the freedom movement would subside. Here Pt. Nehru's assessment was not based on the true study of the Naga mind. It is true that the moderates wanted to get rid of the bloody and anarchic situation and had inclined towards the government of India, but the general Naga mass had not yet forgotten the dream of independent Nagaland. It is evident from the fact that even after creation of Nagaland state, the freedom movement of the Nagas continued. The underground people also intensified their militant activities.

The sixteen-point proposals with a slight modification were finally accepted in the light of the discussions with the Foreign Secretary of India held on the 27th of July, 1960. To give effect to the decision of the Foreign Secretary, the government of India formulated the Nagaland (Transitional Provisions) Regulation, 1961, for the "regulation of Nagaland and for matters connected therewith until the creation of Nagaland as a state under the Indian Union".[27] The Regulation provided for an Interim Body "consisting of forty-two members chosen by election from the tribes of Nagaland". The nomenclature as the Naga Hills Tuensang Area was replaced with the new term as Nagaland. Provision was also made for an executive body to "assist and advise the Governor on the exercise of public order as may be specified by the Governor in this behalf".[28] The tenure of the Interim Body was fixed for three years, and it was to meet at least once every four months. The Executive Council would "consist of such members of the Interim Body, not exceeding five in number, as the Governor may appoint after obtaining recommendation of that Body, and the "Executive

Council would choose a member of the Council to be the chairman thereof". The Interim Body was "assigned the right to discuss and make recommendations to the Executive Council on matters of administration involving general policy and schemes of development and other matters referred to it by the Executive Council".[29]

The promulgation of the Regulation, 1961 was, in fact, a historic turn in the political history of Nagaland because it gave the foundation for a democratically organized government of the Naga people. It opened the way for the Naga electorate to exercise their right to franchise and choose the representatives of their choice. The Interim Body was soon formed, which consisted of the members chosen by the Tribal and Area councils of the Naga tribes. While inaugurating the Interim Body, the Governor, General S.M. Shrinagesh, said that with formation of the democratic body Nagaland moved towards the path of constitutional government, and suggested to the Naga people to forget the bitterness of the past so as to make the future of the Nagas and Nagaland peaceful and prosperous.

Imkongliba Ao who had been instrumental all these years to pave the way for the growth of democratic processes in Nagaland was elected as the Chairman of the Interim Body. While thanking the Governor he assured him that all the efforts would be applied to restore peace in Nagaland and create the avenues for the prosperity of the Naga people. He also invited the underground brothers to come overground and work for prosperity of the Naga people abandoning the path of violence.

The promulgation of Nagaland (Transitional Provisions) Regulation, 1961, was definitely a severe blow to the underground Nagas who not only rejected such move but also decided to fight against the policy of appeasement of the government of India to divide the Nagas. Hence they became more adamant and dangerous to both the government of India and the leaders of the Naga Interim Body. By issuing warning letters to the moderate Naga leaders, they asked them not to infringe on the Naga's birthright to be free. But the moderate Naga leaders paid no heed to their warning and followed the democratic and constitutional course fearlessly. On the other hand, the extremists assassinated Imkongliba, the chairman of the Interim Body, on 22 August 1961, when he was coming back from his dispensary in Mokokchung. The assassination of Imkongliba, which created wide terror and fear all-over the state, was, in fact, a serious matter to the moderates. Moreover, it was a direct challenge to the government of India also.

It is said that those who create history are never afraid of any consequences. The Naga leaders who were creating new history for the Nagas accepted the murder of their leader Imkongliba Ao as a challenge to their courage and spirit. T.N. Angami, another dashing and foresighted Naga leader, accepted the challenge by assuming the responsibility of the chairman of the Interim Body. The government of India assured the Naga leaders to provide all possible protection and assistance to protect their lives and change the economic face of Nagaland. Thus, the Interim Body moved ahead with greater determination to work for the progress and prosperity of the Nagas as a whole.

The 1st session of the Interim Body demanded that the Nagaland (Transitional provision) Regulation should be scraped and the elected Executive council be recognized as the provisional cabinet and the Interim Body should also act as the provisional legislature of Nagaland, and it should have its own secretariat. As a second step, Mr. Shillu Ao, the first Chairman of the Executive Council, reached New Delhi with the memorandum, which emphasized the need to grant the Executive Body and Interim Body the real status as the cabinet and the legislature respectively. At this juncture when the undergrounds were hanging like daggers over the heads of the peace-loving Naga leaders, the government of India had no alternative other than to accept the demand of the Interim Body with the result that the Central government increased the power and status of both the Interim Body and the Executive Council. Thereafter, the Interim Body assumed the status of *de-facto* legislature while the Executive council got the status of *de-facto* cabinet of Nagaland.

Nagaland: from a District to State

The time came when the Nagaland Bill for the creation of Nagaland state was introduced in the Assam Legislative Assembly. B.P. Chaliha, the chief minister of Assam, introducing the Bill said, "This Assembly, however, notes that the government of India is committed to the setting up of Nagaland as a separate state within the Indian Union." A member of Assam Assembly opposed the Bill on the ground that it would not only reduce the size and population of Assam by separating Nagaland from it but it would also encourage other hill peoples, such as Jaintia, Khasi, those of NEFA, Mizo, Tripura to put forward similar demand. Some of the members accused Pt. Nehru, the Indian Prime Minister, of sowing the seed of disintegration in the country. B.P. Chaliha, however, defending the move of the government of India, said, "All of us should share the blame equally." H.E. Posha, the leader of the Hill Leaders Conference, welcoming the Bill stated that "It is the loyalty of the people" that "it is the strength of the country" and "not artificial boundaries". Any way, the Nagaland Bill was passed by the Assam legislative assembly.

After getting approval from the Assam legislature, the Indian Prime Minister introduced two Bills, the Nagaland Bill and the Nagaland the Constitution Amendment Bill, in the Lok Sabha on the 21st of August, 1962. He said to the members of the House that these Bills were in pursuance of commitment made by the government of India to the Naga delegation in July 19€2. He also said that the creation of Nagaland state would be a right step to consolidate and integrate the people of India having different cultures, languages and social backgrounds. Commenting on the nature of the Bills the Prime Minister further stated, "For the time being the Governor will have special powers in regard to law and order and finance, but as soon as the situation is normal, it will not be so. The state is a small one, and for the time being, it will have certain restriction in regard to Tuensang District. Otherwise, it will be a full state of the Union, and it will have all other powers of the state of the Indian Union".[30]

Voices were heard from the opposition bench, which vehemently opposed the move of the government on various grounds. The logic was given that such move of the government of India would definitely encourage various other peoples of India to come ahead with the similar demands at the cost of national integrity. U.M. Tiwari, a Jan Sangh member stated, "We are creating a territory, which we have not been able to administer because of violence that was practised there."[31] He accused Pt. Nehru of leading the country on the path of disintegration. P.C. Baruah, a Assam representative expressed the view that he would accept the Bill with "sorrow and pain" for two reasons. Firstly, the "new state was being created cutting a limb of Assam and secondly, when all efforts were being made to put an end to the "fissiparous and disruptionist tendencies in the country".[32]

A question may be raised here as to whether the step of Pt. Nehru to grant the Naga people was a wrong step. May it be considered as a policy of appeasement of the government of India towards the Nagas? The question is not difficult to answer. Those who have the knowledge of the land and people of the Northeastern region of India may not deny the fact that the region is occupied by different peoples who belong to different ethnic groups and who differed in their language, culture, religion, race and social backgrounds. The tribal people who live in the region were in prolonged isolation where they developed the habit of separation. These people have been sensitive and suspicious about the plains people of India. That is why the Naga people did not like at all to be associated with the people of Assam. The imposition of Assamese language over the tribal people had irritated them. Moreover, the development of the tribal people under the rule of Assam was very much limited. They were determined to have their own separate identity. Hence at this very critical juncture "No other assurances and alternative suggestions could satisfy them and ultimately the political map of North-East India had to be reorganized by forming separate states of Meghalaya and Nagaland".[33]

Hence, what the government of India thought of giving the Naga people a separate state of their own may not be treated merely as a policy of appeasement and a step towards disintegration of the nation. The militant Nagas were determined to fight with the government and they had already opened the front supported with moral and material assistance from the India's neighbouring countries. Had the Naga people not been granted the statehood, the situation there would have become too difficult to handle. Pt. Nehru had visualized the existing situation in the North-East wisely. That is why he thought of granting the Naga people a state under the Indian Union. Rather the step was too late. Had it been taken some years back, not so much blood would had been shed in the Naga Hills and terrorism, perhaps, would have been controlled easily. S.C. Jamir, a Naga representative in the Lok Sabha and also parliamentary secretary to the Ministry of External Affairs, rightly said, "The creation of the Nagaland state within the Indian Union is a matter of pride for India because we have in the Nagas a brave, honest and hard-working set of people. I feel that Nagas have got a right to claim a place in the Union of India."[34] Hem Baruah, a Assamese member of the Lok Sabha, also said that "this political settlement arrived at by the government of India with the Naga people's convention led by Imkongliba Ao is an act of sagacity".[35]

Concluding the debate Pt. Nehru said that all the people in India lived like a family. Hence the creation of Nagaland state would not encourage fissiparous and disruptionist tendencies, it would rather help in bringing the Naga people in the mainstream of India.[36] Pt. Nehru was very much correct in his observation. What he did was the need of the time. Naga public opinion was too much matured. The people had the wish to have a sovereign political status. They had the determination and courage to fight for their cause, too. By creating a full-fledged Nagaland state under the Union of Indian Republic, the government succeeded in protecting the integrity of the nation. The anti-Indian forces were still awaiting the circumstance to separate Nagaland from the rest of the country. The Indian Prime Minister by creating the state of Nagaland supplied a befitting reply to the underground Naga government.

The Constitution (thirteenth) amendment Bill and the Nagaland Bill were adopted by the Lok Sabha on the 29th of August, 1962 and Rajya Sabha approved them on the 3rd of September 1962. Thereafter, the President of India accorded his assent to these Bills on the 4th of September 1962. It shows that every thing was done in quick succession.

The state of Nagaland came into being on the 1st of December 1963 after its inauguration by the President of India. The day was marked as a 'gala day' in the political history of Nagaland. Dr Radhakrishnan, the then President of India, while inaugurating the state expected from the Naga people the return of "normal condition" quickly in Nagaland, and invited the underground people "to participate in the development of Nagaland". He further said that "the highest position in the country is open to every Naga in the parliament, in the central cabinet, in the various services". Lastly, he advised the Nagas to come forward and open a new chapter in the Naga history written with "progress, prosperity and goodwill". Shilu Ao, the care-taker chief minister of Nagaland, greeted the people and thanked the government of India for granting the Naga people a state of their own.

Constitutional Provisions for Nagaland State

The Thirteenth Constitution Amendment Act, 1962 added a new Article 371 (A) to the constitution, which ensured the creation of Nagaland state on the one hand, and made some special provisions for the protection of the customary laws and religious beliefs of the Naga people on the other. The Article laid down that unless so decided by the state assembly, no Act of Parliament shall apply to the state of Nagaland in respect of:

(i) "religious and social practices of the Nagas;
(ii) Naga customary laws and practices;
(iii) administration of civil and criminal justice involving decisions according to the Naga customary laws; and
(iv) ownership and transfer of land and its resources".[37]

Section 3 (1) of the Act assigned the Governor of Nagaland special responsibility with respect to law and order in the state for as long as in his opinion, the internal disturbances continued to occur there. However, such special power was subject to the permission of the Indian President who had the authority to withdraw such provision of special power any time. In regard to the Naga representation in the Indian parliament it was provided that "there shall be allotted one seat to the state of Nagaland in the Council of States (Rajya Sabha) and one seat in the House of People (Lok Sabha)".[38] So far the Nagaland legislative assembly was concerned, the Act converted the *de-facto* interim Naga legislature as the legislative assembly with "the total number of seats sixty to be filled by persons chosen by direct election".[39]

Thus, the democratic processes which were set in motion by the moderate Naga leaders at the risk of their life in the People's Convention in 1957, ultimately culminated in creation of Nagaland state. The creation of Nagaland state is a journey from a district to state, which is full of thrills and enthusiasm of the moderate Nagas. Many people lost their lives in the battle of freedom struggle and numerous people suffered a lot at the hands of both the Indian armed forces and the militant Nagas. The price what the Naga people paid for creation of the state of Nagaland is very high. The loss of properties and lives is irreparable. However, their long-cherished wish was fulfilled. The movement of insurgency yet continued, no doubt, but its biting capacity was reduced considerably. The Naga people got the responsibility to work for the progress and prosperity of the state and its inhabitants. The creation of Nagaland state opened the way for the party politics inviting those Naga leaders who wanted to exercise their political skill and potentialities for the betterment of the Naga people. The democratic and legislative processes, which were laid down, prepared fertile ground for the growth of Naga politics. Democratically spirited Naga leaders found indulging in formation of new political parties on the one hand and the Naga electorate began to exercise their right to franchise to choose their representative fairly and freely on the other. Thus, the state of Nagaland moved fast towards progress and prosperity under the care and control of the loyal sons of the soil.

Working of Democratic System

Once the Naga politics got its firm root established in the state of Nagaland, democratic as well as legislative processes moved ahead despite numerous problems and challenges. The challenges before the Naga political leaders were to lead the people towards the life of prosperity and work hard for establishment of permanent peace in the state. The political leaders, who had been realizing this truth, assumed full responsibility to change the poor economic situation of Nagaland and lead their people towards the life of progress and prosperity. Those leaders, who were yet silent spectators of the political events of Nagaland and away from the party politics, got enchanted and joined politics. With their increasing interest in party politics, the attention of the people declined towards the movement of insurgency. Politics became a means for them not only to work for the people and the state but also to obtain power, wealth and prestige. On the other hand, the interest of the general Naga people in political activities also increased. They began to take more interest in political affairs and activities. As a result, political dimension of Naga politics began to expand unexpectedly.

Timely elections for composition of the Nagaland Legislative Assembly were held. New political parties began to emerge with new objectives and ideologies. Successful working of two terms of democratically installed Naga government convinced the people that the Naga leaders had the wisdom, caliber and tactics to rule and administer their people. They also had the ability to lead their people towards peace and prosperity. What the state of Nagaland needed presently was not violent movement for independent and sovereign status, but peace and economic development, which were possible only when the democratic processes, which were set, must be allowed to prosper. Under this realisation the government of Nagaland worked hard without taking note of the threats of the undergrounds.

Such changing notion of the Naga leaders and the Naga people, in fact, provided stability to politics in Nagaland on the one hand, and detracted the attention of the general Naga mass from violent activities of the underground Nagas. Under such existing circumstances the freedom movement carried on by the underground Naga leaders was bound to suffer and decline. Problem before the Nagaland government was not only to run the affairs of the state but also to adopt the measure to solve the prolonged Naga political problem taking the underground leaders in good faith. The efforts applied by the leaders of the Baptist churches and the peace loving public leaders to maintain peace in the state resulted in the formation of the Peace Mission, comprising the chosen and renowned leaders and social reformers like J.P. Narayan, B.P. Chaliha, Narendara Deb, (both Sarvodaya leaders) Michael Scott (a British national on the request of the undergrounds), came into being in 1964 with the mission to prepare fertile ground for the solution of the Naga issue and preservation of permanent peace in the state. Due to sincere efforts of the Peace Mission the cease-fire agreement between the government of India and the underground Naga government was signed, which gave temporary relief to the Naga people.

Thereafter, peace talks between the representatives of the government of India and the underground set-up began. Despite six rounds of peace talks even at the level of Prime Ministers, no desired result could be achieved. The underground Naga leaders were not ready to accept any thing less than sovereignty while the government of India made it clear that such demand could not be conceded. Thus, the peace talks were bound to fail. It brought immense disappointment to the Naga people who were anxiously awaiting fruitful results of the peace talks. On the other hand, the leaders of the underground began to have conflicts among themselves blaming each other for the failure of peace talks. The personal clashes of the underground leaders in the name of tribalism resulted in sharp division among the undergrounds, which further weakened the strength of the freedom movement. The government of India was not looser because politics of Nagaland had taken deep root in the state under the guidance of the Indian political leaders.

New scenario appeared, which made it clear that the underground movement for freedom would not get the required strength to achieve the goal. Rumours also spread that continuation of armed conflicts with the government of India would add more troubles to the Naga people destroying their peace and progress.

The Naga politicians who had joined the mainstream of politics occupying various ranks in ministries, went ahead to give democracy a successful trial in the state. In such circumstance a number of underground leaders giving up their faith in armed struggle for the achievement of Naga's freedom, decided it better to surrender and join the mainstream of politics with the result that the dawn of peace took place in Nagaland in 1975 soon after signing of the historic Shillong Accord between the underground Naga leaders and the government of India. This is a fact that Shillong Accord could not prove as the final settlement of the Naga peace as the underground leaders who had not accepted the Accord and were out of India, resumed the activities of freedom fighting in 1980 which gave a new turn to the political dimension of the state.

Politics of Defection

The politics of defection has become a national phenomenon of Indian political system. It is a trend, which has affected both Central as well as state parliamentary democracy. Politics of defection may be defined as a political manoeuvering of the dissatisfied and disgruntled politicians of a political party who have either been undermined or whose interests have not been served by the bosses of the political party. Such members generally form a group within the party and look for the opportunity to defect from their own party to the rival party, which not only welcomes the defectors but also encourages politics of defection with the marked objective to assume power by toppling down the democratically installed government. Hence defection may be treated as a revolt against a party or a dirty game of politics, which not only destabilizes the government but also creates a circumstance of confusion and disorder. There may be various reasons behind a defection, but a general observation brings the fact to the light that the basic cause behind defection is lust for political power even at the cost of democratic principles. Defection has paved the way for corruption. Study on politics of defection makes the point clear that the defectors instead of getting punishment have been benefited, which has encouraged the politics of defection to such an extent that even those politicians who have been true to the democratic norms, are inclining towards defection. No viable step has been provided so far to check up such trend. Even the provisions made under the Anti-Defection Act have failed to stop the practice of politics of defection with the result that the government having absolute majority in the House is forced to quit from power without completing its full tenure.

With the rise and growth of multi-party system and also emergence of mushroom regional political parties, the politics of defection assumed such a height that it began to play a decisive role in making and unmaking of the government. With growing lust for power and prestige the Indian politicians forgetting their commitment to the parties, to which they belong and overlooking the principles and the ideologies of the political party, have been found indulging in politics of defection with the result that the stability of the government badly suffers.

Naga Politicians and Politics of Defection

The growing political consciousness and their involvement in party politics made Naga politicians more ambitious for power, wealth and prestige. By 1975, various political parties had come into being. Flow of financial funds for the development of the state and its people made the Naga politics more lucrative and ludicrous. Wealth, power and prestige "became the nuclei of Naga politics around which all the Naga politicians began to evolve putting aside their commitment and loyalty to the party's leadership and discipline".[40] This was the reason which paved the way for the growth of multi-party system and politics of defection in Nagaland. The leaders, who were not accommodated in the power began to form new parties, which offered them chances to serve their purpose.

No doubt, politics of defection in Naga politics appeared from 1975, but the year 1980 was marked as the year of defection and counter-defection in search of power. No political party was left true and committed to their principles and objectives. If there was any objective, it was how to capture power by toppling down the democratically established government. The process of toppling down of the government became so frequent that it was impossible to guess whether a party would run the government even for a month. Describing such confusing situation the Editor of *Nagaland Times* rightly remarked, "In the annual history of Nagaland there is no precedent when the state was ruled by coalition of parties holding no identical views on the problem facing the state."[41] The editor was very much correct in his observation. The leaders, who had been quite contrary to each other in the name of principles and objectives, joined their hands together deviating from all of their commitments only for power. In pursuit of power the enemies became friends and friends became enemies overnight.

It is interesting to note that during 1980s, there were no political parties, which had not enjoyed power even for a week. There was hardly any MLA who had not been appointed as a minister. Arienba Jamir, commenting on such ugly political scenario and dirty political environment of Nagaland, expressed the view, "The Christ-like political preachers are today the defectors of different parties... . Not a single party could implement to fulfill their promises during their tenure of office." In his opinion, "The politicians of Nagaland are a mixture of different weights, their goal of political philosophy differs from man to man and party to party. Except very reasonable view, majority of so-called politicians are too ambitious to become the leader of a party aiming to become the top leader of the government. To them other ranks like minister of state, deputy minister and MLA are negligible and do not welcome to accept such position".[42] What Arienba Jamir said was not the exaggeration of the facts but the reality of the picture, which, in fact, existed at the time. It was difficult to rely upon the sanctity of the ministers and political leaders in Nagaland. They all had become tricky and shaky.

Increasing Lust for Power

The fifth and the sixth general elections were held in Nagaland for the composition of the legislative assembly in November 1982 and November 1987 respectively. Before that the contest for power was between two political parties and the Naga electorate had exercised their right to franchise without much political tumults. As the years rolled down, the political consciousness of the general mass and political interest of the Naga leaders expanded. The politics became a profession for the Naga politicians and also meant to establish their hold not only on power but also on social institutions. The Naga politicians had fully understood that it was politics which could bring them power, prestige and wealth with the result that politics in Nagaland got the dynamic trends, no doubt, but towards the dangerous path. It created serious political rivalries among the Naga leaders. Unbridled ambitions of the Naga politicians, which grew during eighties and nineties of the 20th century, opened a new chapter in the history of Naga politics, which created doubts and suspicions in the minds of the Naga people as a whole about the sanctity and sagacity of political character of their leaders and to their commitment, which they used to make the people during election periods. Defection of political leaders from one party to another with a longing to obtain better ranks in politics, maligned the image of political leaders and dissatisfied the Naga people. The people witnessed mushroom growth of political parties, which appeared overnight, but devoid of principles and ideologies. The process of electioneering became tough and complicated due to increase in the number of candidates and their undue indulgence in unpleasant activities and unrequired interference in the process of election. However, the democratic processes continued. The government was organized and legislature followed its bounded legislative processes with frequent changes of power.

Horse-trading in Naga politics has been a common feature. By 1990, the trend of horse-trading reached at its climax. In the words of Chandrika Singh, "The political parties, either ruling or opposition, left no stone unturned to win over the independent

MLAs offering them money and ranks of their choice .... The parties, which were pole apart and inimical, easily agreed to join their hands with the rivals also, only to serve their interests... the leaders who had been bitter critics to each other became fast friends overnight... ".[43] During nineties, the practice of horse-trading once more created trouble for the government of Mr. Chishi soon after assuming the power. Hardly his government had completed 17 days in power, 17 NPC's MLAs led by Noke defected to the camp of Vamuzo who had defected from the NPC and joined the Congress-I. Thereafter, Vamuzo formed the coalition of the Congress-I and NPC and successfully managed to become the chief minister of Nagaland toppling down the government of Mr. Chishi.

In the words of Chandrika Singh, "In a spell of sixteen months ever since January 1989, fifty-eight MLAs belonging to various parties and groups remained fortunate enough to become ministers by following the trend of defection. During this period only three dominant politicians such as S.C. Jamir, K.L. Chishi and Vamuzo availed the opportunity to become the chief minister of Nagaland even for a few days or for a few months".[44] The study reveals the truth that among the Naga politicians, who played notable role in the politics of defection with the marked objective to become chief minister, were S.C. Jamir, Vamuzo Angami, J.B. Jasokie and K.L. Chishi. They all fulfilled the dream of becoming the chief minister of the state even. These leaders had been bitter critics of each other but getting the benefit of existing circumstance they did not make any delay to become fast friends with the objective to serve their vested interests. The lust for power, money and prestige as well as their personal rivalries made them too blind to see the party's ideologies and people's reaction. Observing such situation Khiren Roy writes, "Most tribal leaders being fresh in politics and without having any sort of commitment to the cause of public benefit often get attempted to indulge in shameless acts of amassing public funds while being in power."[45] The ex-Naga MLA, Huska Sumi remarked that "the legislators of Nagaland have learnt the tactics of defection under the provision of law, reducing themselves to gain opportunism at any opportune time".[46]

Jamir and Vamuzo were bitter critics of one another, but they came near to form the government. It was Vamuzo who had managed defection during the Jamir ministry in 1989 to oust him from the power. Now defending the move in favour of Jamir, Vamuzo clarified that "it is through a unique political experiment that the NPC and the Congress-I have joined hands to provide the state a stable and efficient government". What Vamuzo said was not reality. Jamir and Vamuzo had joined their hands not for giving a stable and efficient government, but it was a 'marriage of convenience'. Such move "made the Naga politics more bitter and sour and intensified the feeling of rivalries strengthening the process of instability",[47] which "adversely affected the Naga life and thinking" and the "mass began to loose confidence not only in their representatives but also in the question of the utility and suitability of the present system of election".[48]

TABLE-I

POLITICS OF DEFECTION IN NAGALAND FROM 1971 to 1990

Leader of Defection	No. of Defectors	Year	From	To	Results
S.C. Jamir	15	1971	NNO	UDF	Fall of Hokishe Govt.
Tokeho Sema	5	1975	UDF	NNO	Fall of Vizol Govt.
Tokeho Sema	6	1977	NNO	UDF	Fall of Jasokie Govt.
S.C. Jamir	13	1980	UDF	ULF	Fall of Vizol Govt.
J.B. Jasokie	5	1980	ULP	NNDP	Fall of Jamir Govt.
K.L. Chishi	5	1980	NNDP	NPC	No effect
K.L. Chishi	13	1988	Cong-I	NNDP	Fall of Hokishe Govt.
Chongsen	12	1989	Cong-I	ULP	Fall of Jamir Govt.
Noke	17	1990	ULF	NPC	Fall of Chishi Govt.

TABLE –II

FREQUENCY OF DEFECTION AND INSTABILITY OF GOVERNMENT FROM 1964 to 1990

Year of formation of Govt.	Chief Minister	Ruling party	Period of rule	Cause of fall of Govt.
February 1964	Shilu Ao	NNO	About 3 years	Defection
October 1966	T.N. Angami	NNO	About 2 years	General election
February 1969	Hokishe Sema	NNO	Five years	General
February 1974	Vizol Angami	UDF	13 months	Defection
March 1975	J.B. Jasokie	NNO	10 days	Defection
Nov. 1977	Vizol Angami	UDF	16 months	Defection
April 1980	S.C. Jamir	Cong-I	49 days	Defection
June 1980	J.B. Jasokie	NNDP	2 years	General election
Nov. 1982	S.C. Jamir	Cong-I	5 years	General election
Nov. 1987	Hokishe Sema	Cong-I	20 months	Defection
Jan. 1989	S.C. Jamir	Cong-I	15 months	Defection
May 1990	K.L. Chishi	ULF	29 days	Defection
June 1990	Vamuzo	Coalition Cong-I and NPC	23 months	

The tables illustrated above presents a clear picture of politics of defection and its impact upon the government and legislative assembly. Table-I reflects that from 1964 to 1990 the government in Nagaland was toppled down not less than eight times before completing the tenure due to politics of defection only. During that period political parties like the United Legislative Party (ULP), United Legislative Front (ULF), Naga People's Council (NPC), the Congress-Progressive and Naga nationalist Democratic Party

(NNDP) appeared and disappeared without having any historical background and ideological base. Their only purpose was to topple down a democratically installed government and assume the power.

Table-II reflects that within such period 13 Naga political leaders availed the opportunity to occupy the chair of chief minister even for a period of ten days. Luckiest among them was S.C. Jamir who occupied the chair of the chief minister thrice while J.B. Jasokie and Vizol Angami managed to become the chief minister twice. The state went under the President's Rule not less than three times within such period where politics of defection reined the state.

Thus, it is obvious that politics of defection as well as horse-trading which began in Nagaland from 1974 onwards and reached its climax during 1980-1990 badly affected the democratic and legislative processes of the state. Premature dissolution of Nagaland legislative assembly and promulgation of the President's Rule three times in Nagaland badly affected the legislative processes. During such period whenever the assembly came in session most of the time was wasted by the honourable members of the House criticizing and blaming each other for the anarchic situation, which existed in the state. Moreover, frequent fall of the government and existing political uncertainty, did not allow the Assembly to complete the process in the interest of the state and people. At such period, neither durable progressive policies were adopted nor could the programmes, which were on run, be completed within the prescribed time. Rather it created mass political confusion among the people loosing their faith in both the political leaders and the democratic political process. The study shows that the Naga politicians either from the ruling bench or from the opposition, during 1980s were found opportunists who were more interested in their own cause. They talked much about public welfare, but did little for public well-being. The self-interested attitude of the Naga politicians during the phase of politics of defection definitely undermined the sanctity and sagacity of democratic spirit and legislative process in Nagaland. It was politics of defection, which forced the state to go under the President's Rule thrice. First the President's Rule was imposed in 1975, second time in 1988 and third in 1992. During these periods the Naga politicians remained away from party politics and the state and its people remained without their elected representatives.

The study makes the fact obvious that politics of defection took deep root in Nagaland because the Naga politicians wanted to improve their lot as quickly as possible. Under such corrupt situation politics became a device to serve the interests of the politicians. The Naga electorate began to fall easy prey to money. It is, indeed, unfortunate that the in-built mechanism within the Naga society has so far failed to check this fast slide of the state into corruption and political opportunism. It is not that the Naga electorate is ignorant, illiterate or innocent, but they have become greedy, selfish and short-sighted. Their demands during elections are "pork, supply orders, government jobs, and this tendency has given birth "to corruption, frustration and social turmoil". The results, in the words of Changkiza , are that the "political drama being staged currently in Nagaland is unfortunate, the reflection of the malignancy of the attitudes, values and trends of the Naga society".[49] The political scenario of the state from 1990 onwards "is an obscene displaying of avarice, an ego-centralism and total disregard for people and state".[50]

References

1. Asoso Yonuo, *The Rising Nagas,* Vivek Publishing House, Delhi, 1974, pp. 18-9.
2. Piketo Sema, *British Policy and Administration in Nagaland* (1882-1947), New Delhi, p. 142.
3. *The Naga Nation,* Vol. I, No. 5, April, 1946, p. 89.
4. Asoso Yonuo, *The Rising Nagas, op. cit.*, p. 89.
5. *Naga Nation,* Vol. I, No. 5, April, 1946, p. 5-6.
6. *Ibid.* vol. I, No. 11, June 1946, pp. 2-5.
7. Asoso Yonuo, *The Rising Nagas, op. cit.*, pp. 159-60.
8. Piketo Sema, *British Policy and Administration in Nagaland* (1882-1947), *op. cit.*, pp. 152-53.

9. *Proceedings of Assam Legislative Assembly*, vol. III, 1947, p. 2133.
10. D.R. Mankekar, *Slippery Slope in Nagaland*, Bombay, 1965, pp. 195-96.
11. Constituent Assembly Debates, *Report of the Sub-committee on Northeastern Frontier (Assam), Tribal and Excluded Areas*, Appendix (C), Part-I, vol. II, No. 1, 1948, pp. 122-26 and 132-33.
12. Sajal Nag, "Construction of Nationhood: Ethnic Minority" in Girin Phukon (Ed), *Political Dynamics of North East India*, New Delhi, 2000, p. 32.
13. *Asian Recorder* (a weekly), January 28-February 3, 1956, Delhi, p. 649.
14. *Ibid.* April 7-13, 1956, pp. 772-73.
15. *Ibid.*, January 28-February 3, 1956, p. 649.
16. *Ibid.* February 16-22, 1957, p. 1307.
17. *Pt. Jawaharlal Nehru's speeches*, vol. III, Delhi, 1958, pp. 448-50.
18. Asoso Yonuo, *The Rising Nagas*, op. cit., p. 219.
19. *Keesing Contemporary Archives*, (a weekly) vol. XI, September 23-October 5, 1957, Delhi, p. 15864.
20. *Ibid.*, vol. IX, September 28-October 5, 1957, p. 15868.
21. *Ibid.*, vol. XI, September 28- October 5, 1957, p. 15864.
22. Naga Hills Tuensang Areas (Administration) Regulation, 1957, published in the Gazette of India, Extraordinary, Part-II, Section I, No. 37 dated 30th November, 1957.
23. *Ibid.*
24. *Ibid.*
25. Cited in Prakash Singh, *Nagaland*, Delhi, 1974, p. 106.
26. *Report of the State Reorganization Committee*, No. 1, Para 694, New Delhi, p. 187.
27. "The Nagaland (Transitional Provisions) Regulation," 1961, Section 2 (2), quoted in P.N. Luthra's, *Nagaland from a District to State*, Shillong, 1974, pp. 92-96.
28. *Ibid.*
29. *Ibid.*

30. *Lok Sabha Debates*, 2nd Series, vol. VII, No. 11, 1962, Cols. 3177-78 and 5407.
31. *Ibid.*
32. *Ibid.* cols. 4507.
33. Sajal Nag, "Multiplication of Nation and Political Economy of sub-nationalism in India", *Economic and Political Weekly*, vol. 228, No. 29-30, July 17-25, 1993.
34. *Lok Sabha Debates*, 2nd series, 1962, vol. VII, No. 11, Cols. 4507, 4520-22 and 4530-31.
35. *Ibid.*
36. *Ibid*, Cols, 4573-74.
37. The Constitution (13th Amendment) Act, 1962, published in the Gazette of India, Extraordinary, Part II, Section 2, dated New Delhi, august 21st, 1962.

    Also see Article 371 of the Indian constitution.
38. *Ibid.* Section 11 (2).
39. *Ibid.*
40. Chandrika Singh, *Naga Politics: A Critical Account*, Mittal Publications, New Delhi, 2004, p. 146.
41. *Nagaland Times*, vol. 10, No. 43, April 30, 1980, Dimapur, Editorial Page.
42. *Ura Mail*, July 26, 1981, daily newspaper, Dimapur.
43. Chandrika Singh, *Naga Politics: A Critical Account, op. cit.*, p. 157.
44. *Ibid.*
45. Khiren Roy, "Nagaland Gang-Opportunism", in the *Assam Tribune*, June 16, 1990. p. 4.
46. Huska Sumi "The anti-Defection Law: Its Impact on Defection in Nagaland", *The Weekly Express Journal*, September 1990, p. 4.
47. Chandrika Singh, *op. cit.*, 2004, p. 158.
48. *The Hill Express*, (daily newspaper), June 26, 1990. p. 5
49. Monalisa Chankiza, "Nagaland Politics with Hopes and Disgusts", in the *North-East Sun*, August 1998, p. 26/xii.
50. *Ibid.*

* * *

6

Socio-Economic Structure

The British occupied the Naga Hills. Till then the Naga society was stagnant, confined to the villages, isolated from the civilized world, relied on minimum needs and depended on tribal customary laws. The Naga tribes were proud of their supremacy and independence, but they were separated, disintegrated and inimical to each other. Their parochial consciousness, traditional social outlook and conventional behavioral attitude were chauvinistic and related to the community life where individualistic thinking had either no place or a little role to play. However, the scenario changed with the establishment of British suzerainty over the Nagas and penetration of the Christian missionaries into their land. Close association of the Nagas with the Europeans and adoption of Christianity as a new faith changed the traditional as well as parochial outlook of the indigenous people bringing them near to the threshold of modernity. Adoption of new educational system and propagation of new social values, to which the animist Nagas were quite ignorant of, opened a new dimension of social change, while their ancient culture and social values were completely eroded.

After India's independence and creation of Nagaland state, the pace of social, economic and political changes became more visible. Introduction of new political structure and laws, the setting up of new administrative headquarters in new towns, advent of new economic and fiscal system and flow of huge amount of funds for development paved the way for the growth of modernization and urbanization of the Naga society. The rural areas, which represented the ugly and vulnerable picture, began to change where the rural people witnessed construction of new roads, running of new buses, opening of new towns, construction of new bridges, and, implementation of various rural development programmes involving the villagers to change and upgrade the standard of life. Kohima, the capital of the state, along with other towns like Mokokchung, Wokha and Tuensang marked notable expansion. Several new towns appeared. Trade and commerce spread all over the state. New avenues for services and business were opened where many of the Nagas availed the opportunities to earn money and change their living style. The Naga people found themselves in the era of modernization, which made them enchanted towards new lifestyle. Their attention was drawn towards material prosperity and they lost no time to become materialist and consumerist at least by behaviour, if not by spirit. At the same time, the development of the Naga society produced a number of social evils along with new civilization. This chapter discusses about the advent of modernization in Nagaland and examines its impact upon the Naga society and its people. The chapter also analyses the factors responsible for income disparities in Nagaland and its consequences.

Meaning of Development and Modernization

Changes are the established rule and constant process of the nature. There is nothing in the universe, which stands beyond transformation. There is no society in the world, which has been static throughout the span of time. Changes may also be understood in the sense of development. Development is a process of gradual change where different component factors work together. So far the social change is concerned, it is the process of social mobilization first in people's attitude, faith and behaviour and then in their social structure. Development, in fact, is a shift from old to new, regarding values, faith and living style. The factors responsible for social change are spread of mass education (both general and technical), growth of mass-media, availability of industrial products, expansion of consumerism as a habit, inclination towards secularism and materialism and the economic capability of the people to meet the cost of new requirement available at their door. Under the process of development "major clusters of old social, economic and physical commitments are eroded or broken and people are available for new pattern of socialization and behaviour".[1] "It implies a complete dichotomy between tradition and modernity. After the breakdown of traditional social and economic institutions, new way is opened for the beginning of modernization".[2] Thereafter, changes take place in position, power and economic strata of the people dividing the society in "permanent groups or categories linked with each other by the relationship of subordination".[3]

The group, which acquires maximum benefits of development, occupies the highest hierarchical ranks of the social stratum and provides leadership to the society in such a manner that their interests are safe and well protected. Moreover, they have enough power to defend their interest if there is any threat to it. On the other hand, the subordinate groups are bound or rather forced to follow the lead provided by the group that is capable and viable both. A belief is created by the class of intelligentsia, which is the product of the well-to-do group, that inequality is the base of civilization and the more the society develops, the more economic disparity takes place. People are informed that social disparity is an inevitable result of development. This is a permanent feature that cannot be eroded even by applying force. On the other hand, the sections, which are deprived of the benefits of development, think that injustice has been done to them and they prepare themselves to fight for justice, which ultimately results in social conflicts and civil-war.

However, theory of development is maintained and spread by the class of bourgeois. The Marxists, on the other hand, regard such theory of development prejudicial, unscientific and based on false consciousness. They also regard it as a trick of the society of the bourgeoisie to perpetuate their rule and maintain their status. Social disparity is not natural, but artificial, which has been created by some vested interests while establishing their hold over means of production at the cost of deprivation, suppression and exploitation of the working class. There is not an iota of doubt that social disparity is dishonesty; verily it is social injustice and a crime committed against the poor. Hence the Marxists ask the proletariat to get organised, fight against the common enemies, overthrow their rule and change the basic pattern of capitalist society where no scope is left for any sort of exploitation. This creates social conflicts, paves the way for the growth of class antagonism and involves people in the class war. To avoid such things new theory of development put emphasis on social and economic justice where everyone is assured at least of his/her minimum requirements available in a developed society, and where everyone is given equal opportunity to develop.

. Modernization as a form of cultural reforms is basically universalistic. Modern social values are 'pan-humanistic', 'trans-ethnic' and 'non-ideological'. It symbolizes attitudes towards social values and their evaluation from universalistic and not particularistic viewpoints as it generally happens with the traditional society. In the words of Yogendra Singh, "Modernization as a form of cultural response, involves attributes which are basically universalistic and evolutionary.... Modernization in this respect should be treated as a kind of cultural, universal... a level at which the institutionalization of a higher order of culture is possible."[4] Here science and technology play greater roles to change the attitude of the people.[5] Modernity is not an exclusive possession of any one ethnic or cultural group, but it belongs to the humanity as a whole. According to Max Weber, emphasis on formal rationality, experiment, codification, verification and rational utilitarian orientation in behaviour and thought are some of the unique substantive questions of western cultural tradition, which come under the category of modern society.

Invention of science and technology has led the greatest revolution in human history. According to Santa Ana, "No revolution has so radically and permanently transformed the social structure of all human societies as the industrial and technological revolution."[6] From 17th century onwards, a number of traditional as well as tribal societies have changed due to advent of science and technology in their areas or their contact with the industrially and technologically advanced nations. Science and technology are the base of industrialization, urbanization, means of communication, new education, new political processes and new economic system. Thomas has rightly remarked, "Social technology had developed the human capacity for engineering with social forces, planning for social change and bureaucratic administration and management.... Mass communication technology has eliminated distance whereby the world is fast becoming a global village. Psychological techniques are able to control the minds and spirit of the people and advertisement as well as education for character."[7]

Development of the Naga Society

The Naga society is one of the oldest tribal societies. Before the arrival of the British the economic conditions of the Naga people were poor and their whole thought process was confined to villages. They had no idea of science and technology. The technology used for production of foods, weaving, dying and construction of houses was primitive. The village iron-smith made tools like daos, axes, hammer, and iron arrows from iron procured from the plains area of Assam. These instruments were used for agriculture, hunting, preparation of food, etc. Clothes were mostly made from cotton yarns with simple looms, and indigenous vegetable dyes were used for coloring clothes. Mode of cultivation was mostly *jhumming* (shifting cultivation) and forest materials were utilized for house construction. No doubt, changes took place in the mental attitude of the Nagas with the arrival of the British and Christian missionaries, but no change in their economic structure was marked. What the Nagas achieved during the British period was "familiarization of these tribes with new ideals, coupled with the subsequent independence and democratization of the polity", which took "them into the modern world with all its strengths and dangers".[8] Christianity served as defence mechanism for tribal interests and identity against threat of dominance and absorption into the larger Hindu society of the plains.

In the Naga Hills the British rulers had utilized two layers of native administrative agencies—the village chiefs and their traditional leadership at the village level for village administration. The village chiefs were earmarked with some special kind of costumes, which was a symbol of British power. The villages, which lacked the system of chieftainship, were provided with Gaon Burah with some powers. Notable thing is that the British authority never allowed these village authorities to exercise their power on the traditional line. They over-exercised their power weakening the village traditional authorities. The Dobhashi acted as informants and personnel of the intelligent department of the government. Nirmal Minz has rightly observed, "The British legal system introduced in the regions of the adibashi/tribal indigenous people, undermined and slowly destroyed the customary laws prevalent among them. A complete new concept of property, and property inheritance was introduced. Land became commodity to be bought and sold. Ownership was changed from the community to private individual."[9] Thus such new legal system served as mechanism to destroy the old social and economic pattern of the Naga society on the one hand, and encouraged the practice of individualism on the other.

Administrators, military and police personnel, technicians, businessmen, engineers, contractors, other workers gave impetus to the growth of urbanization in the Naga Hills. Spread of commerce and trade brought the natives near to the plains people. As a result traditional way of life began to disappear. The newly constructed administrative establishments, houses in bungalow quarters enchanted the rustic Naga people. According to Snaitang, the biggest trauma imposed on the tribal was "the imposition of cantonment with well equipped military powers, guns and ammunitions which had overshadowed the traditional weapons and developed a sense of threat to their existance."[10]

Introduction of money economy enabled the Nagas to enter economy which was self-sufficient and independent. Money economy was introduced with the involvement of tribal people as a labour force in constructionworks like roads, residential houses, office quarters, hospitals and business centers. The World War I had opened the way for the Naga labourers to go to Europe and earn money and return to their native villages bringing huge amount of money which made them more alert and conscious of new lifestyle. The Second World War provided them another greater opportunity to earn money. Thus, introduction of money economy enabled the tribal to adopt non-tribal avenues of work. Such move alienated a number of tribals from land-labour. With the emergence of urban places and introduction of communication and business enterprises, village policy gradually disintegrated. It caused danger to both community and individual identity. Besides, it provided ample opportunity for wider interaction with others. Life gradually became interdependent increasing the scope of social mobilization.

Once the Naga people moved towards modernity, it was not possible for them to look back at their old living style. Their contact with the outside world sharpened their outlook. They bought new tools and borrowed new approach to the human life. Now leaving aside the local loom-made clothes, they began to prefer factory-made clothes. They discarded those things and goods, which were directly produced from the soil and replaced them with factory-made goods. The wooden and bamboo cups and plates and the utensils were replaced by manufactured goods made from aluminum.[11] Lanterns and kerosene oil was replaced by manufactured matches.[12]

Stagnation of Development due to Armed Conflicts between Naga Warriors and Indian Armed Forces

The development, which took place during the British regime, was not in the field of economics, but mostly in the religious field. No doubt, changes occurred in the attitude and behaviour of the Naga people, but they were yet far away from the pace of real economic development. Most of the people specially living in the rural areas were yet in the hold of poverty and scarcity. They were not able to buy the things of their daily needs. Major shift of development took place in Nagaland after the creation of Nagaland state in December 1963. It was unfortunate that soon after India's independence the Naga people found themselves in the whirlpool of cross-currents due to freedom struggle. The Naga warriors fought with the Indian armed forces with the hope that they would achieve freedom soon, but circumstances proved that to achieve freedom was to crack the hard nut, which was not practically possible. Under such tense situation where doubt, fear, suspicion etc. prevailed, the economic development of Nagaland could neither be thought of nor be practised. The year 1963 was the dark phase of Naga history. Instead of getting development, people lost their houses, granaries, prestige and peace.

Peace and development have reciprocal relationship. No development can take place in an anarchic situation. According to Oxford English dictionary, peace means "freedom from mental or spiritual disturbance" or "freedom from disturbance or perturbation". Peaceful situation means 'undisturbed state'. In general parlance, peace means absence of unrest, disorder, chaos and anarchy. For existence of peace, antagonism, clash and conflict have no room at all, because any one of these factors destabilizes first peace and then development. Dynamics of development, which take place under peaceful situation, are multifarious. History bears the testimony that various branches of natural science, different fields of literature, arts, historical monumental architecture, science of engineering, technology etc., have developed during the peaceful era. Whenever peace is allowed to exist, development takes place and when peace is disturbed, annihilation raises its ugly hydra-heads.

After India's independence economic development of the state of Nagaland suffered a lot due to absence of required peaceful environment for reason of constant fight between the underground freedom fighters and the armed forces of the government of India. Such struggle brought with it more miseries, troubles and harassments for the Naga people. However, situation improved by 1957 when a group of the underground Naga leaders came forward with the demand of peace and negotiated it with the government of India. The Naga government during the transitional phase worked hard to usher peace in the region preparing the ground for the creation of Nagaland state. The people, too, realized the significance of peace and helped their leaders who were engaged with setting the ground for permanent peace with the result that peace in Nagaland got the chance to stay and development got its pace covering each corner of the state and its people.

Major Shift in Development

When the insurgency in Nagaland subsided to some extent and the Naga political leaders assumed the responsibility to administer their own state after the creation of Nagaland state in December 1963, the development began. The Nagaland government under the centrally sponsored schemes launched various projects and programmes to change the poor shape of the Naga economy. Urbanization took place due to opening of new headquarters, sub-divisional headquarters and other buildings of various departments of the government. Naga people witnessed the growth of increasing number of new towns and business centers. New roads were constructed and efforts were made successfully to link each village with the main towns and roads.

Before creation of the Nagaland state, agricultural sector remained an untouched sector. The number of schools specially for higher education was miserably limited. Road communication was scarce. The Naga Hills had no industries except small scale cottage industries and that also in limited numbers. The government applied tremendous efforts to improve Naga economy. The government of India, too, assisted the state generously by providing sufficient funds and the required directions. Various ministries and departments for agriculture, soil conservation, medical, physical health, engineering, education, rural development, mining etc., were set up with the determination to work for taking the state on the road of development. The efforts of the government proved successful. During 1964-65, foodgrain production, which was 62,000 M.T., increased to 283.45 thousands M.T. by the end of 1998-99.[13] Use of improved seeds, better agronomic practices, use of manures and fertilizers, plant protection measures, increase in irrigation facilities and use of small farm powers and machineries etc., have not only increased the productivity of the land but also enriched the farmers. The economic status of the farmers has changed to a considerable extent.

Development in Rural Sector

Under the various programmes of rural development, infrastructural assets like housing, roads, community halls, community transports, recreational centers, playgrounds, community latrines, approach roads etc., have been created to meet the basic needs of the rural people in every district of the state. The Development Block, District Planning Board, District Rural Development Agency (DRDA) and the Village Development Board (VDB), which assumed the responsibility to help the villagers in their self-development schemes, are playing remarkable roles to implement the schemes and programmes launched by the central government. Today the state has 1046 functional VDBs. This is a unique developing agency of the state, which has, in fact, revolutionized the process of rural development. The grant-in-aid to the VDBs, which was started in 1980 with Rs. 100-/ only per household has now been increased to Rs. 2250/- per household to make the working of VDBs more viable.[14] The Rural Development Department of the state government is far ahead in implementing the centrally sponsored schemes like the Integrated Rural Development Programme (IRDP), Training for Rural Youth Self-Employment (TRYSEM), National Rural Employment Guarantee Programme (NREGP), Development of Women and Children of Rural Areas (DWCRA), Jawahar Rojgar Yojana (JRY), Indira Awas Yojana (IAY) , JGSY, SGSE etc., All these schemes and programmes have helped the rural people a lot to change their standard widening the scope of social and economic changes of the Naga society. The tables mentioned here clearly indicate the working of these programmes, investment of funds and achievements.

Social Welfare Schemes

Organised social activities in Nagaland began in 1968 and a number of planned social welfare activities have been initiated for improving the lot of the socially and physically handicapped women and children who constitute the weaker sections of the community. The Department of Social Security and Welfare provides supplementary nutrition to children in the age group of 0-6 years and expectant and nursing mothers in the rural areas. Besides that, school-going children in the age group of 6-11 years are covered in mid-day meal centers located in various primary schools. Grant-in-aid is also extended to Non-Governmental Organizations (NGOs) to assist orphans and destitute children in various children homes. There are six women centers located in different districts for imparting training in knitting and tailoring to needy rural women. They are given financial assistance. The Nagaland State Social Welfare Advisory Board, which was established in 1958, has set up seven Border Area Projects in all the districts to cater to the social, health and economic needs of the weaker section of the society. It provides financial assistance, child care and nutrition in the areas.

Schemes such as vocational training programme, condensed course for adult women to facilitate them to appear in HLLC examination, holiday home camps, socio-economic programmes and supplementary nutrition are being implemented by the Board to uplift the socio-economic conditions of the underprivileged, women and children. All these activities have, in fact, improved the economic status of the rural people. Their living standard has increased and their way of living has changed to a great extent.

TABLE-1

STATEMENT SHOWING PLAN EXPENDITURE UNDER RURAL DEVELOPMENT BLOCKS (Rs. in Lakhs)

S.No.	Heads	1998-99	1999-2000	2000-01	2001-02	2002-03
1	2	3	4	5	6	7
1.	SGSY	-	232.62	307.08	124.98	184.01
2.	Integrated Rural Development	173.40	120.00	-	-	-
3.	VDB for CD schemes	1125.00	1125.00	1251.15	1200.01	1200.00
4.	Additional Grant to CD Schemes	15.13	21.28	48.00	30.00	30.00
5.	E A S	820.00	820.50	491.90	343.49	761.63
6.	I R E P	20.29	22,50	40.00	40.00	67.00
7.	BMS (Housing)	594.00	669.00	616.96	452.60	700.00
8.	BMS (Road)	228.00	228.00	700.00	400.00	-
9.	TRYESM	774.00	-	-	-	-
10.	D.W.C.R.A.	24.50	-	-	-	-
11.	I.A.Y.(Rural Housing)	220.00	955.98	616.37	705.00	667.61
12.	J.R.Y./ JGSY	175.00	347.15	454.46	555,48	511.60

Source: *Statistical Handbook of Nagaland 2004*, published by Directorate of Economics & Statistics, Government of Nagaland, Kohima.

Table-II

COVERAGE AND ACHIEVEMENT REPORT UNDER G.I.A.

DURING 1998-2003

Sl/.N	Physical Achievement	Unit	1999-2000	2000-01	2001-02	2002-03
1	2	3	4	5	6	7
1.	Approach road cutting	Kms.	182	209.50	209.50	209.50
2.	Approach road soling & metalling	Kms.	69.6	93.00	93.50	93.50
3.	Approach road Black topping	Kms.	13.75	50.25	50.25	50.25
4.	Rural Housing	Units	503	1743	1743	1743
5.	Tree Plantation	Hect.	1638	4329.50	4329.50	4329.50
6.	Horticulture Farming	Hect.	1397	4498.15	4498.15	4498.15
7.	Community Bus	Nos.	27	73	73	73
8.	Multipurpose Building	Nos.	108	280	280	280
9.	Playground	Nos.	08	230	230	230
10.	Community Centre	Nos.	64	199	199	199
11.	Youth Centre	Nos.	68	184	184	184
12.	Women Centre	Nos.	71	-	-	-
13.	Sports goods	Nos.	-	72	72	72

Contd.

1	2	3	4	5	6	7
14.	VDB Educational Tour	Nos.(VDB)	105	302	302	302
15.	Fishery Ponds	Nos.	114	114	114	114
16.	Piggery Farming	Nos.	86	-	-	-
17.	Dairy Farming	Nos.	36	-	-	-
18.	Cash Crop Farming	Hect.	25	174	174	174
19.	Social Agro Forestry	Hect.	195	-	-	-
20.	Poultry Farming	Units	-	32	32	32
21.	Protection wall	Nos.t	—	55	55	55
22.	Bee Keeping	Unit	-	-	-	-
23.	Construction of F/Step	Nos.	-	59	59	59
24.	Suspension Bridge	Nos.	17	44	44	44
25.	Culverts construction	Nos.	-	33	33	33
26.	Public well	Nos.	27	46	46	46
27.	Urine shed	Nos.	-	16	16	16
28.	Walting shed	Nos.	-	13	13	13
29.	Repairing of School Buildings	Nos.	22	62	62	62
30.	Construction of Community latrine	Nos.	9	2960	2960	2960

Source: *Statistical Handbook of Nagaland 2004*, published by Directorate of Economics & Statistics, Government of Nagaland, Kohima.

Industrial Development

Before 1963, industry was almost non-existent in Nagaland. Since 1964 , the government has initiated several schemes such as establishment of industrial centers, modernization of hand-looms and handicraft sectors, promotion of garment industries, development of agro-forest and mineral based industries. The Department of Industries has continued to promote industrial activities by providing incentives and assistance for the last four decades. Seven District Industries Centers with six sub-centers have been established for promotion of industries at grass-root level. The Department has also set up 18 medicinal and essential oil demonstration farms including one training-cum-production centers. Mini industrial estates have been identified at Chuchuyimlang, Saringm, Baghty and Viswema where all necessary infrastructural facilities are being built to attract entrepreneurs to promote industries. Besides, the government has promoted a few public sector undertakings in the state. The fruit vegetable processing-cum-cold storage plant at Dimapur has been commissioned in 1995 with an installed capacity of 5 MT per day and the Nagaland Mechanized Bricks Company Limited with a capacity of 1,00,000 bricks per day set up for commercial production. Moreover, efforts are being made to review the Tuli paper mill and the Nagaland sugar mill at Dimapur, which have been laid off temporarily. The government has done all these to promote the trade potentials of the state along the Indo-Myanmar border. The border trade centers already established at Longwa and Pangsha are expected to open up a new shift in commercial activities of Nagaland.[15]

Keeping in view the size and population of Nagaland, the industrial growth what has taken place till date is not much encouraging. Only two large industries namely, the paper mill at Tuli and the sugar mill at Dimapur were set up, but both of them are defunct today. There is only one brick making industry at Dimapur. No district of the state has got any industry where people can be employed. The investment of the government in this sector is negligible. Due to disturbed situation no entrepreneur from outside the state is ready to invest money in the industrial field of the state. There is no source of employment in the state except the government jobs in administration, police and educational institutions. However, the government have made a beginning in this area but the result is not satisfactory. Study shows that till 1986-87, the state had altogether 22 types of industries. By 1996-97, the number of variety of industries increased to 47, which have not only opened new avenues for self-employment of the people but also brought about considerable amount of changes in their economic and social standard. Despite of all these activities Nagaland cannot be called as the industrial state. The government has taken initiative to increase the number of small scale industries in rural areas to help rural people to improve their living standard.

Progress in Geology and Mining

The Department of Geology and Mining has discovered and proved some mineral raw materials such as petroleum and natural gas, nickel-cobalt chromium, limestone, marble, coal, clay, slate and dimensional and decorative stones. The Department has established 50 TPD Mini Cement plant at Wazebo under the management of NSMDC Ltd. The semi-mechanized brick plant at Chumukedima is producing ten thousands bricks per day. The North Eastern Council, which is meant to work for economic development of the Northeastern states of India, has recently agreed to sponsor Decorative and Dimensional Stone Plants at Wazebo and Dimapur based on the mineral deposits explored by the Department. Besides that, with active cooperation of the Department, the Oil and Natural Gas Corporation has carried out exploration for oil and natural gas. Since minerals for economic development are available in Nagaland, the government of Nagaland is in the process of building a proper climate for free inflow of technology and investment in mineral and mining sectors.

Power Sector

In 1963, only three towns of Nagaland had the privilege of electric light by diesel generators. Now the Naga people have come a long way in this regard. In 1998, Nagaland became the first state in North East India to achieve 100% rural electrification. From a few hundred consumers in the sixties, the number of consumers has increased manifold. The power consumption per annum has reached 187 million units. The Power Department has completed transmission line of 138 KV from Dimapur to Mokokchung via Kohima, Melori, Kiphere, Tuensang and Mokokchung.

The construction of sub-stations at Wokha, Naginimora, Kohima and Doyang Way is in progress. Besides these, the government has adopted some more devices to improve the position and strength of power in Nagaland, which has involved thousands of workers all over the state. The table mentioned below presents the picture of development in the field of power in Nagaland.

Table-III

GENERATION, CONSUMPTION AND PER CAPITA CONSUMPTION OF ELECTRICITY

Period	Installed	Generation	Consumption	Per Capita
1995-1996	5,260	2.55	111.01	95.56
1996-1997	5,260	2.22	127.36	105.29
1997-1998	4,260	2.35	131.19	108.46
1998-1999	4,260	2.42	129.19	106.89
1999-2000	5,160	2.80	145,75	120.49
2000-2001	4,500	3.05	220.00	118.00
2001-2002	4,500	0.50	238.00	120.00

Source: *Statistical Hand Book of Nagaland, 2004*. Published by Directorate of Economics & Statistics, Government of Nagaland, Kohima.

Table-IV

EXPENDITURE: PLAN AND NON-PLAN

(Rs. in Lakhs)

Sl.	Categories	1999	2000	2001	2002	2003
1	2	3	4	5	6	7
1.	Plan	2847.68	3697.00	4671.00	5615.53	7341.46
2.	Non-Plan	3463.83	3451.97	5891.02	5912.37	5851.83
	Total	6312.51	7148.97	10562.02	11527.9	3193.29

Road Communication and Transportation

Road communication has played a remarkable role in taking Nagaland on the track of modernization. Prior to independence, there was only one road from Dimapur to Mao. Before Nagaland became a state, there were hardly 169 kilometers of surfaced road and 2939 kilometers of unsurfaced road. At present the state has 248 km of national highway, 675 km surfaced and 357.5 km unsurfaced state highway, 1018.4 km surfaced and 1319.5 km unsurfaced major district roads, 11053.37 km surfaced and 1899.13 km unsurfaced other district roads, 2129 km surfaced and 3021 km unsurfaced village district roads, 11020.85 km surfaced and 4082 km unsurfaced road under Border and 81 km surfaced and 1405 km unsurfaced feeder roads. Presently in totals surfaced and unsurfaced roads in Nagaland are 6225.62 km and 7142.83 km respectively.[16] Nearly one thousand villages have been linked with roads. The state highway numbers I and II-Kohima -Wokha and Mokokchung Amguri roads have been upgraded to Nagaland National Highway No. 61 providing a totally new life for the state and people.

The first transport service in Nagaland was inaugurated in June 1965 on the Kohima-Dimapur road. Today tremendous progress has been made in this regard. This is obvious from the facts mentioned here. The Nagaland State Transport operates more than 60 routes with a total of 176 daily scheduled services covering 20696 kms daily. The state has a fleet of not less than 223 buses.

The Department of State Transportation has managed to run buses on inter-state routes connecting Kohima and Dimapur with Imphal, Guwahati and Shillong. The transport and communication avenues for the state have gone a leap forward with the completion of the broad gauge railway line and the introduction of the Rajdhani Express train service connecting Dimapur and Delhi.

Public Health Engineering

The Department of Public Health Engineering of Nagaland has made astounding progress providing drinking water for the people even in the rural areas. Such activities of the Department have not only provided government jobs to a number of people but also has made the life of the people safe and secured from the diseases caused by drinking impure water. The real effort to improve the condition of drinking water supply and sanitation facilities was made since 1970 onwards. Between 1966 and 1990 there was a stage when the Department had a record of having covered up to 90% of all recognized villages. Works have been carried out under Minimum Needs Programme, Basic Minimum Services and Accelerated Rural Water Supply Programme. In urban areas the existing water supply activities have proved inadequate due to rapid increase of population in towns. The Department, keeping in view such problems, is working hard to improve the condition of water supply. A major project is being taken up for Kohima town.

To improve the health of the people and provide them adequate medical facilities the government is taking active part. The table given here clearly indicates the improvement done by the government in the field of healthcare.

Growth in Police and General Administration

Prior to 1963, police administration had only three stations located at Kohima, Mokokchung and Tuensang. After creation of state till 2002, altogether 41 police stations, 29 police out-posts, 20 police-check posts and six police beat-posts were established all over the state. Besides that, there are Naga Armed Police

Table-V

NUMBER OF HOSPITALS, DISPENSARIES P.H.Cs, C.H.Cs, S.H.Cs, SUB-CENTERS IN THE YEAR 2003

Particulars	Kohima	Dmp	Mkg	Tsg	Zbto	Wokha	Phek	Mon	Peren	Total
District Hospital	1	1	1	1	1	1	1	1	1	10
Community/H center	3	2	3	5	2	1	3	1	1	21
Primary H/Center	11	8	11	12	9	8	17	12	5	93
Subsidiary/H centre	2	2	1	2	3	5	6	5	4	30
Dispensaries	-	2	5	2	1	1	3	1	1	16
T.B. Hospital	1	-	1	1	-	-	-	-	-	3
Mental/Hospital	1	-	-	-	-	-	-	-	-	1
Sub-center	39	50	51	69	43	42	46	57	15	412
S.T.D.Clinic	1	1	1	1	1	1	1	1	-	8
O.T.C.	1	-	1	1	1	-	-	1	-	6
Post-Mortem Center	1	1	1	1	-	-	-	-	-	4
Total	61	67	76	95	61	59	77	80	77	603

Table-VI

NUMBER OF MEDICAL Personnels

Year	Particular	Kohima	Dmp	Mokok	Tsg	Zubto	Wokha	Phek	Mon	Total
1	2	3	4	5	6	7	8	9	10	11
1999	Doctors	107	58	49	38	26	26	28	20	352
	Compounders	103	-	63	99	53	49	59	66	492
	Nurses	302	-	189	258	129	96	118	122	1209
2000	Doctors	121	58	49	38	26	26	28	20	366
	Compounders	68	35	63	99	54	49	60	69	497
	Nurses	255	165	243	166	103	84	65	35	1116
2001	Doctors	121	58	49	38	26	26	28	20	366
	Compounders	68	35	63	99	54	49	60	69	497
	Nurses	255	165	243	166	103	84	65	35	1116
2002	Doctors	121	59	49	38	26	26	28	20	367
	Compounders	69	35	63	99	53	49	60	69	497
	Nurses	282	120	203	205	123	100	134	111	1278

Table-VII

NUMBER OF DOCTORS, COMPOUNDERS AND NURSES IN THE YEAR 2003

Particular	Kohima	Dmp	Mokok	Tsg	Zubto	Wokha	Phek	Mon	Total
Doctors	122	59	51	38	26	26	28	20	367
Compounders	69	35	63	102	55	49	61	71	505
Nurses	269	134	205	218	109	95	113	89	1232

Source: Statistical Hand Book of Nagaland 2006.

Battalions, several Village Guards and Indian Reserved Police Battalions. Today Nagaland police is headed by a Director General assisted by Additional DGP, IGP and a host of officers.

Tremendous growth has taken place in the field of general administration. There are 11 district headquarters and 18 Sub-divisions headed by the Deputy Commissioners and Sub-divisional Officers (C) supported by the Additional Deputy Commissioners, Extra-Assistant Commissioners and a host of supporting staff. Besides there are 2336 educational institutions along with 20963 teachers and 421498 students.[17] Out of 1317 villages, 1196 villages have been electrified till March 2000. All together 52 Rural Development Blocks are busy with changing the shape of rural area. By March 2000, the state had 73373 employees working in different departments. Till 2002-2003, the total length of roads in Nagaland was recorded 13369.45 kilometers along with 9,3 km railway line. There are also 5382 cooperative societies which are helping the people in their self-development. Till 2002, 186276 vehicles were registered. Installed capacity of power is 28.5 MW and per capita consumption of electricity, by 2002-2003 was 140.02 KWL. Per capita income at current price was Rs.18911 in 2001-2002.[18] Moreover, the state has one central university divided into three camps—Lumami Headquarters, Kohima and Medziphema. All the camps are imparting teaching in science, arts and commerce. A number of students are busy in doing research in various fields. The multi-storeyed buildings of the state secretariat comprising thousands of government employees have been constructed at Kohima.

Thus, it is evident that Nagaland has totally changed in all aspects. All the development has not only changed the physical shape of the state but also have transformed the social structure. Various development schemes, programmes and economic projects supported with the central finance and aids have involved the Naga people in various development activities. Their economic conditions have improved. The rise in income has opened the door for material prosperity and social dignity. Urbanization, which was unknown to the Naga people four decades back, has taken strong and deep root into Naga society changing their mental outlook and behavioural attitude.

Urabanized Naga Society and its Impact

Modernization of the Naga society has been divided in two sectors—urban and rural. The urban area came under the direct influence of modernization. In the words of Kailash Sharma, "Urbanization is a growth process primarily engineered by human factors either directly or indirectly.... The process of transformation is fostered by a number of socio-economic, administrative and religious factors".[19] Emergence of transportation, communication facilities, establishment of administrative set-ups, educational institutions, development agencies, medical and public health engineering and creation of non-agricultural occupations in trade and commerce are the factors, which served the growth of urbanization in Nagaland. The Naga people have witnessed tremendous infrastructural growth in various fields. The state has moved fast on the road of modernization and urbanization.

Kohima, which was a small town during the British regime, developed fast when it became the capital of the state. The capital today locates a number of government quarters and official buildings including secretariat and various directorates. Though Kohima is not a city, it is more than a city. Dimapur is the second biggest town of Nagaland, which has become the main commercial center of the state. Nagaland ranks the 24th in terms of urbanization of the country. There are altogether nine urban centers. Both the towns of Kohima and Dimapur are well connected with national highways from all sides and with all neighbouring states. Dimapur is also connected with a railway station. In these two towns there are people from all places of the state. The towns also have sizable non-tribal population. Non-tribal people are living in these towns as government officers/employees, teachers, doctors, engineers, traders, shop-keepers, labourers, etc. Due to growth in population and spread of trade and commerce, old towns of the state are expanding in size. The suburbs have been developed mostly in the barren areas and of the towns. The towns have become main centers of higher education, specialized healthcare facilities in government hospitals, cultural contacts, entertainment, sports and games, transport and hotel facilities, etc. Urban centers provide opportunity to the people for interaction with their own people coming from other districts as well as with non-tribals. People exchange their views with each other on different platforms organized and sponsored by different local and outside organizers. Such development has left behind the idea of orthodox and conservative feelings and helped the urban people to adopt new mode of life, understand the cultural and religious life of the incoming groups of people and to learn languages and lifestyle of others.

Naga society may be called as urbanized society due to commendable economic growth. In 1994, the Governor of Nagaland while inaugurating the Assembly and highlighting the development of the state said:

"The state has made commendable progress in the field of development. Since the attainment of statehood, there has been considerable development of infrastructural facilities. Significant improvement has been achieved in the field of education, roads and transportation, health care, water supply, power, agriculture and allied sectors".[20] In 1996, The chief minister of the state, S.C. Jamir, admitting the growth of Naga society said that "all these developments were done "to bring cohesiveness to society and also to make people progressive and modern".[21]

Migration of the People towards Urban Areas

With the rising trend of urbanization in Nagaland many people began to rush to newly developed towns from the rural areas in search of new job opportunities and obtain material prosperity. Sudden detachment from the land made the rural people aware of modern life. In this rush the Naga individuals began to look down upon village life and traditional behaviours. They began to search new avenues and opportunity to settle in towns where modern facilities and amenities are available. Collectivism, which was the established trend of the Naga society, began to convert into individualism. The people began to think in terms of personal achievement and gain. The authority and respect, which the Naga parents used to enjoy under the traditional mores and customs, are being challenged today by the youngsters. Horam agrees that in full many a homes, is rebellion from the children against their parents is reported to have been raising its head under the influence of modernization and urbanization of the Naga society. The educated youths breaking the customary barrier of racial marriage, have begun to prefer inter-tribal marriage for better life partnership in accordance with their choice.[22]

Table-VIII

GROWTH OF URBAN POPULATION IN NAGALAND, 1981-1991

	1981		**1991**		
Total population	**Urban population**	**% of urban population**	**Total population**	**Urban population**	**% of Urban population**
7,74,930	1,20,234	15.52	12,15,573	2,10,095	17.28

Source—Census 1991 (Provisional).

Table- IX

RURAL-URBAN COMPOSITION OF POPULATION IN 1991

Population in 1991			Decennial growth rate of population in %		
Total	Rural	Urban	Total	Rural	Urban
12,15,573	10,05,478	2,10,095	56.86%	53.58 %	74.74 %

Source—Census 1991 (Provisional).

Both the tables mentioned above clearly indicate the substantial rise of urban population. In the year 1981, the percentage of total urban population was 15.52 while the percentage of the urban population in 1991 increased to 17.28 per cent. The decennial growth rate of population in the rural area was 53.86 % while the same in the urban area was 74.74 %. This shows that the urbanization in Nagaland got considerable strength. The growth of population in urban areas became faster as years rolled down.

Sudden rise in migration of the rural population of Nagaland towards the urban areas has some vital factors which are mentioned below. First, Nagaland was a backward area and people there were totally ignorant of modern life. Since 1951, under the five year plans the government of India invested substantial funds to the hill areas with a view to upgrading the living standard of the people. Steps were initiated to set up basic infrastructure, develop human resources and adoption of higher technology. In the words of J.B. Ganguly, "All these have set in motion significant changes in the institutions of organised political, administrative, social, economic and cultural activities of the people".[25] In Nagaland all these changes ushered in an era of urbanization, which attracted more and more rural people towards urban areas for better living. This brought about massive increase in migration to urban areas in the state.

Secondly, better educational, medical and recreational facilities are available in the urban areas. The rural people being aware of the significance of better education are sending their children to the urban areas, whereby urban population has increased. Thirdly, the rural people have no avenues of employment. While in urban areas they have the opportunity to get various types of occupations including government services. This prompts the rural people to migrate towards the town areas. Nessa has rightly observed: "When the tribals come out of their seclusion and participate in the market economy, obviously they get attracted towards urban amenities and prefer to be settled in the towns or their suburbs".[26] Fourthly, educated people migrate to towns for employment. Due to financial assistance provided by the government to unemployed youths through various development programmes and projects, a new trend has developed. According to Saikia, "Educated youths are becoming self-employed by opening schools, hotels, studios, grocery units, variety stores, ready-made clothes-centers, etc. Besides, doctors also have opened clinics for conducting private practices along with pharmacies. A few nursing homes have already been started at Dimapur and at big towns of Nagaland".[27] All these factors are playing a vital role in increasing urban population.

According to Coleman a modernizing state is progressively cut off from other institutions of the society, it becomes more specialized and is "able to operate on a wider spatial scale, covering a wider range of issues to more effectively implement political decision".

Moreover, the state must be supported by "a widely approved secular—non-religious and largely non-traditional—system of political beliefs and goals that stress democracy, open government and involvement and the drive for equality, as move of modernization has to face resistance from traditional groupings with vested political interests".[23] Habermas sees modernization as a product of juxtaposition of three events—the renaissance, the reformation and discovery of a new world. He holds the view that modernity is essentially a mode of thought that refuses to accept tradition unreflectively. He states, "Modernity can and will no longer borrow the criteria by which it takes its orientation from the models supplied by another epoch; it has to create its normativity out of itself".[24]

Fifthly, but not the least, unfolding economic opportunities in towns have attracted rural labourers where they get job-opportunities both skilled and unskilled. Once the rural workers avail the opportunity of living in towns, they hardly like to go back to their respective villages. They prefer to settle in towns with the result that towns expand in area and population both. To quote Saikia once more: "Growth of business enterprises in and around the urban areas gives a fillip for human resource mobilization. The required labour force... compose the first category of migrants from different areas. The inflow of such migrants helps the other entrepreneurs to start their new venture, as they have to pay less wages".[28]

It is a fact that urbanization has taken place in Nagaland and urban areas are expanding in size and population. However, the Naga society is still rural based. Altogether there are nine towns. Except Kohima and Dimapur, other towns are still underdeveloped. The towns lack industrial base with the result that the flow of migrants is very slow. There are no better avenues for self-employment. Nearly 70% people still depend on cultivation. No doubt, there is longing for urban life in the minds of the rural people, but most of them are incapable of either to afford the expenditure of the urban life or to buy land and construct building in towns. The pace of urbanization in Naga society is not fast.

In the case of modernization of the Nagaland state and Nagaland society, modernization renaissance and reformation both occurred. Renaissance and reformation both had begun during the British regime, which changed the thinking pattern of the Naga people on the one hand and forced them to reform their traditional practices in new light on the other. With the growth of material prosperity the Naga people began to loose their faith in their religious norms, as they preferred to be called as Christians. The impact of religious bonds is no more a binding force for the modernized Nagas. No doubt, traditionality may still be discerned in the Naga society, but its effect, which was a binding force once, has lost its compulsion to a great extent. A secular approach has appeared damaging the religious compulsion and paving the way for the growth of non-religious thinking. The people today put much emphasis on secularism, which demands equality, fraternity, liberty, openness of the society, democratic political system and feeling of nation-state whereas the ancient Naga culture and social practices are loosing their base in modern Naga society, which has created irritation of minds and worries to those Nagas who still prefer traditional values and norms.

Stratification of the Naga Society Under the Influence of Modernization

Modernization has enchanted the Naga people no doubt, but a close observation of their present social behaviour and outlook reveals the truth that the culture what the Naga people have borrowed from the western society, has not yet completely shaken off its relations with the past. It is very difficult to say to what extent the Naga society is modern and to what extent it is traditional. But it is obvious that the Naga people still have inclination towards their past social, cultural and religious systems. Whenever they practise their religious ceremonies or social practices, one can mark the imprint of past beliefs on their present activities. Their social as well as political organizations still have the influence of their past life. According to Yogendra Singh, "We cannot easily separate modernity and tradition from some versions which function ideologically as directives. The modern comes to the traditional as a particular culture with its own tradition."[29] The modern style of the Naga people is not the modification of their ancient culture, but adoption of a western culture which was quite alien to them. If the Naga society is not totally modernized, it may not be called traditional, too. In reality the society is the mixture of modernity and traditionality with greater amount of modernity, which has caused social stratification on the one hand and paved the way for economic competition including the rise of corruption on the other. Modernity has complicated the fabric of the Naga society. Modernization has caused social stratification in the society on the basis of wealth, power and prestige. On the other hand, modernization has created a number of problems in the society such as theft, robbery, drug addiction, and HIV, etc.

The bases of social stratification are—power, prestige and wealth. Stratification is division of societal layers of a society on the basis of divisions of works, religions, wealth, power and status. In the opinion of Gilbert, "Social stratification is the division of society in permanent groups or categories linked with each other by the relationship of subordination".[30] Each social stratification exhibits hierarchy of social status with corresponding lower and higher social rules. The class consciousness leads to a lot of impediments in social cohesion. Social stratification is a subject of change according to circumstance and consciousness of the people. It reflects the levels of different peoples or groups of a society. There is no society which has no social stratification, but the advanced society has sharp stratification.

Development brings more divisions in the society. In the words of S.P. Verma, "While social mobilization involves changes in the aspiration of the individuals, groups and societies, economic development involves changes in their capabilities."[31] It is growing literacy, education, mass media, urbanization etc., which help to drop the old attitude of the people and adopt new things. Most of the African and Asian countries have either become modern or swiftly moving towards modernity because of rapid growth in their aptitudes and behaviours due to increase in educational facilities, literacy, communication and industrialization.

The consequences of variation in wealth, prestige and power are most evident in the ways of lives of the rich and the poor. At the top of society is a community of mutually aware families, most of whom inherit a substantial fortune. They possess that much wealth that they can survive comfortably even without work. But it is notable that all rich families do not possess honour and dignity. Honour and dignity come out of the high political or bureaucratic ranks. In modern politics it has been observed that wealth plays a remarkable role in obtaining political power. Wealth is very much related to power. At the same time wealthy families are in position to influence powerful authorities by giving donation to the political parties or by bribing the big authorities. The most vulnerable position is of those who are poor or manual workers. Generally such people remain deprived of the benefits of development. Moreover, the rich and socially high ranking people do not hesitate to either neglect or exploit the poor sections of the society with the result that class antagonism takes place. The lifestyle of the rich becomes luxurious while the living standard of the poor remains vulnerable.

Status is a position in a social system. An individual assumes the status as per his /her role performed in society. Status may be high and low. Some individual assumes high status on the basis of his or her birth in high caste or in wealthy as well as reputed family. Social status has become the symbol of prestige and it plays an important role in social activities. It has been observed that people prefer to fix marriages always either in the same status or higher status. Since high status brings prestige and honour in the society, every one likes to obtain high social status either by being wealthy or by entering into political power and win the election by hook or crook.

Naga society was classless and casteless, but the advent of modernity has changed the scenario to a great extent. In ancient Naga society there were some chiefs or village elders who enjoyed high social status based on customary laws. However, there was no division of labour. Every one was a farmer and cultivation was the only profession where there was no scope for growing rich. Moreover, the land system was not individualistic, but collective.

But under the impact of modernity, the whole social fabric of the Naga society has changed. Too much development in economic and political field has taken place attracting the people to grow rich and maintain luxurious life. The development of the Naga economy under the five-year plans and also implementation of various centrally sponsored development schemes and programmes have yielded two major consequences in Nagaland. First, the approach and attitude of the people are much inclined towards materialistic prosperity, and secondly, the society has been stratified on the basis of work, prestige, status and wealth.

Income Disparities in Naga Society

Development means improvement in the well-being of the general mass and upliftment of people's living standard. The minimum level of well-being must "include the satisfaction of the basic needs". The purpose of the rural development has been "providing maximum job opportunities and new direction of changes".[32] The Naga society, which was classless till yesterday, has become modern today where social stratification has taken place on the basis of power, wealth and prestige. Today economic development and status consciousness have, in fact, divided the Naga society into higher and lower social stratum. The growth of education, mass media, urbanization and consumerist attitude has enchanted every Naga towards attraction of modern lifestyle. The Nagas, who have been alert enough and aware of social changes, lost no time to avail the opportunity for enriching themselves. This has resulted in emergence of a class of affluence. Such conscious people have succeeded in amassing huge amount of wealth. On the other hand, the majority of the Naga people have remained deprived of actual benefits of the development. Thus, uneven distribution of economic benefits has divided the Naga society into two groups—the haves and the have-nots. The first group, though in minority, has managed to avail maximum modern facilities either through fair or unfair means. It is that group, which has assumed political power and provides leadership to the society. The living style of this group has totally changed. They have more than enough to lead the life of luxuries and comforts. Such people "are capable of enjoying aristocratic life style possessing multi-storeyed buildings fitted with the latest facilities in towns and maintaining big bank balance" even in foreign countries.

Factors Responsible for Social Disparities

Professor Wali has rightly observed that despite encouraging the growth of Indian economy in post-independent period, poverty has continued to grow at a faster rate because of high concentration of wealth in the hands of the few. The western capitalist model, which India has followed under the guise of democratic socialism, in fact, is anti-people model with low-income growth and worse economic distribution.[33] Nagaland, which is the integral component of Indian federal system, is moving towards the same model of economy creating increasingly polarized nature of society where the few affluent Nagas are real beneficiaries of development. It is because "the income distribution, flow of capital, concentration of economic power continues to be in favour of the upper income brackets in the rural and urban areas".[34] Such trend of development, which has converted the whole nation in a capitalistic pattern of society, will not achieve the decided goal of the constitution and it "will polarize the social fabric."

In the words of Mahajan, the prevailing of no tax policy in Nagaland has provided for the rich house-holds "to be more affluent and rich ... a sort of income multiplier process has emerged because of the present tax policy".[35] Secondly, indulgence of the Naga elites in party politics and the involvement of the Naga bureaucrats in implementation of development schemes and programmes have created new avenues for them to acquire both money and power. Politics in Nagaland contributes less ideological differences and more economic consideration and lust for power.[36] Every Naga politician after electoral victory is desirous of obtaining the rank of ministership even at the cost of politics of defection. Stating the nature of the Naga politicians, K.V. Krishsna Rao, the ex-Governor of Nagaland, rightly said: "Those who are already ministers wanted so-called better portfolio and those who are mere

MLAs wanted to be ministers."[37] This is all because the ministership is the best source of earning easy money and to enjoy the status.

Observing the defective economic as well as political system of the Naga society, V.K. Nuh writes, "The prevailing situation in our society is that the rich are becoming richer, the educated becoming more educated, but the poor become poorer." "Most of the MLAs turn millionaires when they become ministers. Most of the party workers become rich within a year or two. Government is no longer 'people's government, but it has become party's government...." Commenting on favouratism in the government jobs he further writes, "Government job is now on public sale, not on merit, but on party favour. The privileged classes are destroying the under-privileged people." Pointing out the activities of the corrupt bureaucrats, he writes, "Many bureaucrats misguide their masters if it is not in their favour... . The public money siphoned out left and right from the schemes and projects in the name of the poor unprivileged"[38]

Third reason for expanding gap between the rich and the poor in the Naga society is that the blind copying of the western lifestyle by the affluent Naga people has multiplied their needs. According to Mmhonlumo Kikon, it is the current 'westoxication' in the Naga society which "determines the psycho-historical factors governing basic principles" and "external forces have consistently shaped our historical accounts and has managed to shift our focus from 'becoming' as a gradual process to 'acquiring' as an escalating process".[39] According to Nuh, "It is because of philosophy of secularism and materialism in the educational concept of life—the moral aspect of life is completely ignored and as a result of this the society is fragiled into atheistic culture where the purpose of life is largely ignored".[40]

Thus, it is evident that the growing lust for material satisfaction, unquenchable thrust to obtain maximum wealth and high ambition to be honoured by others among the educated and well settled Nagas have caused corruption in every aspect of life. In the words of Thomas, the ex-Governor of Nagaland: "It is the social change that has brought wide spread corruption" and which has "hindered economic development seriously and brought about class differences destroying the traditional egalitarianism of society and a culture of consumerism and easy money." He has rightly observed: "Funds available through the years were enough to push Nagaland's standard of living... but they have been cornered by a few self-seekers."

Newly emerged Naga intellectuals getting close contact with the Indian political leaders, fully realized the significance of wealth and property in modern life. Hence they left no stone unturned to earn and accumulate wealth by any means. Following the style of the politicians, the bureaucrats, too did not remain behind in the race of wealth accumulation. As a result, corruption in the Naga society becomes rampant. It was the politicians who first began the money-making affairs. Thereafter, their agents, party workers, contractors, top level village leaders and government servants joined the money-making affairs openly with the result that a class of affluent in the Naga society appeared with all the facilities and undue privileges. On the other hand, the poor people specially living in the villages became the victims of sufferings, miseries and scarcities. They have no money to buy seats for their children in good academic institutions either within or outside of the state. They are bound to live in perpetual poverty. Observing economic scenario and corruption in the North East India, Rajani Kothari maintains that corruption will not stop and rather it "will instead polarize the social fabric".

The Naga society under the charm and enchantment of modernity has changed to a great extent no doubt, but at the cost of destroying its ancient social, cultural and political values. The culture what the early Naga people had has totally replaced with new culture. The culture, which the modern Naga people has adopted is neither their own nor their ancestors. Mr Kikon has rightly observed that the Nagas have no definite roots of their social and cultural accounts which they have today. In his own words, "After the British occupation and the work of the Christian missionaries, external forces have consistently shaped our historical accounts and has managed to shift our focus from 'becoming' as a gradual process to 'acquiring' as an escalating process." The trend of present Naga culture has been shaped by the forces who are rich enough materially and cultured enough educationally. In fact, it is an individualistic pattern of civilization based on self-adoration, self-perfection, self-centralism. Materialism is mounting over moralism. Such culture has given birth to social diseases like alcoholism, goondaism, drug-addiction, pauperism, etc. The development process has widened the gap between the rich and the poor. The state has developed and society has changed, but real beneficiaries are those who have successfully maneuvered to exploit political, administrative and economic mechanism of the state. The poor sections are still deprived of even essential daily requirements. No doubt, the groups standing between the rich and the poor, namely, the white colour workers like teachers, doctors, small rank officers, small businessmen posters etc., have managed to avail the minimum needs developing their link with the people who are well-to-do or who are in power. Though they are conscious of such unjustified development, they have neither the will nor courage to raise their strong voice against such prevailing socio-economic injustice in Nagaland. Rather they are also 'hobnobbing' with the present scenario to serve their own interests having close contact with the powerful authorities of the state. It is surprising to note that corruption has entered even in churches.

It is heartening to note that there are some native thinkers and writers who dare to talk about such issues and bring the facts to the light through their writings in books, journals and weeklies and newspapers. But their number is very few. The Naga society immediately needs the courage and will to criticise such ominous happenings in the name of social change. The corruption and injustices must be fought courageously. The society has a number of non-governmental organisatisons, such as the Naga Students' Federation, All Nagaland Students' Federation, Naga Mother Association, Nagaland Human Rights Association, Naga Hoho and others, but all these unions and associations have not developed any viable device to fight against the mounting corruption in the state. They have not yet acquired the required courage to challenge anti-social forces and control the growth of high-handedness in Naga politics. Their leaders are either self-centered like others or they lack the tactics as well as energy to fight corruption and to oppose violation of rules and regulations by the vested forces. The agents of socialization in Nagaland are weak. Moreover, the leaders of the NGOs mostly from the students' groups are misguided and misutilized by the politicians and vested interests. Here money and temptation for jobs play the vital role.

References

1. Karl W Dweutsch, "Social Mobilization and Political Development" *American Political Science Review,* vol. XL September 1961, p. 494.
2. S.P. Verma, *Modern Political Theory,* Vikash Publishing House, New Delhi, 1975, p. 303.
3. R.N. Sharma, *Principles of Sociology,* Modern Promoters and Publishers, Bombay, 1993, p. 277.
4. Yogendra Singh, *Modernization of Indian Tradition,* Rawat Publications, New Delhi, 1996, p. 61.
5. Morhon J Levy, *A Setting for International Affairs,* Princeton University Press, New Jersey, 1996, p. 11.
6. J De Sanata Ana, *Separation without Hope: The Church and the Poor during the Industrial Revolution and Colonial Expression,* Geneva WCC, 1978, p. 9.
7. M. Thomas, *The Nagas towards A.D. 2000,* Madras Center for Research of New Industrial Economic Order, 1972, p. 204.
8. B.P. Singh, *The Problem of change: A Study of North East India,* Oxford University Press (2nd imprint), New Delhi, 1997, p. 51.
9. Nirmal Minz, "Crisis in Indigenous People in India", *Ecology, A Theological Response,* p. 204.
10. O.L. Santang, "Christianity and Tribal Solidarity in Meghalaya India", *Church Historical Review,* June 1994, p. 26.
11. W.C. Smith, *The Ao Nagas: Tribes of Assam,* London Oxford University Press, 1936, p. 182.

12. J.P. Mills, *The Ao Nagas*, London University Press, 1873, pp. 97-99.
13. *Souvenir* (Commemorating 35 years of Statehood), published by Directorate of Information & Public Relations, Government of Nagaland, Kohima, 1999, p. 21.
14. *Ibid.*
15. *Statistical Hand Book of Nagaland 2004*, published by Directorate of Economics & Statistics, Government of Nagaland, Kohima, 2004, pp. 190-206.
16. *Ibid.* p. 275.
17. *Ibid.* pp. 24-25.
18. *Ibid.*
19. Kailash Sharma, *The Pace of the Growth Center in the process of Urbanization in Asia*, Deep & Deep Publications, New Delhi, 1995, p. 184.
20. *The Warrior* (a monthly magazine), vol. 23, No. 4, published by Directorate of Information and Public Relations, Government of Nagaland, Kohima, January, 1994, p. 13.
21. *Ibid.*, vol. 25, No. 2, February 1996, *op, cit.*, p. 9.
22. M. Horam, *Naga Polity, op. cit.*, p. 109.
23. *Encyclopedia of Social Sciences,* Fitzroy Dearborn Publications, London 2001, pp. 1061-62.
24. Habermas Jargon, "The Philosophical Discovery of Modernity, Lectures, Twelve Nassa Chasetts," MIT Press, Coimbatore, 1987, p. 7.
25. J.B. Ganguly, (editor), *U I Banker and Development in North East India: Trends and Policy Implementation, op. cit.* p. 105.
26. S. Nessa, "The Social Consequences of Migration and Urbanization" published in J.B Ganguly (Ed), *op. cit.*, p. 56.
27. K.K. Saikia "Process of Urbanization in Nagaland: A Case Study of Kohima and Dimapur" in J.B. Ganguly (Ed) *op. cit.*, p 280.
28. *Ibid.* pp. 281-82.
29. Yogendra Singh, *Modernization of Indian Tradition, op. cit.* p. 121.

30. Cited in R.N. Sharma's, *Principles of Sociology*, Media Promoters and Publications, Bombay, 1993.
31. S.P. Verma, *Modern Political Theory, op. cit.*, 1975, p. 203
32. A.L Ao, *Rural Development in Nagaland*, Har-Anand Publications, New Delhi, 1993, pp. 24-25.
33. R.L. Wali, "Indian Development Process: Parameters of Development in North East India", in V.S. Mahajan, (Ed.) *Emerging Pattern of North East Economy*, Deep Publications, New Delhi, 1987, pp. 52-53.
34. *Ibid.*
35. V.S. Mahajan (Ed), "Widening Income disparities in Mizoram: Its Socio-Economic Implications and Alternative approaches", *op. cit.*, p. 265.
36. Chandrika Singh, *Political Evolution of Nagaland*, Lancers Publications, New Delhi, 1981, p. 188.
37. *Nagaland Times*, vol. 10, No. 42, Dimapur, April 30, 1980.
38. *Nagaland Post*, September 4, 2006, p. 6.
39. Mmhonlumo Kikon,"Did Naga Live in Darkness", in *The Nagaland Page*, February 28, 2000, Dimapur, p. 5.
40. Rev. (Dr), V.K. Nuh, "Education from Christian Point of View", in *The Nagaland Page*, August 2, 1997, p. 5.

***

7

Problems and Pangs

After the creation of Nagaland state in December 1963, Nagaland has covered a long-distance of progress and development no doubt, but the people have neither got rid of biting pangs of insurgency nor enjoyed permanent peace. Soon after India's independence the Naga society lost many of the Naga lives falling in the grip of insurgency and highhandedness of the Indian armed forces. The society has been bleeding profusely. The question which has been causing concern to every reasonable Naga mind is how to regain a wholesome permanent peace in the Naga society and how to set the state in motion of progress and prosperity without interruption where every Naga may avail the fullest opportunity to enjoy life and upgrade their personality. The Naga issue, which is related to the future political status of the state, is very much grave and complex. All the efforts hitherto applied to resolve the issue have not yielded the desired results. Rather differences of opinions and views among the Naga leaders—both underground and overground—have made the problem more difficult and complex causing serious worries in the mind of the general Naga people. At the same time emerging dangerous trends such as increasing factional fighting among the underground set-ups, nexus between politicians and criminals, use of money and muscle power during election and amalgamation of public funds by the corrupt ministers and officials are the factors which have multiplied constant worries and fear in the mind of the people on the one hand, and have created hurdles on the path of progress and prosperity of the state on the other. Various social problems, which have taken place in the Naga society after modernization, are the other challenges to the Naga people and the society.

The Naga society is a modern society based on its traditional as well as conventional foundation, but development, which has taken so far, has created rift in the society on the basis of wealth, power and prestige. The vested forces that have emerged today establishing their hold over social, economic and political systems are active to perpetuate their hold by using dirty maneuverings where they have established their close link with the underground forces. The people who are in the government service holding big responsibility, lack working culture with the result that the offices and establishments have the sufficient number of servants, but responsibilities are not disposed of satisfactorily.

This chapter critically analyses and examines the challenges and emerging trends of the Naga society, which have not only posed serious danger to the growth of the society and the people but also has caused disunity and division among people on the line of tribalism. It also presents a critical account of sufferings of the people under the existing circumstances of political uncertainty, fear-psychosis, high-handedness of authorities, and cheating and fraud by the party workers and government servants.

Political Issue and the Naga Leaders

The Naga leaders, specially after India's independence, have remained divided in their opinions and views regarding the political status of their land. The differences of opinion among the Naga leaders for shaping future political shape and status of their land has always been found in confusion and conflicts resulting in formation of different rival groups. It may be the case of the underground or overground Naga leaders, whenever they differ in their way, they prefer to form a separate group. To dominate one group and establish their hegemony they hardly hesitate to resort to violent means to exterminate the rival. This has resulted in factional feuds and killings. The factional fighting among the underground groups is mostly due to personality clash and difference in the opinion of the underground Naga leaders. The most unfortunate thing, which has remained as a big hurdle before the Naga leaders, either underground or overground, is division of their opinions and views regarding future political status of Nagaland right from India's dependence. The Naga National Council (NNC) was divided first in 1956, on the issue whether the Nagas should accept India's suzerainty or should they fight for its independence. The moderate decided to remain under the Indian constitution while the extremists opted to fight for independence. No doubt, the moderate leaders of the NNC succeeded in having a full-fledged state for the Nagas under the Republic of India, but at the cost of displeasure and wrath of the extremists who straightway condemned such move of the former on the logic that it was 'a sell-out of Naga's right to self determination'. On the other hand, the moderates who dissociated from the path of violence argued that to work under the constitutional framework of India was the need of the day. Any way such difference of opinion led the Naga people towards whirlpool of cross current which still exists.

The moderate Naga leaders took the creation of Nagaland state as the triumph of the peace loving Nagas while the extremists considered it as the success of the government of India's policy of divide and rule and they branded the moderates as the 'puppets' in the hands of the Indian political leaders. Thereafter, the underground government did all to futile all the activities of the government of Nagaland by creating hurdles on its path and declaring a war against the government of India, but all in vain.[1] At the initiative of the Baptist Church leaders of Nagaland, the Peace Mission was formed to normalize the situation and stop fighting between the nationalist forces and the armed forces of the government of India.[2] The government of Nagaland supported the effort by passing a resolution in the Assembly.[3] The Peace Mission successfully persuaded the underground Naga government to sign the agreement of ceasefire which brought about cessation of armed struggle with effect from 6 September 1964. Thereafter, the people were found rushing to the churches and ringing the bell to express their happiness over such move. Describing the happiness of the Naga people over ceasefire, Gundevia, the then Foreign Secretary of India and the representative of the government of India for peace talks, writes:

"The singing of the hymns in that little church in Kohima by our Naga boys and girls in their choir, was superb; it was beautiful and brought tears to many eyes ... that September afternoon, sung by so many with uncontrolled tears running down their chicks, was an unforgettable experience.... There was street light in Kohima after the first time in seven years. Kohima Mokokchung and all the little towns had been under dust to dawn curfew, years after years, almost continuously".[4]

Peace talks between the representatives of the underground government and the government of India began with great expectation that the Naga issue would be resolved once and for ever and the state would have permanent peace. The peace talks were held even at the level of Prime Ministers of both the governments, but the fate of the peace talks resulted in its failure bringing utter disappointment to the people and too much resentment to the undergrounds. Despite various rounds of peace talks, the Naga issue remained unresolved.

Who are responsible for failure of peace talks? Is it the government of India or the underground Naga leaders? The blame for the failure of the peace talks in 1967 must be shared by both the parties because both adopted stubborn attitude throughout the talks. Moreover, the policy of the government of India to appease the undergrounds even at the cost of displeasure of the democratically installed Nagaland government boosted the morale of the underground leaders who remained determined to accept nothing less than a sovereign independent Nagaland. On the other hand, the government of India was ready to give them any thing except sovereignty. It is evident from the statement of B. K. Nehru, the then Governor of Nagaland. He writes, "Delhi had from the very beginning, adopted the attitude of appeasement towards the insurgents, trying to give them what they wanted, irrespective of the national interests in an effort to get them to give up their insurgency."[5] Expressing his view about the increasing morale of the underground leaders due to the policy of the appeasement, Hokishe Sema, the then Finance Minister of Nagaland, said that the Prime Minister's talks with the underground leaders yielded contrary result. In his own words, "a section of the underground is flirting with China to obtain arms and assistance from that country as well as from Pakistan".[6] Agreeing to the same fact, T.N. Angami, the then chief minister of Nagaland, while talking to the Nagaland governor, expressed his view that his authority was undermined by the government of India, because the real attention of the government was towards the underground Naga leaders and efforts were being applied to please them even at the cost of displeasure of the democratically installed government of Nagaland.[7]

Thus, the peace talks under such situation were bound to fail. The failure of peace talks caused disunity among the underground leaders. Peace talks discontinued and the Naga freedom fighters resumed once more their freedom struggle at full length overlapping the provisions of the ceasefire, which officially came to an end in September 1972 causing utter confusion and disappointment to the Naga people who had enjoyed a temporary relief.

The failure of peace talks resulted in division in the underground set-up. Kughato Sukhai, the prime minister of the rebel government and representatives for peace talks, was blamed for having a secret deal with the government of India. This infuriated the Sema tribe to which Kughato belonged. Kaito Sema, a rebel Naga leader and brother of Kughato, revolted against the Angami's hegemony over the Naga rebel government. With the help of his close associates he ransacked the underground Naga army headquarters at Gaziphema and looted the arms, ammunitions and money that were kept there. On the allegation that Kughato was assisting his brother, he was forced to resign from the Prime ministership of the underground federal government. Mhiaseui, an Angami and close associate of Phizo, was appointed as the prime minister of the federal government which resulted in bitterness between the Angamis and the Semas. The climax of the revolt was that Kaito was assassinated by an unidentified gunman. The Sema leadership suspected the hand of underground Angamis in such a drastic and inhuman act. Thereafter, scenario took drastic change. All these activities set the stage for internal feuds and conflicts among the undergrounds. At the same time another section of the undergrounds in Tuensang area came out with a resolution that the solution of the Naga problem had to be found "within the framework of the Indian Union".[8] Speaking about the futility of freedom struggle Saniba said, "All that we have achieved over the years of our struggle in Nagaland is untold miseries for our own kith and kin".[9]

Shillong Accord as a lull before Storm

Weakening strength of the undergrounds due to their internal disputes and feuds enabled the government of India to have commanding control over the undergrounds. A number of underground militants including their top ranking leaders were arrested. The realisation by the undergrounds that to fight with the Indian armed forces was not possible, opened a new phase where the process of surrendering of the undergrounds along with their arms and ammunitions to the government of India began. Saniba Ao, the Major General in the Federal government along with Mepyangdang, the Vice President of the NNC, and his secretary, Tajen Ao, surrendered in the middle of 1975.[10]

Thus, it is obvious that the declining strength of the undergrounds and successful working of the democratic processes in Nagaland created a new environment where people preferred peace and development. This paved the way for the advent of historic Shillong Accord whereby the underground people decided to surrender in bulk along with arms and ammunition and join the mainstream of the Indian nationalism. The Accord which was signed on 5th September 1975 ushered in an era of understanding peace and tranquility in this strife-torn state. It brought insurgency to an end. The underground organizations and their movements, thereafter, ceased to exist, as all had agreed to be peaceful citizens of India to function in accordance with the Indian constitution. The general mass heaved a sigh of relief because the prolonged struggle and armed conflicts had come to an end.[11] The government, on the other hand, assured the undergrounds of their rehabilitation after their surrender. The Accord also provided the opportunity to those undergrounds that were across border to come back to their land and to join the mainstream under the Indian constitution with their colleagues.

The surrender of the undergrounds along with arms and ammunitions following the provisions of the Shillong Accord, in fact, created a congenial atmosphere in Nagaland. The Government of India suspended all operations and actions against the underground people under the Unlawful (Prevention) Activities Act, 1967. The governor declared that he would release all persons who had accepted the Shillong Accord and would refund to the villagers all collective fines imposed after September 1972.[12] Sentences against those who had already been convicted were remitted. The cases against the undertrial prisoners were withdrawn and cases pending in investigation were closed down.

It is sad to note that Shillong Accord could not bring all the underground Nagas in the mainstream under the Indian constitution. There were many underground soldiers of Naga army who were either in China or Pakistan The appeal of the Indian Home Minister to these people to surrender and accept the Indian citizenship made no effect upon them because they were hard core and they had not given up their hope to achieve the Naga's freedom. Though for few years they remained inactive, by 1980s their activities became more apparent. They, condemning the Shillong Accord, charged the signatories of the Accord for selling out the Naga's right to self-determination to the government of India. Thereafter, they resumed hostile activities against the governments of India and Nagaland both. The government of India, being alert of their activities did all to suppress the Naga rebellion. Thus, the peace which appeared in Nagaland from 1975 hardly lasted till the resurgence of freedom movement.

The resurgence of freedom movement from 1980 onwards followed by the newly organised forum, namely the Nationalist Socialist Council of Nagaland (NSCN) proved that the silence, which prevailed in Nagaland after Shillong Accord, was nothing, but a lull before the storm. A group of Naga freedom fighters headed by Thuingaleng, Muivah (Tankhul Naga), Issac Chishi Swu (Sema Naga) and Khaplang (Burmese Naga), rejecting the Shillong Accord formed a new organization called as the NSCN instead of NNC on first January 1980. All these three leaders were trusted lieutenants of Phizo and the authorities of the NNC. Issac was the Vice President and Muivah was the General Secretary of the NNC. Breaking away their relations with the Naga Federal Government (NFG), they formed a new government of their own. According to the constitution of the NNC it "is the only legitimate political party to seek the mandate of the Naga people and settlement of the Naga issue is reached with the Central Government of India".[13] Since both the leaders of the NNC (Phizo and Muivah) were not the signatories to the Shillong Accord, they were not bound to accept it. When the Shillong Accord came into being, Phizo kept mum while Muivah condemned the Accord and finally rejected it. It is learnt that Muivah had tried to contact Phizo and persuade him to condemn the Accord, but no response was received from Phizo.[14] It is also learnt that Muiva and Issac had invited Phizo to come back from London and accept the leadership of the NSCN, but Phizo again remained silent.[15]

Appearance of NSCN and Resumption of Freedom Movement

On January 31st 1980, the NSCN was formed under the chairmanship of Issac Swu. Muivah was chosen as the General Secretary and Khaplang as the Vice-President of the newly formed NSCN. The NSCN also set up the Government of People's Republic of Nagaland (GPRN) replacing the old Federal Government of Nagaland. The NSCN soon declared that it had come into being for Naga sovereignty and to constitute Nagaland into a Christian socialism. Thus the NSCN having its own government and expressing its hard determination to fight for the cause of the Naga people revived the Naga freedom movement from 1980 onwards, which opened a new chapter in the history of Naga freedom movement.

The objective of the NSCN/GPRN was to work for Christian socialism based on the principles of Marxism-Leninism and Maoism. However, inclusion of the new term 'Christian socialism' had special meaning. The model of the Naga society, which Muivah and Issac have in their mind, is neither purely based on the principles of socialism on the Marxist line nor related to democratic socialism practised in India. They want a society, whose structure should be socialist, no doubt, but based on religious and moral principles. Muivah knows it well that the emerging Naga society under the leadership of India has developed elements of a class-society; its super echelons have been swept by consumerism. Muivah has been inclined towards Chinese society from the beginning. In his opinion the "West would only give some assurances, just to ensure that the Nagas did not go over to the Chinese totally". While living in China from 1966 to 1971 as the representative of the NNC, he was very much influenced by the Chinese revolution and also the philosophies of Mao Ze Dang. In the opinion of Muivah the Chinese leaders were "great who changed the lives of the millions". Muivah wanted to set an egalitarian society. Muivah believes that teaching of Bible would certainly protect the Nagas from falling easy prey to the rising western concept of materialism and consumerism.

As a strategy to make the Naga people aware of their right to self-determination and create a favourable circumstance, the leaders of the NSCN adopt the propaganda policy reiterating the old stand that Nagaland had never been a part of India and that the Nagas had forcibly been occupied by the "Indian occupationist forces". A claim was made that the NSCN was the only authentic body of the Naga people to fight for the cause of Naga's sovereignty. The aim of the NSCN was to "drive out Buddhism and Hinduism from Nagaland and Nagaland will stand for Christ".[16] Thereafter, the men of the NSCN fully equipped with modern arms and ammunition and developing close links with other anti-Indian organizations in the Northeastern states moved fast on the way of confrontation with the government of India.[17]

Resurgence of Naga Insurgency

Due to wrath of Muivah against the Burmese, Khiamniungan Tuensang became the home of refugees in September 1980. A report came that hundreds of the Khiamniungan people in the Myanmar were exterminated by the men of Muivah. According to Rev. Imti, the Field director of the Khiamniungan area of Nagaland Baptist Church Council, the Naga militants killed about one hundred Khiamniungan including eight church leaders in September 1980.[18] Noklu Konyak, a Congress (I) MLA from the Tuensang area was murdered along with two other persons in an ambush on April 27, 1981, by some unknown assailants.[19] Though the real culprits could not be arrested, the murder of Noklu created fear in the minds of the Naga politicians. It was the first murder of the Naga political leader after the Shillong Accord.

During 1990s, the anti-Indian and anti-Nagaland government activities of the NSCN increased to a great extent. The Naga freedom fighters began to attack and ambush the Indian security forces openly. The Superintendent of Police of Mokokchung district was shot dead in broad day light in the main market. Thereafter, the Deputy Commissioner of Kohima was killed by a group of the undergrounds when he was going to attend his office. In retaliation the government of India again promulgated the Disturbed Areas Act with a view to controlling the situation and checking the unlawful activities of the Naga militants. The promulgation of Disturbed Area Act and Maintenance of Law and Order Act empowered the Indian armed personnel to raid every household of the Nagas at anytime to search the rebels and arrest them. Such military operations disturbed total peace of the state. While dealing with the civilian Nagas during operations the security personnel harassed the people. The public began to demand immediate withdrawal of such draconian Acts.

The government of India accepted the truth that significance of the Shillong Accord had been totally lost. The direct armed tussle between the Naga militants and the Indian armed forces continued where the most sufferers were the people. The peace and progress of the state once more came to question.

Division in the NSCN

As stated earlier the Naga leaders can not remain united if their personality comes in question. In June 1988, Khaplang and Dalley, parting their way with one-time close associates Muivah and Issac, formed a new group, namely the NSCN (K). Khaplang assumed the responsibility of new group as the Chairman while Dalley Mongro became the General Secretary. On the other hand, Muivah and Issac termed their group as the NSCN (IM). Thus, the leaders of undivided NSCN, who had taken a vow to fight for the cause of the Naga's independence till the last drop of their blood, got splintered causing bitter enmity. This put the Naga people in utter surprise. The big shock which came to the Naga people was not the division of the NSCN, but appearance of bitter enmity between these two splintered parts because the enmity pushed back the major Naga issue like freedom and struggle against the Indian government, on the one hand, and brought forward unbridled factional fighting among the Nagas on the other.

Asoso Yonuo is of the view that the Nagas have not come out "altogether from the clutches of the traditional feuds, headhunting and tribalism deleterious to unity, and it is the fratricidal conflict among themselves into which they had been politically divided".[20] Confirming the same view Charles Chasie says, "The fabric of Naga unity and society... are being torn. Every issue is seen through the prism of personality clashes."[21] Personality clashes among the Naga leaders hardly allow them to stand united and work collectively. Tribalism in the Naga society has been a ruinous factor among the Naga people. It is this factor which has jeopardized Naga unity again and again. During the period of ceasefire—1964-1967—considerable amount of efforts were applied to settle peace, but it all failed causing serious setback on the part of underground organization due to tribalism. Shillong Accord failed due to differences among the undergrounds. When Muivah and Issac revived freedom movement in 1980, the unity of the underground leaders once more got shattered due to personality clash between Muivah and Khaplang. Vashum has rightly remarked, "The Nagas have been badly divided on factional political parties cutting across tribal solidarities and allegations... . Today Naga tribe, big or small, is observed to have been divided as to their loyalty and affiliation to one underground political group or the other. Dominion of one political group/faction with their counter-parts among the tribes is also prominent".[22]

Unlimited aspirations of the Naga leaders form another cause of disunity among them. In the words of Chaisie, "Naga history has only too frequently been reduced to personality clash of the leaders, whether underground or overground. This often eluded the thing borderline between the subject and the object of the ultimate goal. And in the name of the people, the leaders frequently expected, even demanded that the people (should) follow wherever they lead, right or wrong."[23] The only alternative they are given is that if you are not with me, you are against me. Study reveals the fact that the Naga leaders are power hungry and they consider nothing when their power comes in danger.

Personality Clash and Levelling of Allegations

The basic reason of the rift and division in the NSCN in April 1988 was the personality clash between Muivah and Khaplang. None of them was ready to compromise their differences at the cost of their personal superiority. In view of Muivah and Issac, Khaplang "desired to be pumped with special power and position". According to Muivah on the initiative of Khaplang "he was given second in command and his men were accommodated in several high positions".[24] Muivah further said that Khaplang belonged to such a community where there was no place for democratic elements. Khaplang suffered from "superiority complex" and he preferred "power and status".[25] In the words of Muivah, "He (Khaplang) did not hesitate to stop any thing when it came to the point of his self-gratification. He was never guided by scruples. Most of the time he abused power and placed himself above the organization—he was a law unto himself.... He was averse to democratic practices."[26]

On the other hand, Khaplang is of the view that Muivah being a Tangkhul Naga, was very much against the Burmese Naga tribes to which Khaplang belongs. That is why Muivah committed heinous crimes against the Konayaks and the Burmese Nagas. In the opinion of Khaplang, Muivah did not allow other to supersede him. Both the leaders after division in the NSCN have been levelling number of dirty allegations against each other with a purpose to malign the image of the adversary among the public. Thus, it is obvious that both the leaders had personal cause related to their ego that ultimately divided the NSCN and made the divided factions bitter enemies of each other damaging the expectations of the Naga people.

Muivah and Issac believe that the group led by Khaplang is nothing but a 'puppet' of the Nagaland government led by S.C. Jamir while Khaplang called the Muivah's faction as 'blood sucker' to the Nagas. Since Muivah is a Tangkhul Naga, Khaplang maintains that he is not a Naga. According to him "the Nagas did not know about the Tangkhuls because they never participated in Naga's struggle against the Indian armed forces from 1954 to 1956".[27] There has been no place in the Naga soil where the Tangkhuls have not killed and murdered innocent Nagas".[28]

Blaming Khaplang the faction, NSCN (IM) says, "Mr. Khaplang, the false self-proclaimed freedom fighter with intent to mislead the people, throws his immature and impulsive whims of accusations, allegations, defamations, libels, derogatory statements etc., and has been vying to enunciate a bad image of the Nagas."[29] On the other hand, the Secretary MIP/GRNP NSCN (K) writes, "Issac Swu, Th. Muivah and their men have committed genocide on the innocent Nagas in the name of Naga sovereignty. They have also massacred hundreds of pro-Shillong Accordists." The NSCN (K) maintains that the Naga struggle and sovereignty does not belong to the NSCN (IM). The NSCN (IM) begs for "packages, autonomies like the Bodos, Cacharis, Dimasas, and Kookis within the Indian constitution". The leaders of the NSCN (IM) "are making luxury trips to Europe and America to impress upon those people with terrorist visions than the general views".[30] It further alleged, "The NSCN (IM) and NISC (Naga International support Centre) collect millions of rupees from Neiphiu Rio and innocent Nagas and bribe the Indian armed forces."[31] The leaders of the NSCN (K) are of the view that the NSCN (IM) have close links not only with the Rio government and Indian security forces but also with NGOs like NISC, Naga Hoho, Naga Mother Association, NIBCC, CNBC "who are under the pay roll of the terrorist Indianism and fratricide".[32]

Y. Wangtin Naga, Central Council Member of the NSCN/GPRN (NSCN (K), expressing his sorrow over mass killing of the Nagas by the men of the NSCN (IM) writes, "No family is safe from today's abnormality and none is secure. The freedoms of life and liberty that had been once enjoyed has gone very far away and no Naga is certain of what his life will be." He further writes, "Issac group should explain to the Nagas the purpose of their killing of Naga leaders for no cause who after dropping sovereignty issue slipped down for integration but failed."[33]

It may be noted that Muivah wants that the districts of Manipur inhabited by the Nagas (Tangkhuls) should be integrated with Nagaland. It is this move of Muivah which is irritating the mind of Khaplang and his men because they think that the Tangkhuls are not Naga citizens and their inclusion in Nagaland as Naga citizens would create more problems. That is why the NSCN (K) served 'quit notice' to the Tangkhuls living in Nagaland immediately or to face the consequences. Such move of the NSCN (K) has added another challenge to the Naga society. Many sections of the society have come forward with a request to the Khaplang's group to withdraw such notice and reduce the atrocities on the Nagaland.

It is very much difficult to say which faction of the underground is on the right track. The NSCN (K) alleges that its rival faction the NSCN (IM) is related to the present DAN government led by Rio while the NSCN (IM) blames the Khaplang group that it has been maintaining close link with the government of India and all of its activities are supported by the Indian government with a view to divide the Nagas and weaken the freedom struggle. It is evident from the statement issued by MIP, GROPN, NSCN (IM). The statement says, "The patronage and hospitality of the Indian armed forces shared by the Khaplang group explains in itself that they are on the side of the Indian forces against the Naga people's aspiration".[34]

Division in the NSCN and enmity have resulted in severe inter-factional clashes where thousands of the activists from both sides have been killed despite the request of the public leaders, students' leaders, Naga Hoho, NMA etc., to stop such bloody activities. The question is not which faction is more responsible for killing of Nagas, but the issue which is much more vital is the factional fighting which has pushed aside the main issue that is Naga nationalism and freedom struggle. In the words of Timoths, "The underground factions totally ignored the voice of people by killing their own brothers and sisters in the state. Naga Hoho, Naga Association of Mothers, Naga Student's Federation and other NGOs appealed to the undergrounds not to kill each other, but to no avail. Random killing in public places without caring even the innocent people, even not sparing the students and children is on."[35] S.C. Jamir, the previous chief Minister of the state, writes, "They (Naga freedom fighters) are fighting for the same cause, but they are killing each other... . The main objective has taken the back seat whereas ego problems and personal issues are dominating the present action".[36]

According to the present chief minister of Nagaland, Neiphiu Rio, disunity among the Naga people and factional fights were the main obstacles for peace and reconciliation and for a lasting solution to the vexed Naga issue. The Editor of *Nagaland Post* has rightly remarked, "The greatest challenge is on how to end the vicious cycle and bring about human reconciliation... . The hurdles to reconciliation are bitterness and blame shifting which give rise to a spirit of unwillingness to reconcile."[37] Talking about the problem related to factional fight K. Soho, a citizen of Phek area, says, "Factional clashes in and around civilian places became the fashion of their day...damaging civil properties in the most unwanted ways, killing, injuring, harassing the innocent civilians was their aims and objectives for the struggle for Naga sovereignty."[38]

Thus, allegations and counter-allegations leveled by both the rival factions and their factional fights have created not only troubles for the Nagas but also confusion among the general mass. It has also brought tribalism on the fore front. The Tangkhuls who are mostly living in some districts of Manipur, are more advanced. Since 1970, the Tangkhuls increased their influence in the underground activities and came near to the overground activities also. Muivah, the leaders of the Tangkhuls, has put the condition for peace talks with Delhi to consider greater Nagalim (greater Nagaland) including the Tangkhuls, which is not acceptable to the leaders of the NSCN (K). This is one of the vital reasons, which is hampering the unity of the Naga people. One more reason of their disunity has been, in the words of Vashum, "Some feelings of discontentment and jealousy among others which are sometimes manipulated by some politicians/leaders of respective tribes for vested interests to create confusion among the Naga mass... . These crises have been a great stumbling block for the Naga national movement as they are divisive in nature".[39]

Split in Naga National Council (NNC)

No doubt the significance of the NNC led by Phizo declined after Shillong Accord but its existence could not be denied. After the death of Phizo on April 30, 1990, the question was who would lead the NNC. The issue to appoint a new President of the NNC caused split in it. There were two groups of the NNC—one led by Adeno, the daughter of Phizo, and another led by Khodao Yanthan, the Vice President of the NNC, till the split occurred. These two leaders did not come to the point of unity with the result that the oldest Naga organization was bifurcated into two groups—NNC (A) and NNC (K) in 1995. The NNC led by Khodao merged with the NSCN (IM) while, the NNC led by Adeno gradually lost its voice among the people under the shadow of the NSCN. Presently the NNC and FGN are much inclined towards the NSCN (K). It supports all the moves of the NSCN led by Khaplang.

Underground Issue

The division of the NSCN into two factions i.e. (NSCN-IM) and NSCN-K) and their growing differences and enmity, which resulted in factional fighting, killings and abhorrence for each other, not only annihilated the peace and progress of the state but also spread mass terror and fear among the Naga people. The situation became so grave that the members of the Nagaland Legislative Assembly raised such issues on the floor of the House again and again and showed their serious concern about deteriorating law and order situation in the state. Both the members of the treasury and opposition benches, blamed each other for siding with the undergrounds and taking their assistance during general elections held in the state. Even the Naga electorate did not remain unaffected of the underground issue. The voters were divided on the line of the factions of the undergrounds.

By 1994, the issue of the undergrounds became so severe that the House spent much of its time on discussing and debating the problems caused by insurgency. The government of Vamuzo was charged by S.C. Jamir who had been the chief minister of the state. First of all, he raised the issue of the undergrounds and their interference in the villages. He said, "Now we have more than 1,020 villages and in all villages you will find underground unit there. You cannot move freely; I cannot move freely because there is no security of life. People are afraid, businessmen are afraid because there is no security; there is no law and order. It is in a chaos because the present chief minister is following the double standard policy." He further said, "In the presence of government another parallel unseen government is running and they are demanding two lakhs rupees from each minister and one lakh from each MLA. Is it the kind of government that you are running today? Why are you turning a blind eye to these affairs?"[40]

It is not that the underground problem was new in Nagaland. Even during the regime of Jamir the state faced acute problems created by the underground. But that time he was the chief minister. Now he was the opposition leader. Hence it was easy for him to raise such issue dashingly and blame the government. Moreover, what he was talking was a reality. Resurgence of the insurgency in Nagaland had once more paved the way for the growth of troubles and miseries for the Naga people specially living in villages. The terrorism created by the undergrounds was such that even the government officials including the ministers and MLAs could not deny meeting the demands of the militant Nagas. With the emergence of the NSCN the problem of law and order specially in the areas of Mon and Tuensang had badly deteriorated and the problem of refuges, which appeared in 1980 was the creation of the NSCN people.[41]

S.C. Jamir could not maintain silence over such anti-social and anti-national activities of the undergrounds. Hence, he became vocal and blamed the Vamuzo government for not taking stern action against such elements. Since entire government machinery was under the direct threat of NSCN, which had emerged as the most powerful organization in comparison to other underground sections of Nagaland, the government found itself helpless. Jamir apprehended: "The bureaucrats who are sitting in the gallery and even in the secretariat must have paid the amount as has been demanded from them. They are keeping silent as they are helpless. They are helpless because government cannot take any steps for protection of their lives and the situation is not normal"[42]

However, Vamuzo, the leader of the House, was not ready to accept the fact that law and order situation was bad in the state. He agreed to the view-point of the opposition members: "All underground factions must unite. They should sink their differences as also any tussle for the leadership in the long term interest of the Nagas and should come together on the same platform."[43] He said that it was unfortunate that each faction claimed "to be better than the other, stronger than the other and the claims to be moving in the right direction and others in the wrong direction". He agreed to the fact, "It is painful to see that in the process of splitting, many promising youth have been lost through bloodshed. This must be stopped." He asked the underground factions to join their hands together and form a single platform in order to bring early solution to the problem.

The basic cause of defeat of the government of the NPC was deteriorating situation of law and order all over the state of Nagaland. It was all due to spreading influence of the NSCN and their terrorist activities among the people. The government, in fact, had become merely a spectator of the activities of the underground. There was no pocket left in Nagaland, which was not under the impact of the NSCN directly or indirectly. A parallel government was running all over the state and the militants had spread openly in all towns and villages.

Thus, it is evident that growth of the resurgence of insurgency in the state and increase in factionalism among the underground leaders not only created the problem of law and order but also brought numerous troubles and miseries before the people. Life of the general people once more became insecure. There was no safety of any body. No one knew at what time and at what place factional fighting would erupt making the situation panicky. People were afraid of coming out of their homes. Even homes were not safe. President rule was imposed and after that when election was held in February 1993, the NPC was defeated. The Naga people once again reposed their faith in the Congress-I leaders and expected from them not only economic development but also protection of life and property and gurantee of durable peace in Nagaland. However, bitter reality is that no government in Nagaland dare to challenge the undergrounds and control their activities.

Money and Muscle Power in Naga Politics

Another challenging trend of the Naga society, which has damaged the political image of the state, is the use of money and muscle power by the Naga politicians to serve their interests. The lust for power became so strong among the Naga politicians that they have become expert in using money and muscle power during election and managing to capture the polling booths, threatening of polling officials, bogus voting and plundering of ballot papers. Geoffrey has rightly remarked, "Those indulging in election malpractices graduated from ordinary muscle power to gun power by hiring services of gun-men to scare away voters so as to effect a coup of government. These elements got involved committing various types of crimes openly because they had official patronage. The trend once set in motion perpetuated its strength and it is still present in influence of muscle power that can easily be discerned during the period of election".[44]

The Naga politicians spend enough money during election. That is why the ministers when they are in power make all efforts either right or wrong to earn money. The Naga voters who come from the rural areas and who are illiterate and poor are in need of money. They do not pay attention to the character of the candidate or the nature of the party. What they want is money from them. Disregarding the democratic value, they are ready to sell their valuable votes to the candidates who give them more money. The youths are employed with the help of money to work on behalf of the politicians. Even the government officials, who are supposed to be neutral, are influenced through money. It has been observed that the Naga electorate, generally, vote the party's candidates or independent candidates not for their principles, ideologies and character, but for their money. The electoral law has the limit to spend money during election and it has the provision for keeping accounts of expenditure during the election period. But money spent during election more than the limit has polluted entire system. Money has become the viable source to manipulate elections and manage to win them. Vohra Committee has rightly remarked, "Our experience of fifty years (of democracy has taught us that rules and regulations are known merely for violation than for compliance."

Trend of Corruption

Free flow of money in Nagaland in the name of development of the state and its people attracted new set of politicians to join the rank of the politics and tempted the old politicians to serve their own ends. The leaders with the intention to earn money and power either joined a political party or founded a new political party to suit their personal choice and serve their vested interests. Under such notion no political parties in Nagaland remained true to their adopted ideologies and principles nor did they remain committed to the membership of the party. They changed the party and joined the other one with the only objective to serve their own interests. A political party became an instrument in the hands of such politicians who utilized it as per their own personal ideologies. They began to interpret the things in such a manner that could defend their personal view-points. The party became the self-centered and the fortune of the leaders began to determine largely the prospects of the party. Under such circumstances, in the words of Reddy, "The increasing number of candidates contesting the polls, bewildered voters ... the declining number of voters, winning by an absolute majority of votes polled, fractured mandates and hung house and unstable governments are all attributes to the party structure and their unprincipled leadership".[45] In Nagaland, the growing number of political parties and polarization of Naga voters paved the way for the growth of hung assembly and coalition governments comprising the political parties having no affiliation to ideologies and programmes. They all joined their hands to form the government and serve the interests of the party leaders.

Under such emerging situation in Nagaland where politics lost its real ethos of public service and the bureaucrats began to side with the ministers giving up their bond of neutrality, corruption on large scale was bound to take place. The money, which was earmarked for the development under various new projects, could hardly reach the people. No doubt, the number of departments of the government increased with sufficient infrastructure, but they are hardly true to the assignments which have been given to them. The funds from the Central government to give effect to the centrally sponsored programmes under the IRDP, RLEP, RLEGP, JRY, Indira Awas Yojna, Gramin Vikas Yojna, Gramin Swarojgar Yojná etc., for the rural development are mostly misutilized. All these programmes, which came into being from time to time, has opened the flood gate of money in Nagaland. But it is sad to note that the development specially in the rural areas has not taken place on the expected line due to mismanagement of the funds by the ministers and the bureaucrats. The members of the opposition parties raised the issues related to bungling of the funds with greater voice on the floor of the house, but the situation remained as it is. Reality is that the opposition, which criticized the government for such mismanagement and embezzlement of the funds, did nothing to stop such practices when they came in power. Rather their ministers, too, have been found indulging in such black and ugly practices.

According to Ntsalumo Kyong, "political powers and ministerial offices were abused and completely misused for the personal pleasures and material gains by the politicians and the state bureaucrats at the expense of the common public of the Nagas".[46] Those Nagas who got such opportunity began to avail of it giving up all sorts of morality, honesty, sincerity, etc. Their life and living style changed overnight. They joined the rank of elite. Their children availed the opportunity to obtain better education outside the state. Most of such politicians are addicted to liquor though the state has been declared as a dry state. They have enough money and influence to buy the best quality of liquor from outside the state. To quote Kyong once amore, "Whatever development and progress that have taken place in Nagaland is in reality the sole development of the politicians and the bureaucrats and their family members .... Only 10% of the Naga population have enjoyed and been benefited by the state development programmes and the mass remains untouched by the various state development activities".[47]

The Naga people have justly been viewed as a people known for directness and simplicity, but flow of politics in Nagaland is such that the Naga people are being provided "with one corrupt government after another by their own leaders, while public money in that state has been squandered in such proportion that the Reserve Bank of India was forced to stop all Nagaland development payments in April 1990."[48] Making the fact public, the *Ura Mail* editorial wrote, "With effect from March 29, 1990, till further instructions, the Reserve Bank of India has instructed the various Branches of the State Bank of India located in Nagaland not to honour any cheques issued by the departments of Nagaland government except for salaries".[49] The issue of non-payment of the cheques issued by the departments of the government of Nagaland was raised and strongly debated on the floor of the assembly. The government found itself in embarrassing situation due to financial crisis. Observing the cause of bankruptcy of the Nagaland government the editor of the *North East Politics* wrote, that "the side downwards in Nagaland began ever since the Centre decided that the best way of controlling insurgency was by pumping money".[50] The government of India siphoned money in Nagaland to please the Naga elites and the undergrounds. Hence it was natural that the misappropriation of money would have corrupted the people concerned.

There may not be two opinions about the fact that the government of India pumped huge amount of money in Nagaland with a view to winning over the insurgent Nagas and also take up some viable projects, which could provide jobs to the unemployed youths. But no attempt was made by the government to utilize these extra funds for the sustainable development. As a result, a small class of affluent Nagas who was either directly or indirectly associated with the government established its hold over politics and managed the affairs in such a manner that they became the main beneficiaries. Today the Center's policy of softening the edge of the insurgency with the help of money seems to have paid large dividends in the shape of rank, political opportunism and corruption in the state. It were the personal rivalries among the Naga politicians and the lust for power which resulted in politics of defection on the one hand, and paved the way for the growth of mushroom political parties on the other.

Nexus Between Criminals and Politicians

In Indian politics the most dangerous trend which has recently emerged is a nexus between criminals and politicians. Vohra Committee appointed by the government of India has affirmed that "there is nexus between crime syndicates and political personality and this has got deep root in the election system of India".[51] In Nagaland, the nexus between these elements is not so deep, but a trend is coming up. The Naga politicians are inclined towards the criminals. There are several incidents where the criminals hired by the politicians disturbed the fairness of election. Till 1974, the Naga politicians had been fair and committed to the public service. With the rise and growth of politics of defection and entrance of new set of corrupt politicians, trend of criminalization of Naga politics has badly affected soundness and fairness of elections. Such nexus between criminals and politicians has traveled to Nagaland from other parts of the country. Today the criminals are hired in Nagaland during elections by the political parties or by the candidates. They create terror among the people and frighten them to caste their votes in favour of the candidates whom the criminals support. Capturing of polling booths, plundering of the ballot boxes and disturbing the polling process are all the result of the nexus between the criminals and politicians.

Decay of Political Morality

Decay in political morality is another trend which is rooted deeply in the Indian party politics including Nagaland. The political morality of the Naga politicians has degenerated to a great extent. Machiavelli, who for the first time strongly pleaded for separation of politics from ethics and religion, opened the way for deterioration of moral standard of the rulers. He allowed the politicians (Prince) to be immoral, no doubt, for their personal interests, but for common interests. Declination of morality in politics from that time onwards has become a permanent feature. Today, politicians think that morality is not a bond for them and they are exempted from any moral obligation with the result that they hardly care for common good. They have become not only liars but cheaters also. They hardly hesitate to speak lie and use immoral tactics to win over the power. Politics to them is a device to earn more money and prestige which ultimately make them corrupt. Passing a comment on deteriorating moral standard of the Naga politicians, Arienba Jamir remarked, "The Christian-like political preachers are today the defectors of different parties... . As a matter of fact politicians are a mixture of different weights".[52]

The growing irresponsibility of the Naga politicians and their inclination towards corruption has caused a great danger to decency and decorum of Naga politics. The moment the politicians come in power, they find themselves above all rules and regulations and in the areas of their activities they least hesitate to break decency and decorum that they are supposed to uphold. They feel that there is no moral bond to control their behaviours and conducts, which are harmful not only to political system as a whole but also to the well-being of the people. *The North East Time's* editorial has rightly remarked in the context of the absence of moral constraint, "The kingly gestures like feudal lords of Europe are not rare among them. When they move out, they throw the impression that they are rulers and as such they are not governed by the laws rather they are above them".[53]

Even the Naga electorates are not free from the flow and influence of moral degradation. Monalisa Chankiza remarking on degrading moral standard of the Naga people said, "They are greedy, selfish and shortsighted. They demand pork, supply order, government jobs and become blind. This tendency has given birth to corruption, frustration and social turmoil." He further writes, "The Naga electorates "do not question their leaders because they have sold themselves. They hardly care for their (leader's) qualities.... They (Naga people) pose as ignorant villagers for personal gains." Result is that the "political drama being staged currently in Nagaland is unfortunately, the reflection of the malignancy of the attitudes, values and trends of the Naga society".[54] Thus, in the absence of moral dignity of both the people and their representatives the political scenario of the state from May 1990 became "an obscene display of avarice, ego-centralism and total disregard for people and state".[55]

There may be some exaggeration in the aforesaid statements of Changkiza, no doubt, but it is the truth that politics in Nagaland has lost its earlier meaning and purpose. It has badly affected healthy growth of political system in Nagaland. On several occasions the Naga legislators raised such issues on the floor of the House and blamed each other. They discussed the issue of corruption and defection very seriously, but did a little to stop them because what they talked on the floor hardly they followed in their life.

Money Extortion Drive

No underground or terrorist organization may run without support of money. The only source of money for them is voluntary donation of money by people or imposition of taxes over people and extortion of money from them. To meet this need first they contact big business houses and then they tax government officials, private and public firms, shopkeepers, contractors and lastly the general public. At denial they are punished or harassed. The habit of extortion of money from the people aggravate their thirst for money and money, ultimately, becomes their object.[56] In Nagaland, at the beginning, the drive of money collection from the people by the undergrounds was not harsh and forceful. As the years rolled down and interest of the undergrounds in money developed, the method of money collection became rough and painful causing "untold miseries" for the people living in Nagaland. The extortion drive for money from government servants, businessmen, contractors, teachers, every Naga household etc., created panic all over the state. In the words of Timothy, "They (undergrounds) taxed the businessmen and in return the businessmen recovered the taxes paid to the undergrounds, from public by increasing the prices of their commodities in the markets. Taxes were imposed on vehicles, goods or essential commodities and all items in the state."[57] Imposition of taxes by the undergrounds has become an established rule of the underground organisatisons in Nagaland. Someone has rightly remarked, "The Naga National movement has turned to something like the welfare of the underground activities.... Their accountability to the people is very much lacking.... The money they collect is too heavy for the public. Moreover, the collection is usually harsh and there is nothing like 'voluntary payment' now-a-days. Every thing is compulsory or one has to risk one's life."[58] Kidnapping has also become the method to collect money.

Such activities of the freedom fighters in Nagaland has not only created doubt about the sagacity and sanctity of freedom movement among the people but also increased the wrath of the public against the Naga militants. It is another fact that most of the people are so fearful that they do not like to express their mind in this regard. Naga freedom movement has become so fearful, terrible and destructive that people do not talk much about it today. Expressing such reality, one of the university students of Nagaland, namely, Kezhalesa, wrote, "The Naga nation is torn by internal dissention into several factions, illegal taxes, rapacious intimidations, tribalism, heartless corruption and plaguing economy of outland". He raises the question, "Are these the signs of struggle for sovereignty and do Nagas believe that through these means we can achieve our goal?"[59] Kaka Iralu, the famous author of Nagaland, asks, "Have we Nagas surrendered our life to these leaders and to their law of gun? Is the Naga army uniform a license for its bearers to abduct us, terrorize us and even beat us to death or shoot us to death?"[60] Being annoyed with such terrorist activities of the undergrounds, another Naga scholar says, "They (undergrounds) cannot be given the name of terrorists with their threats, intimidations, violence, kidnapping and factional clashes, but they can be rightly termed as terrorist group".[61]

A common feeling is emerging among the general mass that "national work" has become a "money making industry, a kind of mafia, specific to our situation". One of the causes of factional rivalry and fighting is to put effective control over areas to have freedom to collect money. The general people are more disturbed because the spate of violence is now taking place in the busiest and crowded areas, exposing the entire innocent civilian population to "become human shields". According to Naga Mothers' Association, "The factional fighting "has forced the Naga mothers to mourn deep on the deaths of our children regardless of their faults or innocence... . Bloodshed cannot solve any problem rather it will only create more troubles". Thus, it is very much obvious that increasing lust for money among the undergrounds, underground Naga leaders are losing their control over the greedy soldiers who are indulged in money collection drive even without the permission of their commanders. This is a big challenge to the Naga society.

Ceasefire and Peace Talks

Under the tense and fearful situation peace has become a universal cry for the Nagas. Every section of the Naga people began to talk about peace, not conflict. At this very critical juncture S.C. Jamir, the then chief minister of Nagaland, declared the year 1997 as the year of 'Peace Offensive' making an appeal to everyone including the underground outfits to observe the year as 'the year of peace' by stopping factional fights and anti-government as well as anti-social activities. New Delhi also became active to preserve peace in Nagaland. Initiative to bring peace in Nagaland was first taken by the former Indian Prime Minister Narasimha Rao. Thereafter his successor, H.D. Deve Gowda personally met Muivah and Issac Swu in Switzerland in February 1996. I.K. Gujral, the successor of Deve Gowda, favoured peace talks with the leaders of the NSCN without any precondition. The Naga Tribal Hoho came forward with the proposal to have 'Mass rally processions and prayers'. S.C. Jamir issued the statement stating, "Unless factions unite, there is grave threat to the well-being of the Naga society which would possibly witness a civil war among factions and which could pit one tribal group against other."[62] Thereafter, the Indian Prime Minister informed the members of the parliament, "In recent talks with the Issac-Muivah group of NSCN, it has now been mutually agreed to the ceasefire for three months with effect from 1st August 1997 and initial discussion at political level." Ceasefire was extended after every three months till 31st July 1998 and from August 1998 it was extended on annual basis which still continues.

Thus, the stage for ceasefire and peace talks between the government of India and the government of the NSCN (IM) was set creating a lot of hope among the Naga people. Resumption of ceasefire and peace talks again changed the environment of the Naga society giving some relief to the people. However, the people were yet worried because the NSCN (K) was not included in the peace talks. The government of India, however, declared unilateral ceasefire against the underground group led by Khaplang. Unfortunately the NSCN (K) did not join the process of ceasefire with the result that its struggle against the IM group continued and several Nagas belonging to both the groups have been killed. On the occasion of 125 years of advent of Christianity in Nagaland the Baptist Fellowship of North America organised eight-day Atlanta Meet from 28th July to 4th August 1997 with the purpose to "thrash out a solution to the 50-year old Naga insurgency problem". Several of Naga leaders including the representatives of NSCN (K) and FGN attended and the conference called upon all the Naga people "irrespective of affiliations to relinquish old antagonism, give up old grudges and build up the best of the Naga heritage".[63] But it is sad to note that the NSCN (IM) boycotted the Meet.

The appeal made to the underground sections by the Atlanta Meet did not bring the underground factions to the common platform. Rather the NSCN (K) denounced the ceasefire agreement between the government of India and the NSCN (IM) as "treachery" to divide the Nagas while the NSCN (IM) expressing the reason for their boycott of the Atlanta Meet, said, "They would not team up with its rival faction led by S. Khaplang and the 'puppet' chief minister, S.C. Jamir". Issac Swu blamed Mr. Jamir for forming Naga Hoho federation, Naga Mothers' Association and Church leaders ... paying money to every one."[64] Mr. Jamir wanted to include the representatives of all these organizations in the process of peace talks which was not liked by the IM group.

Thus, despite all the efforts to bring these two dominant sections together, no success has been achieved so far. However, it is heartening to note that the NSCN (K) signed an agreement with the government of India to go for ceasefire. A peace talk between the leaders of the NSCN (IM) and the representatives of the Indian government is still on, but without any solid achievement. No doubt, the armed tussle between the Naga militants and the Indian security forces has reduced, but factional fighting and tension between the groups led by Muivah and Khaplang has increased "creating sense of confusion, fear and despair among fellow Nagas everywhere". According to Shishak, reliance of the Naga freedom fighters on AK-47 rifles, "will lead the Nags to self-destruction". He further says, "I am persuaded that all the Naga freedom fighting groups at one time or another have indulged in shedding innocent blood. It is only a question of which group shed more blood."[65] Shishak doubts whether the Nagas would be able to maintain a new nation under such prevailing situation of internal feuds and flights. Answering his question he replied in negative. He added, "The Nagas know how to suck the blood of others."[66]

For the last five decades the freedom struggle in Nagaland has been continuing despite various splits and divisions among the leaders not for any ideological differences, but for personality clashes and in the name of tribalism. There is no denying the fact that the Naga freedom fighters have suffered a lot for achievement of Naga freedom. What political achievement has gone to the pocket of the Nagas today is due to constant pressure upon the government of India to consider the their historic demand, but very little efforts have been made to prepare national background, create effective national feelings among the people and preserve Naga unity. No one can deny that the Naga people as a whole are conscious of the right to self-determination. They have enough courage to fight for the cause, too. But it is sad to note that their entire efforts to achieve freedom have been victim of disunity and disintegrity. No one knows for how long the people of Nagaland have to face the pangs of factional fighting and live under the shadow of constant fear-psychosis.

The Naga issue has become more complex today. Bitterness and enmity among the various underground factions are so serious that no device is applicable to reconcile them. All the efforts hitherto made by the public leaders, political leaders, church leaders, students' leaders, leaders of the Naga Hoho, leaders of the Mother Association etc., have remained futile to bring them to the sense of unity and maintain unity. Regretting about the present scenario of the Naga society, Charles Chasie says, "What has our society become today? We have reached a stage where no one can say anything to anyone anymore. Power and strength and wealth ... are the only things we understand, threats and intimidations are the only languages we speak and deep suspicion has become the hallmark of our inter-personal relationship whether between individuals or between groups or parties."[67] He further says that "suspicion, fear, exclusiveness, assassinations, bitterness etc., have all led to the present state of affairs." According to Chasie, the Naga society is wounded today which "needs healing, not further wounding". According to him the Nagas today have become "de-sensitized and de-humanized".[68]

What Chasie says is not only his feelings and voice, but it is the feeling of the reasonable Nagas who are suffering from the unbearable pangs. They are sufferers and witness of deteriorating social conditions and dangerous trends, but they are unable to control it. They are fed with such anarchic and painful situation, but they are unable to get rid of it. A question may be raised here as to who are responsible for all this. The question is not easy to answer. Someone may know the correct answer, but they are afraid of expressing their mind freely specially against the undergrounds. The Naga society is democratic in structure, but there is no freedom of expression due to widely prevailed fear-psychosis. The spread of fear is such that even the natives do not dare to move in towns after sun-set. Shopkeepers prefer to shut down their shutters early afternoon. The police or the paramilitary forces have to watch towns whole night. The anti-social elements are active to fish in the troubled waters. The government does not dare to take up decisive action against the law-breakers. Police is also afraid of the threats of the underground and this is evident from the dictates given by the underground forces to the Superintendents of Police of eleven districts of Nagaland. The police asked the undergrounds "not to venture into civilian areas with fire arms". Reacting strongly, the chief administrative officers of the NSCN (IM) issued threats to the SPs "to leave their respective towns within a week". The authorities of the NSCN (IM) also said that the state government has "no right to ask Naga people not to move around in their own land".[69]

The youths of the society are not on the right track. The biggest problem for them is unemployment. The state lacks the avenues to employ them. The problem of unemployment where thousands of jobless youths in Nagaland "are left in the lurch, poses a potential threat to the society".[71] Each year at least two or three thousand graduates from various educational institutions swell the ranks of the educated unemployed. There are several thousands not registered with the employment exchanges. It is a desparate situation that has to be seriously addressed. Those who are unemployed and have no sources of income are under compulsion either to join the underground set-up or to rely upon anti-social activities such as theft, robbery, extortion, etc.

The ceasefire and peace talks have been going on in Nagaland since August 1997. Some positive results have also come out. But the conflict and armed struggle between the men of the NSCN (IM) and the NSCN (K) has not come to an end with the result that the peace of Nagaland is still bleeding. In the words of Chasie Nagas: "People are "fed up with the extortions and high-handed ways of the various underground factions... this is the melting point that Naga society is today and all sides have become mutual props in keeping the 'militant' alive and going without any path-breaking initiatives that would change the situation".[70]

Time has come for retrospection and self-analysis of the Naga society, role of the Naga leaders and attitudes of the Naga people without any fear and prejudice. The Naga people whosoever may be, shall have to rise above the confinement of tribalism, parochialism, chauvinism and false propagandas. If the Naga society is to prosper in right direction, each section shall have to join their hands together forgetting and forgiving its ill-wills against each other. They shall have to think seriously, act judicially and proceed unitedly. Before the Nagas go for a nation of their own, they shall have to have a broadened mindset and farsightedness so that they are not disturbed by petty differences.

References

1. *Lok Sabha Debates,* 3rd series, vol. XLI, No. 8, 1964, pp. 1306-07.
2. *Efforts for Peace in Nagaland,* a pamphlet issued by the Directorate of Information, Publicity and Tourism, Government of Nagaland, 1965, 1974, pp.1-2.
3. *Ibid.* pp. 33-4.
4. Y.D. Gundevia, *War and Peace in Nagaland,* New Delhi, 1974, p. 121.
5. B.K. Nehru, "Mediators of Naga Issue were pro-extremists in North East India," 1970, p. 2.
6. *Proceedings of Nagaland Legislative Assembly (NLA),* March 1968, p. 38.
7. B.K. Nehru, *op. cit.*, p2.
8. Y.d. Gundevia, *War and Peace in Nagaland, op. cit.*, p. 193.
9. *Naga News* published by Directorate of Information, Publicity and Tourism, Government of Nagaland, Kohima September 1975.
10. *Ibid.*
11. *Dawn of Peace in Nagaland,* a booklet published by Directorate of Information, Publicity and Tourism, Government of Nagaland, Kohima, 1975, p.3.
12. *Speech* of L.P. Singh, governor of Nagaland, delivered on 26th January, 1976.
13. Horam (1988), *Insurgency in Nagaland–the Last Thirty Years,* Gosomo Publishers, New Delhi, 1988, pp. 188-89.
14. Tajenyuba Ao, *British Occupation of Naga Country Mokokchung,* p. 299.
15. T. Amongla's Thesis, "Naga Nationalism and National Movement," submitted to the Nagaland University, for Ph.D. Degree in 2004. p. 109.
16. *Nagaland Times,* vol. XI, No.1, July 16, 1980, p. 4.
17. Francis Kikon, "NSCN and allies from STUF" in the *North East Update,* vol. I, No. 6, Dimapur, February 1995, p. 8.

18. *Nagaland Times*, vol. VI, No. 9, September 3, 1980.
19. *The Platform*, No. 3, May 7, 1981.
20. Asoso Yonuo, *The Rising Nagas*, New Delhi, 1974, p. 283.
21. Charles Chaisie, *The Nagas Imbroglio*, Standard Publications, Kohima, 1981, pp. 137-38.
22. Vashum R. *The Nagas' Right to Self-determination*, Mittal Publications, New Delhi, 2002, p. 139.
23. *Daily Review*, November 4, 1997, p. 3.
24. The Joint Statement of Muivah and Issac, published in *The Hill Express*, February 6, 1990.
25. *Ibid.*
26. *Ibid.*
27. *The Threat*, a booklet published by Information and Publicity Affairs, GPRN of Nagaland , p. 5.
28. *Ibid.* p. 13.
29. *Nagaland Post*, 23 July 2006, p. 4.
30. *Nagaland Post*, July 22, 2006, p. 4.
31. *Ibid.*
32. *Nagaland Post*, July 21, 2006, p. 4.
33. *Nagaland Post*, September 18, 2006, p. 4.
34. *Nagaland Post*, September 3, 2006, p.4.
35. *Daily Review*, vol. XII, No. 153.October 24, 1998, p. 2.
36. S.C. Jamir, *Realities of Naga Political Problems*, a booklet issued by Government of Nagaland, Kohima, 1988, p. 5.
37. *Nagaland Post*, September 8, 2006, p. 4.
38. *Nagaland Post*, July 12, 2006, p. 4.
39. R. Vashum, *Nagas' Right to Self-Determination*, Mittal Publications, New Delhi, 2002, p. 140.
40. *Proceedings of NLA*, 1st session, March 1993, pp. 168-70.
41. *Ibid.* p. 192.
42. *Proceedings of NLA*, 8th session, 2nd series, January 1994, p. 5.
43. *Ibid.* p. 159.

44. Geoffrey Yaden "Election Reforms", paper presented in a seminar held on 7th March 2001, Kohima.
45. P. S. Reddy, "Parliamentary Polls and Polls Reforms", in *The North East Times*, Jorhat, September 17, 1999, p. 10.
46. Ntsalumo Kyong, "Commercialization of Poetics" in *Nagaland Post,* July 24, 1995.
47. *Ibid.*
48. *North East Politics,* vol. I, No. 6, Jun-July, 1990, p. 1.
49. *Ura Mail,* April l4, 1996 daily newspaper published from Dimapur.
50. *North East Politics,* vol. I, No. 6, June-July 1990, p. 2.
51. "Review of the Elections," *Law and Processes and Reform Option,* a consultative paper by National Commission to raise working of constitution, Vigyan Bhavan, New Delhi, 2001, p. 37.
52. Natsalumo Koyan, *Commercialization of Politics, op. cit.*
53. *North East Times,* vol. I, No. 34, September24,1999, (editorial page)
54. Monalisa Chankiza, "National Politics with Hope and Disgusts", in *North East India,* August 11, 1990, p. 20/XII.
55. *Ibid.*
56. Archana Goel (1997), *Terrorism: Causes and Consequences,* New Delhi. 1997, pp. 75-80.
57. *The Daily Review,* vol. XII, No. 153, Dimapur October 24, 1998, p. 2.
58. Vashum's *Naga's Right to Self-determination, op. cit.* p. 142.
59. Kezhalisa, "The Naga Struggle Today: Incredible", in the *Annual Magazine,* published by the Post-Graduate Students Union (PGSU), Nagaland University, Lumami.
60. *Eastern Mirror,* Vol. I, No. 111, Dimapur, November 28, 2002, p. 5.
61. *Daily Review,* November 4, 1997, p. 3.
62. *Nagaland Post,* April 27, 1996 editorial page.
63. *The Telegraph,* August 5, 1997.

64. *North East Sun*, vol. 3, September 14, 1997, pp. 8-9.
65. "A. Shishak, Sign of Readiness to welcome the New Naga Nation", *Nagaland Post*, January 9, 1999.
66. *Ibid.*
67. Charles Chaisie, "Quit Notice and the Deeper Issue", in *Nagaland Post*, August 31, 2006. p. 6
68. *Ibid.*
69. *Nagaland Post*, September 14, 2006, p. 4.
70. Charles Chaisie, *The Naga Imbroglio, op. cit.* p. 71.

***

Bibliography

PRIMARY SOURCES

DEBATES (Government)

1962-1963—*Lok Sabha Debates.*, New Delhi.

1962-1963—*Proceedings of Parliamentary Debates*, New Delhi.

1963—*Provisional Parliamentary Debates*, New Delhi

1946-1947 and 1948—*Constituent Assembly Debates*, New Delhi.

Proceedings of Nagaland Legislative Assembly from 1963 to till date. Secretariat Library of NLA, Kohima.

Proceedings of the Assam Legislative Assembly, vol. III, 1947 Guwahati.

ACTS AND CONSTITUTIONAL DOCUMENTS

The Nagaland Hills Tuensang Area, (NHTA) Act, 1957.

The Nagaland (Transitional Provision) Regulation, 1961.

The State of Nagaland Act, 1962.

The Constitution of India, Law Agency of Allahabad.

Transforming Rural India: Programme for Change, published by Government of India, New Delhi, 1999.

NAGALAND LEGISALTIVE ASSEMBLY'S PUBLICATIONS

1964-2004—*Official Reports of Proceedings of Nagaland Legislative Assembly.*

N.D.—*Unique Feature of Sixth Assembly.*

Who is Who (details about the members of the Assembly and ministers from 1962 onwards).

25—Years of Nagaland Legislative Assembly.

"Report on the 7th General Election to the NLA—1988-89."

Souvenir (Commemorating 35 years of statehood).

PUBLIBLISHED DOCUMENTS BY THE GOVERNMENT OF NAGALAND

1976—*Dawn of Peace in Nagaland.*

1985—*Hand Book for Members 1985,* 8th edition.

1989—25 Years of Nagaland Legislative Assembly (1964-1989).

1980—*A Year of Prosperous Nagaland,* a booklet issued by the Department of Information and Publicity and Tourism, Government of Nagaland, Kohima.

1990—*Nagaland,* a booklet issued by Directorate of Information, Public Relations, Government of Nagaland, Kohima.

N.D.—*The Warrior,* a monthly magazine published by the Government of Nagaland, Kohima.

1988—*Government News,* a booklet issued by the office of the Governor of Nagaland, Kohima, August.

1999—*Souvenir* (Commemorating 35 years of statehood, published by Directorate of Information & Public Relations, GON.

1997, 1998, 2000, 2002, 2004—*Statistical Hand Book,* Published by directorate of Economics, and Statistics published by the GON, Kohima.

SECONDARY SOURCES

BOOKS

1974—Asoso, Yonuo, *The Rising Nagas*, Vivek Publishing House, New Delhi.

1975—Aier, L. Imti, *Ao Naga Social and Customary Genealogy*, Jorhat.

1970—Alemchiba, Ao, *A Brief Historical Account of Nagaland*, Kohima.

1999—Akong, Ao, *Practicing of Naga Customary Laws*, Dimapur.

1967—Anand, V.K, *Nagaland in Transition*, New Delhi.

1993—Ao, L.N, *Rural Development in Nagaland*, Har-Anand Publications New Delhi,

1986—Bendangnagshi, *Glimpses of Naga History*, Guwahati.

1929—Bowers, A.C, *Under Head-Hunter's Eyes*, Judon Press, Philadelphia.

1855—Butler, J., *Travels and Adventures in the Province of Assam*, London.

1956—Campbell, A., *A Siege from Kohima*, London.

1974—Chakravarty, P.C., *British Relations with Hill Tribes of Assam* 1873-1974, Shillong.

1973—Chaube S, *Hill Politics in North East India*, Kolkata.

1883—Clark, E.W., *Ao Nagas*, Shillong.

1907—Clark, M.M., *A corner of India*, Philadelphia.

1967—Clod, A., *The Future Government of Assam Tribal People*, Kolkata.

1986—Dao, S.T., *The Tribals of North East India*, New Delhi.

1971—Down, F.S., *The Mighty Works of God—Christian Literary Centre*, Guwahati.

1983—*Christianity in North East India*, C.L.C., Guwahati.

1969—Elvin, V., *Nagas in the 19th Century*, Bombay.

1991—(Reprint), *Nagaland,* Shillong.

1929—*Philosophy of NEFA,* Shillong.

1957—*A New Deal for Tribal India,* Faridabad.

1984—Ganguly, G.B., *A Pilgrimage to the Nagas,* New Delhi.

1975—Gundevia, Y.D., *War and Peace in Nagaland,* Delhi.

1962—Ghosh, B.B., *History of Nagaland,* New Delhi.

1912—Hamilton, A., *In Abor Jungles,* London.

1976—Haimendrof, C.V., *The Naked Nagas,* New Delhi.

1975—Horam, M., *Naga Polity,* New Delhi.

1977—*Social and Cultural Life of the Nagas,* New Delhi.

1988—*Nagas' Old Ways and New Trends,* New Delhi.

1986—Hokishe, Sema, *Emergence of Nagaland: Socio-Economic and Political Transformation and the Future,* New Delhi.

1967—Hutton, J.H., *The Angami Nagas with some notes on Neighboring Tribes,* London.

1921—*The Sema Nagas,* London.

1921—*The Angami Nagas,* London.

1974—Jennings, Sir Ivor, *Parliamentary Laws,* Cambridge University.

1996—Jonstone, James, *My Experience in Manipaur and the Naga Hills,* London.

1975—Kapen, S, *Tradition, Modernity and Counter Culture: An Asian Perspective,* Visther, Bangalore.

1995—Kiramwati, *Education in Nagaland,* Eastern Book Agency, Mokokchung.

1956—Lal, A. B., (Ed) *The Indian Parliament,* Chaitanya Publishing House, Allahabad, 1956.

1972—Longkumar, Nuklu, *The Growth of Baptist Churches and Ao of Nagaland,* Dimapur.

1976—Liyod., L., *Mr. Speaker Sir,* Jonathan Café, London.

1922—Luce, Robert, *Legislative Procedure,* Boston.

1974—Luthra, P.N., *Nagaland from a District to Sate,* Guwahati.

1979—Mackenzie, A., *History of Relations of the Government with the Hill Tribes of North-East Frontier of Bengal,* Delhi.

1965—Mankekar, D.R., *Slippery Slope in Nagaland,* Bombay.

1913—Merriam, E.F, *A History of American Baptist Mission,* American Baptist Publication Society, Philadelphia.

1922—Mills J.P., *The Ao Nagas,* London.

1937—*The Rengma Nagas,* London.

1922—*The Lotha Nagas,* London.

1971—Morris Jone W. C., *Government and Politics in India,* Bombay,

1960—More, S. S., *Practice and Procedure of Indian Parliament,* Thakur and Co. Mumbai, 1960.

1973—Mills, J.P., *The Ao Nagas,* London Oxford University Press. 1973.

1978, Neville Maxwell, *India and the Nagas,* Delhi.

1970—Nirmal Nivedan, *Nagaland: The Night of the Guerrilla,* Delhi.

1986—Nuh, V.K., *Nagaland Church and Politics,* Kohima.

1992—Piketo, Sema, *British Policy and Administration in Nagaland (1882-1947),* New Delhi.

1960—Phizo, A.Z., *The Fate of the Naga People: An appeal to the World,* London.

1982—Philips, P.T., *The Growth of Baptist Church in Nagaland,* Guwahati.

1993—Imchen, Panger, *Ancient Ao Naga Religion and Culture,* Har-Anand Publications, New Delhi.

2000—Girin Phukon (Ed), *Political Dynamics of North East India,* New Delhi.

1984—Puthen, Purkal Joseph, *Baptist Mission in Nagaland,* Vendrome Musicological Institute, Shillong.

1976—Rao, V.V., *A Century of Tribal Politics in North East India 1874-1976,* New Delhi.

1969—Rao, V., *Social Change and the Tribal Conflicts,* Kolkota.

1942—Reid Robert, *History of Assam Frontier Bordering on Assam (1883-1941),* Shillong.

1841—Robinson W., *A Descriptive Account of Assam,* Calcutta.

1996—Sangyu, *A History of Nagas and Nagaland: Dynamic of Oral Tradition in Village Formation,* Commonwealth Publishers, New Delhi.

1991—Saraswati, B., *Tribal Thought and Culture,* Delhi.

1914—Shakespeare, W.L., *History of Upper Assam, Upper Burma and North East Frontier,* London.

1993—Sharma, R.N., *Principles of Sociology,* Media Promoters, Bombay.

1997—Singh, B.P, *The Problem of Change: A Study of North East India,* Oxford University Press, (2nd imprint), New Delhi.

1981—Singh, Chandrika, *Political Evolution of Nagaland,* Lancer Publishers, New Delhi.

2004—*Naga Politics: A Critical Account,* Mittal Publications, New Delhi.

1974—Singh, Prakash, *Nagaland,* New Delhi.

1925—Smith, W.C., *The Ao Nagas,* London, Oxford University Press.

1996—Singh, Yogendra, *Modernization of Indian Tradition,* Rawat Publications, New Delhi.

Sinai, N.D., I.R., *The Challenges of Modernization,* London Chatte and Windus.

1968—Stracey, P.D., *Nagaland Nightmare,* Mumbai.

1994—Sanaitang, O.L., "Christianity and Tribal Solidarity in Meghalaya India", *Church History Review,* June.

1986—Shriniwas, M.N., *Social Change in Modern India*, Allied Publishing house, Bombay.

1993—Sword, V.H., *Baptist in Assam: A Century of Missionary Service–1836-1936*, Chicago.

1984—Ao, Tajen, *Christianity versus Ao Nagas*, Tribal Gospel Mission, Mokokchung.

1976—Ao, Tajenyuba, *Nagas' Customary Laws,* Mokokchung.

1958—*A History of Anglo-Naga Affairs*, Guwahati.

1935—Thompson, E. & Grrat G.T., *Rise and Fulfillment of British Rule in India*, London..

1992—Thomas, M, *The Nagas towards A.D. 2000*, Madras Center for Research on New International Economic Order.

1968—Tracey P.D, *Nagaland Nightmare*, Mumbai.

1986—Verma S.P., *Indian Parliament: A Study of the Socio-Political Background*, New Delhi.

1975—Verma, S.P., *Modern Political Theory*, Vikash Publishing House, New Delhi.

2002—Vashum R, *Nagas' Right to Self-Determination*, Mittal Publications, New Delhi.

1970—Yaden, L. L., *Nagaland*, Kohima.

1968—Wilding, Norman & Philip, Laundy, *An Introduction to Encyclopedia of Parliament.*

1979—Zinyu, Mhiesizokho, *Phizo and the Naga Problem*, Dimapur.

ARTICLES

1989—Ao, Tajen, "Naga Customary Laws and its Influence on Legislation in Nagaland" in 25 Years of Nagaland Legislative Assembly, Assembly Secretariat, Kohima.

1989—Ao, Chubatemjen, "Speaker and his Relations with Legislature", in 25 Years of Nagaland Legislative Assembly, Kohima.

1952—Banerjee, D. N., "The Role of Indian Speaker", *Modern Review,* vol. LXXXII, No. 2.

1989—Barpujari, H.K., "Trends of Nationalism and sub-Nationalism in Assam: A Study of the context of Socio-Cultural Syndrome", in B.C., Bhuyan (Ed), *Political Development of North East,* Delhi.

1960—Chaudhry, B.N., "The Nagas and their Tribes", *Mankind,* July 4.

1944—Elwin, V., "The Aboriginals", published in *Oxford Pamphlet on Indian Affairs.*

1995—Fransis, Kikon, "NSCN and Allies From STUF", in *North East Update,* vol. 1, No. 6, February 6, Dimapur.

1961—Franda, M.F., "The Naga National Council: Origin of the Separatist Movement", *Economic Weekly,* February 4.

1986—Ganguly, G.B., "Socio-Economic Problems of Transition from Shifting to Sedentary cultivation in North East India", in D.N. Majumdar (Ed), *Shifting Cultivation in North East India,* New Delhi.

2001—Geoffrey, Yaden, "Electoral Reforms", published in *Nagaland Post,* March 9.

1990—Huska, Sumi, "The anti-Defection Law : Its Impact on Defection in Nagaland", in the *Weekly Express Journal,* September.

1989—Jamir S.C. "The Naga Tribal Society and Democratic Character", *25 Years of Nagaland Legislative Assembly,* Kohima.

N.D.—Jogmaya, K.K. Saikia, "Process of Urbanization in Nagaland: A Case Study of Kohima and Dimapur",in Ganguly, G.B., (Ed) *Urbanization and Development in North East India.*

1975—Johari, J.C., "Creation of Nagaland State: Triumph of Ebullient Infra-nationalism" *Indian Journal of Political Science,* vol. XXXVI, No.1, January-March.

1961—Karl, W. Dweutsch, "Social Mobilization and Political Development" *American Political Science Review,* vol. XL, September 1961.

1989—Kedtisu, K.V., "Executive Accountability to the Legislature in the Democratic Polity", *25 Years of Nagaland Legislative Assembly,* Kohima 1989.

1990—Khiron, Roy, "Nagaland: Gang-Opportunism" in *Assam Tribune,* June 16. 1990.

2000—Lal Bhure, "Tribal Development in India", in *Nagaland Page,* Vol. 1, No. 262, February 25.

1959—Luthra, I., "Development of the Naga Hills", *March of India,* vol. II, March.

1971—Luthra, P.N., "North East Frontier Agency Tribes: Impacts of Ahoms and British Policy", *Weekly,* vol. 6, No. 23, June 5.

Mahajan, V.S. (Ed), *Widening Economic Disparities in Mizoram: Its socio-Economic Implications and Alternative Approaches.*

1926—Mills, J.P., "The Wild Tribes of Naga Hills", *Discovery,* vol. 7.

N.D.—Certain Aspects of Naga Culture", in *Journal of Royal Anthropological Institute,* vol. LVI,

Mmhonlumo, Kikon, "Did Nagas Live in Darkness?" in the *Nagaland Page,* February 28, 2000, Dimapur.

1987—Morani, A.G., "Crisis in Speaker's Office", *The Indian Express,* 3rd September.

1972—"The Speakers and the Constitution", *The Indian Express,* 9th December.

1962—Nag, A.K., "The Nagas' Sociological Background and the Impact of Civilization", *Quest No. 35,* October.

Nirmal Minz, "Crisis in Indigenous People's Life in India", *Ecology: A Theological Response.*

1999—Nuh, V.K., "Education from Christian Point of View", *Nagaland Page,* August 2.

1963—Robert E. Ward., "Political Modernization and Political Culture in Japan", in *World Politics,* vol. XV, No. 5, July.

2002—Sajal, Nag, "Construction of Nationhood: Ethnic Minorities Secessionism and Legitimization in North East India" in Grin Phukon (ED), *Political Dynamic of North East India,* South Asian Publishers, New Delhi.

1990—Singh Chandrika, "Party Politics in Nagaland, Part- I-II," *The North East Politics,* vol. 1, No. 7 and vol. 1, No. 6 August -September.

1980—Singh Chandrika, "Nagaland from a District to State: Culmination of Democratic Political Process" in *Journal of Political science Association,* vol. 41, No. 4, December.

1969—Snup, E.T., "a Glimpse at the Impact of Christianity on Naga Culture", *The Warrior,* vol. IV, No. 1, Kohima.

2000—Susmita, Sengupta, "Regionalism in Meghalaya and Question of Perception of National, Political Politics", in Grini Phukon, (Ed), *Political Dynamics of North East India,* New Delhi.

1972—Terhuja, K., "The Christian Churches among the Angami Nagas" in *Tribal Situation in India,* vol. 13, edited by K.S. Singh, Simila.

1866—Thomas, M.M., "Modernization of Traditional Societies and Struggle for New Cultural Ethos", *Ecumenical Review,* vol. XVIII, No. 4, October.

1987—Wali, R.L., "Indian Development Process: Parameters of Development in North East India", in Mahajan V.S., (Ed) *Emerging Pattern of Northeastern Economy,* Deep & Deep Publications, New Delhi.

JOURNALS, MAGAZINES, WEEKLY AND NEWSPAPERS

The Indian Journal of Political Science Association.

Modern Review, Calcutta.

The Journal of Parliamentary Information, New Delhi.

The Journal of Constitutional and Parliamentary Studies, New Delhi,

The Journal of Society for the Study of State Government, Varanasi.

The Naga Nation, Kohima.

The North East Update, Dimapur

The Warrior, Government of Nagaland, Kohima.

The Man in India

The Northeastern Politics, Guwahati.

The Platform, Dimapur.

The Political and Economic Weekly, Bombay.

The Highlander, New Delhi.

The Asian Recorder, New Delhi.

The Keesing Contemporary Archives, London.

The Statesman, New Delhi.

The Indian Express, New Delhi, The Times of India, New Delhi.

The North East Express, Dimapur.

The Hill Express, Dimapur.

North East Sun, Dimapur.

The Telegraph, Calcutta.

The Naga News, Kohima.

The Nagaland Times, Dimapur.

The Nagaland Post, Dimapur.

***

Index

***